THE DiGiTAL CATHEDRAL

Networked Ministry in a Wireless World

KEITH ANDERSON

Foreword by Elizabeth Drescher

D1456917

 Morehouse Publishing
NEW YORK

Morehouse Publishing, 19 East 34th Street, New York, NY 10016

Morehouse Publishing is an imprint of Church Publishing Incorporated.
www.churchpublishing.org

Cover design by Laurie Klein Westhafer
Typeset by Rose Design

Library of Congress Cataloging-in-Publication Data

Anderson, Keith, 1949–
 The digital cathedral : networked ministry in a wireless world / Keith Anderson.
    pages cm
 Includes bibliographical references.
 ISBN 978-0-8192-2995-3 (pbk.)—ISBN 978-0-8192-2996-0 (ebook) 1. Pastoral care—Data processing. 2. Internet in church work. 3. Social media. I. Title.
 BV4011.9.A53 2015
 253.0285'675—dc23
                              2014047353

Printed in the United States of America

Contents

DEDiCATiON

"In thanksgiving to the living God for all ministers who have borne
the hot coal of [God's] Word upon their lips and in their lives."
—*Inscription at Washington National Cathedral*

Foreword

PiLGRiMS TO THE DiGiTAL CATHEDRAL

SOME YEARS AGO, in my late twenties, I worked for a while in England as a management consultant. I had a little basement flat in London, on Dorset Square, just around the corner from Sherlock Holmes' digs at 221B Baker Street. I was an easy walk away from the enchantments of Regents Park and at least a half a dozen amazing Indian take-away shops. My London pied-à-terre had all the makings of a remarkable locale for a young woman abroad were it not for the fact that I traveled outside of London most weeks to dank office buildings or soulless industrial parks in Birmingham, Blackpool, Coventry, Lincoln, Liverpool, Manchester, Sheffield, and so on. And I worked such long hours that I was almost always exhausted by the time I got back to my humble flat, very late most Friday evenings. As I dragged myself to bed, I barely felt the rattle of the underground trains as they passed beneath me on their way from Baker Street to Marylebone Station.

It turns out that, while jumbling up corporations across the globe can sound like an exciting job, it was something of an overwhelming grind—days following around hapless middle managers to see where their work might be made more efficient (and they might be rendered redundant); hours coaching executives on everything from globalization strategies to modes of leadership that would improve employee productivity; late nights pouring over organization charts, financial reports, and personnel files. All of that made the experience for me, even then in my decidedly unreligious and only vaguely spiritual days, profoundly soul sucking. The only salvation from this was, ironically, Sunday.

Sundays truly were Sabbath for me. Having caught up on sleep and done sundry chores and errands on Saturdays, I'd wake early on Sunday mornings and take the train to Canterbury. I did it almost every week for the better part of a year—an hour and a half of tea and quiet through the countryside from London to Kent. Once I got to the station in Canterbury, if the weather was reasonably fair, I'd wend my way into the center of town to the famed cathedral, varying my routes to take in more of the storied city where the blood of Thomas à Becket was shed and, on route to which, more famously, Chaucer's fictional pilgrims spun their many wondrously tawdry tales. Most Sundays, I'd stop at one of any number of small bookshops that dotted the city back then—they all seem to have become Starbucks these days—where I'd pick up (yet another) pocket copy of *The Canterbury Tales,* or perhaps something from the anonymous Pearl Poet of *Sir Gawain* fame, or a dry bit of something from Chaucer's less celebrated friend, "moral Gower." Every so often, I'd come upon an ancient seeming illuminated psalter or a slightly mildewed *Book of Common Prayer*, but I seldom took the bait—too overtly religiousy for my tastes at the time, though I would take a spiritual lean once in a while. I found Julian of Norwich for the first time in Canterbury that year; and, the strangely compelling lay mystic and pilgrim Margery Kempe literally jumped off a shelf in a little shop on Longmarket, nearly smacking me in the head. Mostly, it was Chaucer, though, who I'd take with me to some nook in the cathedral, where, often as the boy's choir rehearsed, I'd let the round, guttural Middle English syllables roll with whispered ineptitude off my tongue.

One particularly stunning Sunday morning in August, as I sat outside in the Cloisters reading, as ever, from *The Tales*, I was greeted by a young cleric. He invited me to the Holy Communion service that was to begin shortly. "No thank you," I said. "I'm just reading my book."

"Oh," he smiled, "we have lots of books. We're a very bookish sort of church."

"Well, yes," I sighed a little, "I suppose that's true. But I'm not really religious."

"Ah," he said finally, smiling still as he turned back toward the cathedral, "and yet here you are with your pious pilgrims."

I shrugged off his quip at the time—it would be a few more years before my pilgrimage would take me, a wobbly sort of "believer," into a church for services proper. As the bells rang for the service, I gathered my things and made my way to a nearby tea shop, where I would commit the heresy of insisting on weak American tea (bag dipped briefly into the steaming water rather than steeped robustly in it for long minutes) and eavesdrop on the tales of random fellow pilgrims. Most weeks, someone would strike up a conversation with me as I doodled in a notebook or looked up from my reading. Our stories would weave together for a few moments over a simpler communion of tea and scones that, nonetheless, held a certain air of the holy.

It was, indeed, a religious practice, these regular trips to Canterbury, if by "religious" we mean something vaguely ritualized in time, locale, and the general order of activities. It was "religious," too, as a claim on sanctuary—on a place where one is immune from the persecutions of everyday life, especially the constant pull of "progress" and "improvement" that were so much a part of my profession at the time. The reflective quiet I found within the precincts of Canterbury Cathedral; the freedom to amble around the town through secreted gates and back alleys cobbled with centuries old stones; the hours spent sipping tea while listening in on the lives of strangers from around the world; and, not least, the strange and alluring voices of medieval English poets and the occasional spiritual writer were all as much a part of my religious formation as any inquirers class in a drafty church hall might have been. When I eventually made my way to an Episcopal church in Pennsylvania several years later, it was clear to me that I owed my conversion, such as it was, as much to Chaucer as to Christ, as much to Canterbury as to Calvary. Canterbury—the cathedral; the history, legends, and literatures that emanate from it; and the city in which it is centered at a busy intersection of past, present, and future—connected me to an idea of the past, to a rich tradition, and to a widely distributed and diverse community that reached into and well beyond the particularities of my personal experience. Sociologist of religion Danièle Hervieu-Lége refers to such connections as links on a religious "chain of memory."

Hervieu-Lége argues that, rather than succumbing to modern secularism, science, and rationality, religion "re-emerges, revives, shifts ground, becomes diffuse"[1] in postmodernity. While religion in its institutional forms declines, religiousness—what we more often label as "spirituality" today—continues in new ways, within new forms of elective community. We sit contentedly in various cathedral grounds, that is, with whatever resources seem to offer the comfort of a familiarity that we count as "spiritual" without feeling compelled to worship at the altars of traditional religion. Still, Hervieu-Lége suggests, without tradition, including some deference to traditional authorities, spirituality has no real depth or substance with which to approach the complexities and uncertainties of everyday life from which we seek the refuge of religion. At the same time, without the vitality of new spiritual imaginings and practices refitted to the contours of contemporary experience, traditions are merely dusty idols from the past—museum pieces that are quickly forgotten amidst the challenges of postmodern life. The ability to link tradition to innovation through practices of shared remembering creates the "chain" that, for Hervieu-Lége, constitutes and sustains religion in the postmodern world—or at least it *could*.

The idea of religion as a "chain of memory" has been compelling to many scholars of religion because it helps to explain how, despite the efforts of an often strident cheering section, secularism has not succeeded in replacing religion, especially outside of Europe. Even with the much discussed "rise of the Nones"— people who answer "none" when asked with what religion they identify or are affiliated—and the decline of many Christian denominations, religion carries on with increasing diversity (including less attractive expression of harsh fundamentalism). Even as Nones step away from traditional religions—most of these Christian—the majority retain a belief in God or a higher power, and many continue to engage in some ways with institutional religions and their spiritual treasures. What religions are now being made through this bricolage of religious memory and postmodern spiritual practice, only time will tell. But—and here I fear that Hervieu-Lége is constrained by her own metaphor from seeing the fullness of the implications of her insight into the shift from premodern to modern to postmodern religiousness—I am fairly sure that new religious expressions are held together not so much by chains, as by networks. For Hervieu-Lége, postmodernity is characterized by a kind of fracturing of everyday experience that breaks the chain of religious memory held together by tradition. But networks are not chains—linear technologies of sequence, of binding, of immobility. Rather they are defined by multi-directionality, mobility, diversity, and expansiveness. They are formed not of individual links connected along a line, but of interrelated clusters that may change in relationship to one another and in overall significance over time. Chains break, as Hervieu-Lége laments. Networks reconfigure.

This is the paradoxically premodern-postmodern insight Keith Anderson finds in cathedrals. Cathedrals, he will explain in the pages ahead, are profoundly networked structures, reconfigured through geographical, historical, religious, and spiritual space. My pre-digital age pilgrimages to Canterbury made this all too plain. The journey itself each week depended upon regular movement from one network to another—from the cosmopolitan bustle of London to the pastoral expanse of Kent; from the maze of streets and shops on the walk from the train station to the cathedral grounds; across the time-space continuum entered through one Middle English tome or another; within the tableau of conversations I had with sundry shopkeepers and visitors. Unknown to me then, and perhaps unknown as well to the kindly priest who (more than once) invited me into the cathedral for Sunday services, was that each hub on the network was an opportunity to engage the holy, to open my heart to it and carry it with greater awareness into my work week.

The complexity and reach of these networks is of course vastly expanded by new digital social technologies that give us the ability to connect to others across the globe in less than seconds. These technologies have created no small amount of anxiety among many in the Church, and not entirely without reason. Even as we become more digitally connected, many worry, are we becoming less connected in local spaces where we encounter one another as embodied beings? As religious ideas and practices are increasingly shared through digital texts, images, videos, and so on that can be endlessly adapted and shared again . . . and again . . . and again, are our traditions dissipating to an extent that will ultimately render them unrecognizable?

In an either-or world, such worries are surely well founded. But the hybrid metaphor Keith Anderson has crafted in *The Digital Cathedral* invites us to explore the way Christian practice can play out in a networked world. It calls us to value the richness of our traditions and, in particular, to honor their adaptability and robustness as they are plugged into new digitally integrated ministries. Yes, chains are broken here—perhaps chiefly the hard and fast link between the local church building and what has traditionally been counted as "real" religion. But new relationships are developing, new memories are being formed, and new pathways to the holy are opening in a world set to hear the meandering tales of so many new digital pilgrims. Keith Anderson is to be congratulated for helping us to navigate this changing landscape by clicking on the cathedral—one of the most significant icons of Christian tradition that endures today as a symbol of the holy, as a sanctuary, and a spiritual hub in widely networked, digitally integrated world.

—Elizabeth Drescher

Acknowledgments

> "There is a great distance between the words we speak uninhibitedly to a friendly audience and the discipline needed to write a book."
>
> —GASTON BACHELARD

LIKE ANY CATHEDRAL, this book represents the contributions of numerous people made over a span of many years. I am deeply grateful for the many gifted colleagues and good friends, who have generously shared their experiences, wise counsel, and support throughout the writing of this book. It is my privilege to share their compelling stories and innovative ideas in the pages that follow. They continually inspire me and give me hope for the future of the ministry and the Church. Like the master craftspeople that built the great cathedrals, each has left their own unique mark on this project. In particular, I want to thank the following people, who have been instrumental in helping to build *The Digital Cathedral*.

My great thanks to my publisher, Church Publishing, for believing in this project—and to my editor, Nancy Bryan, for her sharp insights and well-timed reassurances throughout the writing process. For the entire Church Publishing team from editorial through production to marketing whose work supports this book and especially for Laurie Westhafer, whose excellent cover design that captures so well the spirit of this book, I am very grateful.

I am hugely indebted to my friend, co-author, writing partner, and collaborator, Elizabeth Drescher, for her sharing her own cathedral pilgrimage in the foreword as well as her assistance in conceiving, drafting, and editing this book. Elizabeth's original research on the religiously unaffiliated and her perspective on the changing contours of American Christianity have informed my writing throughout.

I give thanks for my late friend, The Rev. Dr. Ronald Thiemann, until his premature death the Bussey Professor of Theology at Harvard Divinity School, who instilled in me a love for the theology of the everyday and encouraged me to write a book about it. There were many times during this project that I wish I could have picked up the phone or emailed Ron for his advice. He is greatly missed.

My thanks to The Rev. Jodi Houge and the people of Humble Walk Lutheran Church in St. Paul, Minnesota for letting me continue to tell their story. It's a great story and I'm honored to share it.

Thanks also to Dan Endicott, Gerard Olson, and the staff and regulars at Forest & Main Brewing Company in Ambler, Pennsylvania for their hospitality for our monthly God on Tap theology pub group and for what they've taught me about third places and sacred space.

I am grateful to those who generously assisted me behind the scenes, including Jim Naughton and Rebecca Wilson, The Rev. Dr. Wendel "Tad" Meyer, Bishop Dan Edwards, Dean John Downey, The Rev. Kirk Berlenbach, The Canterbury Cathedral Archives, and the Trinity College Library. Special thanks go to Bethany Stolle for creating the graphics in chapter three.

I have been honored to serve as pastor to the people of Upper Dublin Lutheran Church in Ambler, Pennsylvania and the Lutheran Church of the Redeemer in Woburn, Massachusetts. I give thanks for the wisdom, inspiration, and support they have given me throughout my ministry. I am also grateful for the encouragement of my bishop, The Rev. Claire Burkat of the Southeastern Pennsylvania Synod of the ELCA.

I have had numerous opportunities to rehearse and test material for this book. My thanks go to the Lilly Endowment Website Consultation, the Northeastern Pennsylvania Synod of the ELCA, The BTS Center, Andover-Newton Theological School, The Lutheran Theological Seminary at Philadelphia, the New England Synod of the ELCA, the Episcopal Diocese of Rochester (New

York), the South Dakota Synod of the ELCA, the Southeastern Pennsylvania Synod of the ELCA, and the New Hampshire Conference of the United Church of Christ.

My thanks to The Rev. Verity Jones and the New Media Project for their continued support of my work and for allowing me to share some of the earliest ideas for this project on their blog. My writing about life and ministry in *The Digital Cathedral* has also appeared in *Faith & Form: The Interfaith Journal on Religion Art and Architecture* and The BTS Center blog.

Finally, I want to thank my loud, loving, and creative family for giving me the time and encouragement to write this book. Thanks go to my wife Jenny for letting me turn our dining room into my writing studio for the last year and for the countless other accommodations she has made during this project. My children, Ellie, Finn, Dulcie, and Tess, constantly remind me of the enduring value of everyday moments and that my first and best calling is to be their dad. My kids already demonstrate a love of writing. As my nine-year old son, Finn, enjoys reminding me, "Dad, I've already written ten books!" in his third-grade class. I look forward to seeing the world they will create, the church they will help to shape, and what they will have to say about it all.

—Keith Anderson
Transfiguration Sunday 2015

Introduction

BUiLDiNG A DiGiTAL CATHEDRAL

"The Christian movement is always the recognizing of a particular situation—and the necessity of a new step forward. There is always a necessary risk in being different. It requires simultaneously a 'place' and a 'further,' a 'now' and an 'afterwards,' a 'here' and an 'elsewhere.' . . . Boundaries are the place of Christian work, and their displacements are the result of this work."

—MICHEL DE CERTEAU

"The medium, or process, of our time—electric technology—is reshaping and restructuring patterns of social interdependence and every aspect of our personal life. It is forcing us to reconsider and re-evaluate practically every thought, every action, and every institution formerly taken for granted."

—MARSHALL MCLUHAN

WE HAD COME TO NEW YORK CITY to celebrate my wife's birthday. It was a quick overnight visit—just enough time to see a Broadway show and squeeze in a little sightseeing. The morning after the show, we made the typical tourist rounds through Times Square, Central Park, and finally, to Rockefeller Center. But as we walked along Fifth Avenue on that crisp March day, the place I was most excited about visiting was the storied St. Patrick's Cathedral. St. Pat's, as it is affectionately called, is a famously beautiful church, the seat of the Roman Catholic archdiocese of New

The covered facade of St. Patrick's Cathedral, March 2014. *Photo: Keith Anderson*

York, and greatly beloved among New Yorkers. However, when we turned the corner, the famed neo-gothic facade was nearly unrecognizable. It turns out St. Pat's was in the midst of a $175 million restoration project, and nearly every inch of the church was covered in some kind of scaffold or white plastic sheeting. Although I was disappointed, I couldn't help but think it was an apt symbol for a book about cathedrals and how the church needs to renovate and reconstruct itself to meet the demands of twentieth-century ministry. As if to dispel any doubt of that, the wrapping around the scaffolding at the corner of Fifth Avenue and East 50th Street read, *"Check-in on Facebook. Follow us on Twitter @ stpatsnyc."* Perhaps it would be too much to call this a sign from God, yet I couldn't help but feel it was an auspicious beginning on this first of many cathedral visits for this book.

We entered St. Pat's beneath that sign, through the western doors, from the vestibule—the small portal just inside the doors—into the nave—the main part of the cathedral—which was covered in an astounding latticework of aluminum scaffolding. In yet another sign of our digitally integrated age, we tapped our names into the touch-screen digital guest book. The main part of the nave was closed off due to the construction, and so, along with other pilgrims there that day, we walked along the ambulatory—the walkway along the sides of the nave. I lighted a candle at the shrine of St. John the Evangelist, and then walked across the front of the nave. From there we could see the Bishop's chair—the word cathedral comes from the Latin *cathedra*, meaning chair—as cathedrals are the seat of the bishop. Beyond that rose the high altar, considered the most sacred place in any cathedral.

We found a seat in the pews near the front of the nave and, as the sounds of workmen restoring stonework echoed down from high above, I contemplated this combination of metal and stone, the juxtaposition of the medieval form and modern repair. The study in contrasts at St. Patrick's went beyond just the architectural renovation, I realized. There was also a renovation in practices of relationship happening. I watched as people talked to one another in hushed tones, prayed, and gazed around the cathedral, as any medieval pilgrim would have. But they also snapped pictures and took videos on their smartphones. As I had, I expect that many others checked-in on Facebook or posted pictures on Instagram. Indeed, it seems that St. Patrick's has become something of a "digital cathedral" that engages a diversity of visitors—Christians and others who appreciate the beauty and respite offered in the cathedral—by inviting connection in both local and extended digital social spaces.

I had come to St. Patrick's searching for inspiration for this book and, as so many others have before me, spiritual insight. I pondered the unique place cathedrals have in the religious landscape and the enduring hold they seem to have on the spiritual imagination. Indeed, a recent study of English cathedrals reported that in the first part of this new century, even with significant declines in religious affiliation and church membership, cathedrals are receiving significant renewed interest as well as increased attendance.[1]

Surely one of the reasons cathedrals capture our imagination is simply because they are often so old and so big. To stand in the nave of a medieval gothic cathedral, like Notre-Dame in Paris, completed in 1272, is to be awed by what was accomplished by generations of medieval craftsmen with rather primitive tools. Because a cathedral of that era took decades to complete—years that would typically extend across the lifetimes of many craftsmen—their construction by the hands of ordinary masons, stone carvers, joiners, and common laborers seems even more grand and complex, almost defying imagination. As renowned cathedral historian Robert Scott writes, "One of the defining qualities of the Gothic style is that it made the doable seem impossible."[2]

But there is much more to cathedrals than their age and their size. They are known for the beauty of their architecture, liturgy, music, and the arts. Those who minister in cathedral are also deeply rooted to their local communities, often advocating for social justice, and engaged in secular and civic partnerships. Tracey Lind, dean of Trinity Episcopal Cathedral in Cleveland, Ohio, shared with me, "I like to call the urban cathedral at its best a *piazza,* a place of celebration and culture and conversation and collaboration and even commerce." Their unique ministry is distinct from parishes, though, as we will see, much of it can be adapted to the parish context. Importantly, cathedrals welcome people with a wide range of beliefs and practices, and those with none at all. They have a sense of openness that mimics gothic architecture with its spaciousness, light, and flying buttresses. They serve as a corrective to a church that has, in many ways, closed in on itself.

THE RISE OF THE NONES, AND FACEBOOK

Today, the church in America, and particularly the mainline Protestant church, is in crisis. These denominations, including Episcopal, Lutheran, United Methodist, Presbyterian, and the United Church of Christ, have all experienced dramatic declines in membership, attendance, and financial giving. Churches that thrived in the post-World War II boom period of American civic religion, and that once occupied a central and privileged place in American culture, have struggled to find their voice and role in today's less formally religious culture. This book seeks to address two of the most important challenges confronting the church today, both of which have emerged over the last twenty-five years. First, is the rise of the so-called "Nones," that is, the religiously unaffiliated, those who check "none" when asked for their religious or denominational affiliation. Today 20 percent of Americans and 30 percent of people under thirty are Nones, and those numbers are growing by about 20 percent year over year.[3] The second is the rapid advance in internet technologies, most especially digital social networks and wireless mobile devices that have fundamentally changed the way we live our lives and conceive of communication, relationships, community, leadership, and authority, and therefore have profound implications for ministry in a digital age.

THE DIGITAL CATHEDRAL

This book is not a study of cathedrals, but it does draw on the distinctive elements of cathedral ecclesiology to help imagine a model for ministry in a digitally integrated world. Nor is this book, as the title might at first suggest, a case for solely online or digital church. Rather, the idea of a Digital Cathedral is intended to evoke an expansive and holistic understanding of church—one that extends ministry into both digital and local gathering spaces, recognizes the sacred in everyday life, and embodies a networked, relational, and incarnational approach to ministry leadership for a digital age.

The Digital Cathedral is an invitation to a more expansive understanding of church, and ways of being church, at a time when our definitions of church have become all too narrow, too parochial—when evangelism is reduced to membership, faith formation is narrowed to Sunday morning education classes, and sharing the Gospel has been reduced to marketing rather than sharing the free and abundant grace and love of God. This more expansive understanding encompasses a range of people, practices, and beliefs. It takes seriously our digitally integrated lives, where what has been called the "triple revolution" of the internet, mobile devices, and digital social media is revolutionizing the way we lead our lives and live out our faith.[4]

However, it is not just about using digital social media platforms for ministry, which Elizabeth Drescher and I discussed in *Click2Save: The Digital Ministry Bible*, but about being meaningfully and consistently present in local *and* digital gathering spaces—being where people are physically and virtually. In a time when fewer and fewer people are finding their way into the church, it is essential that we intentionally seek out and connect with them rather than waiting for them to show up at our doors—and help them to discover the sacred, not just inside our church buildings, but in everyday places and experiences, honoring the holy in the midst of their daily lives. The Digital Cathedral needs leaders whose ministries are networked, relational, and incarnational. These leaders must speak and act in ways that are culturally resonant in today's digitally integrated world, and in order to be meaningfully engaged with those around us, that requires that they also be technologically fluent. Like cathedral builders of old, we must harness the latest technologies of our time to share the Gospel.

Cathedrals were often built upon historic sites considered sacred ground for centuries and utilizing materials salvaged from previous iterations of holy spaces. St. Patrick's, for instance, was built to replace the old St. Patrick's Cathedral in downtown Manhattan, but the current site was once the home to Jesuit, then Trappist, communities, and later a parish church. Likewise, the Digital Cathedral is built upon many of the best traditional practices of ministry and being church, with some new ideas to go along them, as we seek to share the Gospel in a rapidly changing world.

BUILDING THE DIGITAL CATHEDRAL

In the conversational spirit of social media, I have included a range of voices—over fifty ministry leaders—from varied ministry contexts from across the church. My hope in bringing these stories together is to create an overarching narrative for ministry in a digitally integrated world that includes theory and theology, spirituality and practice—a narrative that describes the contours of digitally networked living, and offers stories and ideas for how to engage it. As Robert Scott writes in his study of gothic cathedrals,

> A cathedral-building project provided a potentially defining focus, a master narrative, for collective identity among members of the community in which it was built. . . . Building a cathedral entailed an ongoing, difficult, yet energizing form of collective enterprise in which people could take enormous pride and around which they could rally as a community.[5]

I hope this book can do the same as it weaves that narrative from the stories of the ministry leaders and faith communities building their own digital cathedrals.

Part 1: Life In Cathedral

Cathedrals are not just stand-alone monumental buildings. They are deeply connected to their cities, regions, and the people who live there. Cathedrals are networked, relational, incarnational communities that include people with a surprising range of beliefs and practices. Chapter one describes this historic character of cathedrals by looking at twelfth-century Canterbury and the ways in which the cathedral was deeply integrated into daily life. It will introduce us to a variety of everyday people who lived life fully "in cathedral." Chapter two describes how people are reclaiming that sense of cathedral in our own time and making their neighborhoods their cathedrals through ministry in local and digital gathering spaces. From the West End of St. Paul, Minnesota, a farmers' market in California's Salinas Valley, a café in Maryland, to Twitter and other social media platforms, ministry leaders and faith communities are experimenting with expansive, holistic, and contextual approaches to ministry. In the process, they are expanding our notions of what constitutes sacred space.

Part 2: Ministry Leadership in a Digitally Integrated World

Doing the work of making our local and digital neighborhoods our cathedrals necessitates three key qualities or proficiencies of ministry leadership. Today's ministry leaders should be networked, relational, and incarnational.[6] Chapter three describes our networked reality and how we can effectively operate within those networks. Chapter four highlights the importance of tending the relationships at the heart of those networks. Chapter five explores the incarnational quality of leadership, which is not content to leave relationships on the screen but creates or seeks out opportunities for face-to-face connection.

Part 3: The Humble Sublime

Cathedrals are large enough, in both their architecture and their ministry, to hold seemly dichotomous categories and peoples together. In doing so, they create a welcoming, open, and flexible spiritual space. As Jane Shaw, former dean of Grace Episcopal Cathedral in San Francisco, writes, "cathedrals are often the least 'churchy' of churches, reaching out to a wide audience beyond strict believers."[7] This section provides much of the theological underpinning of *The Digital Cathedral* by looking at the spirituality and theology of the everyday, and deconstructing the false dichotomy we place between sacred and secular, between religiously affiliated and unaffiliated, and between the digital and face-to-face.

Chapter six suggests a spirituality and theology of everyday life, drawing on Martin Luther's understanding of vocation, and then exploring how cathedrals and other ministries and ministry leaders are engaging people as together they seek and find God in daily life. As we see in chapter seven, this is a critical element for how we navigate ministry amidst the rise of the Nones. Much of the church's response to the rise of the Nones has been to ask why they don't like us, or how we might rebrand and re-market ourselves.[8] This approach has been misguided. Instead of asking why Nones don't like us, we need to understand and appreciate the ways in which both Nones and the religiously affiliated make meaning—many of which, it turns out, are deeply rooted in daily life—and find ways to respond and participate alongside them.

Part Four: Third Places and Sacred Spaces

That meaning-making increasingly happens through conversation in local and digital gathering places. Chapter eight looks specifically at local gatherings like theology pubs, and coffee shops, and digital gathering spaces like Facebook and Twitter. It offers practical examples and suggestions about how ministry leaders can host these conversations in their own contexts. The conversations that happen in these settings are often profoundly theological, but it is theology done in a different mode. Chapter nine will suggest a model of theological reflection that is effective for gatherings in the pub, the coffee shop, on the sidewalk, and in social media.

Part Five: Forming Faith and Sharing the Gospel in the Digital Age

The expansive character of cathedrals invites and encourages us to think more expansively about our own ministry practices. The shifts described in this book touch on all aspects of life and ministry. In particular, I believe they call us to reevaluate the way we understand how faith formation and evangelism happen—and what exactly we mean by those terms. Chapter ten extends the previous chapter's reflection on how we do theology to look at how we form faith more generally—advocating for an approach to faith formation that, like a cathedral, is visual, immersive, experiential, and participatory. Chapter eleven suggests an understanding of evangelism that has a broader understanding of what it means to belong to a faith community beyond membership. It also suggests practical advice for sharing the Gospel in a digitally integrated environment.

Part Six: A Digital Rule of Life

In a time of great change, it is essential for ministry leaders to remain spiritually grounded and avail themselves of the great wisdom of the Christian tradition. Inspired by monastic rules of life, from the ancient *Rule of St. Benedict* to more contemporary rules like *The Rule of Taize*, chapter twelve offers A Digital Rule of Life—fifteen rules for effective and spiritually rooted ministry in a digital age. Finally, the conclusion will transport us to the last stop in our pilgrimage, ChristChurch, New Zealand, where a Cardboard Cathedral offers a final point of final reflection on the future of the church.

A CATHEDRAL IS ALWAYS UNDER CONSTRUCTION

Finally, a cathedral is always a work in progress. As Robert Scott suggests above, the sheer length of time it took for the cathedral to be built made it seem—especially in eras of limited life expectance—that they were never finished. Indeed, cathedrals are always under construction. That goes for the building as well as their historic ministries of hospitality, mercy, liturgy, prayer, music, and education. The same goes for *The Digital Cathedral*. I invite you to keep the learning and the conversation going online. Connect with me on Facebook, Twitter, Instagram, and my website, pastorkeithanderson.net.

1

CANTERBURY CATHEDRAL
C. 1167

"The story begins on ground level, with footsteps."

—MICHEL DE CERTEAU

THE VIEW FROM THE TOP of Canterbury Cathedral is absolutely breathtaking. Looking out from Bell Harry Tower, the view
extends to the horizon in every direction, with the English Channel to the south and London to the west. From the top of the
235-foot tall bell tower, even the enormous nave of the cathedral seems small. Further down below the nave lies the town of
Canterbury, founded by the Romans nearly two thousand years
ago. The Roman walls still mark the circumference of the city center, encompassing a street plan that largely dates from the Middle
Ages. There is layer upon layer of ancient, medieval, and modern
history in Canterbury, and at the center of it all, just as it has been
for more than fourteen hundred years, is the cathedral. After soak-
ing in the view from the tower, I headed down inside the cathedral, entering through the western portal, moving slowly eastward
through the nave, the transept—where the two axes of the cathedral intersect, the choir—where wooden stalls serve as seating for
worship leaders, the high altar, and finally to the Trinity Chapel.
The cathedral interior is jaw-droppingly beautiful. The vaulted
ceilings seem to rise all the way up to heaven as light pours into
the space through the tall stained glass windows. Every surface is

covered with highly detailed artwork, which all together proclaim the glory of God and reflect the beauty of heaven. It nearly overwhelms the senses and the soul. After taking in this celestial experience, I exited the cathedral and meandered through the streets surrounding the cathedral precincts checking out the local shops and cafés, marveling at how the modern rhythms of life pulse through this medieval town.

Like other pilgrims in this digital age who can't make a physical journey to the storied religious site, I took this excursion through Canterbury online—from my laptop, sitting at my dining room table—taking a virtual tour on the cathedral's website[1] and checking out the city on Google Street View. It is a far different pilgrimage than that of Chaucer's pilgrims to Canterbury: the knight, the miller, the cook, the pardoner, the wife of Bath, and the parson, of *The Canterbury Tales* fame, traveling to venerate the shine of the murdered archbishop, Thomas Becket. Nonetheless, the advanced technologies used to create the virtual tour make the cathedral accessible for digital pilgrims like me. There's another important difference: Chaucer imagined the *fictional* characters of the *Tales* in Canterbury. My pilgrimage was neither fictional nor, in the sense of grounded, embodied experience on High Street, exactly entirely "real" in any conventional pre-digital sense. It's not quite the same as being there with travelling companions, hearing choral music echo through the great building, but the high resolution and three-hundred-sixty-degree views of the cathedral provide some sense of immersion and the ability to linger over the fine details of the cathedral's art and architecture.

Canterbury Cathedral is one of the greatest and most beloved cathedrals in all the Church. It is the mother church of the Church of England and the Anglican Communion. And, subtly to remind you of that, Canterbury Cathedral's Twitter handle is @No1Cathedral. When I learned that, I tweeted "Love that Canterbury Cathedral's Twitter handle is @No1Cathedral #werenumberone . . . ,"[2] which the cathedral favorited, and to which the dean of Durham Cathedral, Michael Sadgrove, replied

"But NB[3] this cathedral has six times as many Twitter followers. It's not a competition. @durhamcathedral"[4] Not a competition at all! Here, at the outset of this project and in the spirit of my digital pilgrimage, I was able to cross three thousand miles with a single tweet and connect with both Canterbury and Durham Cathedrals, which became, then, an occasion for them to engage in some playful digital ribbing.

This brief exchange had the effect of making this book project and cathedrals themselves much more personal for me. These were no longer distant, historic buildings and institutions to be studied, but real places and real people to be understood and engaged. It engendered in me a genuine affection, which sustained and informed my work. Months later, as I was finalizing my manuscript, I had the occasion to correspond with the staff of the Canterbury Cathedral archive. They were incredibly helpful and gracious. And so, nearly six months to the day after that first exchange, I tweeted back to Canterbury once again, this time expressing my gratitude: "Cool book writing moment: corresponding with the very helpful @No1Cathedral archives today for research on @thedigcathedral."[5] Our relationship, like this project, had come full circle.

PLEASE PARDON OUR APPEARANCE DURING CONSTRUCTION

Exploring these sorts of digital relationships draws on the ethos of cathedral life that goes back at least to the early Middle Ages. Although the origins of Canterbury Cathedral can be traced as far back as 597 CE, we will look particularly at the era from the eleventh century through the end of the twelfth century. It was a defining time for Canterbury. In 1067 the Anglo-Saxon iteration of the cathedral was burned and completely destroyed by Vikings; it would take a decade to rebuild it under the direction of Archbishop Lanfranc. When he arrived in Canterbury from France in 1070, "Lanfranc found a community in a ruined church holding their services by the tomb of St. Dunstan, huddled under the eleventh century equivalent of a tarpaulin."[6] The new Romanesque-style cathedral was completed seven years later, and a series of building improvements immediately ensued under the direction of Prior Conrad and Prior Wilbur.

Prior Wilbur is not one of the great legendary figures in the history of Canterbury like Lanfranc or Thomas Becket, but he made enduring and important contributions to the cathedral and its history. One of those contributions is a drawing of the system that supplied the cathedral precincts with water. Known as the Waterworks Drawing from the *Eadwine Psalter*, it dates from around 1167, the last year Prior Wilbur was Abbot of Christ Church, and illustrates how water was piped in from a spring outside the city walls to the water tower that still stands on the northeast side of the cathedral to be distributed throughout the precincts.

The color-coded plan, using green for fresh water, orange-red for used water, and red for sewage, shows how the water flowed into the cathedral precincts first to the water tower and from there to the infirmary, then to the great cloister, where monks could wash before services, on to the *lavatorium*, and then out to the kitchen, bakery, and brewery, before being deposited into the fishpond. From there it was carried back to flush away the waste at the *necessarium* (the monastic latrines) and finally emptied into a city ditch.[7] Looking at the drawing today, the lines indicating the location of pipes seem more like lines of fiber optic cable networking the buildings to one another. Indeed, the Waterworks plan shows just how interconnected the cathedral was to its precincts—the buildings immediately surrounding it—those who worshipped and worked there, and the town of Canterbury itself.

The Waterworks may not have been remarkable in its engineering compared to other monasteries. However, "what is exceptional is the quality of the cartography by which they are recorded. Decorative and apparently accurate, it constitutes most of the evidence for the disposition and architecture of the

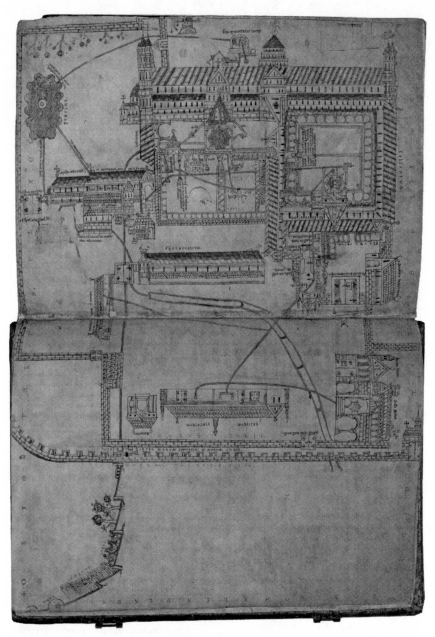

The Waterworks Drawing from the Edwine Psalter, c. 1167. *Courtesy: Trinity College Library, Cambridge, UK*

cathedral and monastic buildings in the mid-twelfth century."[8] It is so accurate that "if we were to cut around each building, the drawing would become a pop-up model for the monastery."[9] But it's notable for more than just its accuracy. Maps—especially, as French philosopher Michel de Certeau notes, medieval maps—are not just static documents, but communicate movement, an active story. He writes, "What the map cuts up, the story cuts across."[10] The Waterworks Drawing opens up for us a larger story of life and people in Canterbury.

Take, for instance, the story of Ingenulph the plumber, who worked for the monastery during this time and probably helped to maintain the Waterworks. He made twenty-five shillings a year as the staff plumber, a trade he inherited from his father, Norman. He lived near Burgate with his wife Eldrith, herself a brewer (a common job for women at the time). She supplied the monastery with beer for eight pounds a year, four times her husband's annual salary.

Or, meet Feramin the master physician, who tended to sick monks in the infirmary, also served by the Waterworks. He was among the wealthiest citizens of Canterbury, one of only about thirty residents who could afford to live in a stone house. He is reported to have had two religious visions of St. Thomas Becket—one in the cathedral crypt, which he saw filled with young queens weeping for Thomas' approaching death, the other near the former bell tower as the monks made their procession at Pentecost riding through the precincts of Canterbury, again foretelling Thomas' future glory. Later, he would found the hospital of St. Jacob for leprous women near the part of town called Wincheap.

Then there is the story of Godefrid, who worked in the bakery indicated on the Waterworks, along with his co-workers Roger and Walter. He lived on Orange Street not far from the Christ Church Gate, and tended a couple of acres outside the city walls. He was married with three sons. His family was also touched by the cult of St. Thomas. It is said that his sons were cured by the touch of a rag that had been dipped in Thomas Becket's blood when he died. In fact, "one of the early Miracles of St. Thomas is the recall to life of the dying child of Godefrid the baker, by virtue of the holy blood, while the saint saved two other children in this somewhat sickly family."[11] Godefrid was also the notorious ring-leader of a revolt by the monastery servants against the cathedral monks in 1188.

These snapshots of the real and complex lives of average people in Canterbury are not the ones typically found in official histories of Canterbury or other cathedrals. These stories are compiled from medieval rental records of the priory of Christ Church dating from the late twelfth and early thirteenth centuries. Canterbury was administered by Christ Church Benedictine monastery until the mid-sixteenth century, when King Henry VIII dissolved the monasteries during the English Reformation. The monks were responsible for the construction and care of the cathedral, as well as the administration of the cathedral properties.

It is estimated that the monks of Canterbury Cathedral were the lords over between one-third and one-half of all the domestic property in Canterbury, collecting rents and recording payments—and they kept all their receipts. Thus, many of the three thousand or so residents lived as tenants of the cathedral.[12] The stories of Inguelph, Feramin, Godefrid, and their families begin to open up for us the life of this thriving town of three thousand souls, which,

> By 1234 had at least two hundred shops, ranging from "holes in the wall" to more substantial edifices, of which over a hundred owed rent to Christ Church. There was a full range of markets—cattle, butter, fish, timber, oats, salt, and perhaps wine—some of which have left traces in the present day topography (Wincheap, Oaten Hill, Salt Hill) and the various trades and professions necessary to service the monastic communities within and without the city walls as well as the citizens: butchers, bakers, brewers, mercers . . . saddlers, wool merchants, weavers, plumbers, masons, glaziers, and carpenters.[13]

Along with the cathedral and Christ Church monastery, there were two other monasteries, a convent, twenty-two parishes with eighty priests, and even a synagogue spread throughout the city. There were potters, masons, millers, bakers, spinners and weavers, mercers (cloth traders), metalworkers, tanners, butchers, shop-keepers, the poor, goldsmiths, and government officials. Although marriages and baptisms and much of the worship life in Canterbury were celebrated in local parishes, as we have seen, many of these people were connected to the monastery and cathedral through rental obligations. Many others were also connected by their work constructing or servicing the cathedral building, commercial dealings, family ties to particular monks, or religious and spiritual devotion. Throughout the cathedral's history, it and the town have had a symbiotic relationship. Today, the city's identity and self-understanding continue to be shaped by the cathedral.

It's almost impossible for us today, cloistered and separated as we are in our private homes and widely distributed workplaces, to imagine the expansive and profoundly interconnected nature of life in a cathedral town such as Canterbury (or, of course, Durham). Here, people lived life fully "in cathedral"—in relationship to one another within an expansive, everyday understanding of "church." The phrase "in cathedral," coined by Elizabeth Drescher, is a play on the term *ex cathedra*, literally "from the chair" of the bishop installed in the diocesan church—that is, speaking from his official station. By contrast, "in cathedral" speaks to the often overlooked spirituality of everyday life in Christian community in distinction from the formal spirituality of the institutional church. As we begin to see all of life as "in cathedral," we move from the historical equivalent of the virtual tour on the cathedral website, standing high atop the cathedral bell tower, looking at the surrounding town from a distance, to something more akin to Google Street View, taking in the everyday life that surrounds and shapes the cathedral.

This all became embodied for me as I was sitting at a table in the sidewalk patio of the Hungarian Pastry Shop, a small café, at Amsterdam and 111th Street in New York City. I had stopped

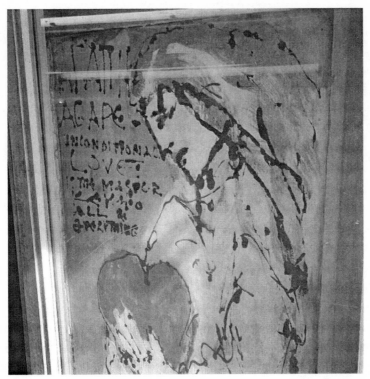

Mural at the Hungarian Pastry Shop, Morningside Heights, Manhattan. *Photo: Keith Anderson*

at the café for a quick bite before a day of exploring the Cathedral of St. John the Divine, the seat of the Episcopal Diocese of New York and the third largest church in the world. As I enjoyed my coffee—and an utterly life-changing cheese Danish—while gazing across the street at the massive cathedral, I watched the neighborhood of Morningside Heights on the Upper West Side of Manhattan spring to life. Delivery trucks and tour buses had already begun stopping outside the cathedral. So had the traffic cops who were keeping tabs on them. Dog walkers were on their beat, as were young parents outfitted with chest-mounted baby carriers. A fruit and vegetable stand was set up just across the street to entice visitors and locals. Early morning cathedral visitors were flowing back and forth to the pastry shop, taking in both spiritual and physical nourishment. The cathedral and pastry shop offered something of both. In fact, the first religious artwork I saw that day was not at the cathedral, but the pastry shop itself, as paintings of angels and the mystical covered the exterior of the shop.

This would be my first visit to St. John the Divine and I planned to spend the entire day absorbing life "in cathedral" here. I took two tours and attended the daily noontime Eucharist, but, mindful of Wilbur's Waterworks, I was equally interested in exploring the surrounding neighborhood. Like Canterbury and its cathedral, St. John and the neighborhood of Morningside Heights grew up together, the development of both dating from the late nineteenth century. For some time the neighborhood was referred to as Cathedral Heights. Still today, West 110th Street, and the subway stop along it, is known as Cathedral Parkway.

Just outside the doors of the cathedral—its modern-day precincts—are Mt. Sinai St. Luke's hospital and emergency room, the Engine 47 fire company, a convalescent home, and an assortment of apartment buildings, restaurants, and cafés. In the surrounding blocks, students from nearby Columbia University hustled off to class. Homeless people with shopping carts stuffed with bags sat at the entrance to Morningside Park. During my tour of the neighborhood, I would walk past a small neighborhood street fair, a farmers' market, and softball games in the park—people and places that all fell "in cathedral."

The stories I heard on my tours inside the cathedral—stories of its history, art, and architecture—continually pointed outside the cathedral to the city. There were stories of local artists and work they had done not just in the cathedral but also throughout the city, such as the famed Guastavino tiles that also adorn the Oyster Bar at Grand Central Station, public bath houses, and subway stations. With my companions on the cathedral tour, I learned that the crypt below the nave of the great cathedral was home to, of all things, a basketball court where children from the cathedral school played and where meals for the homeless were served. We heard how in the 1970s and 1980s young adults from the neighborhood were trained in cathedral construction and helped to build the cathedral for a time. **What I learned from our tour guides at St. John the Divine was that the story of a cathedral, any cathedral, cannot properly be told without telling the story of the neighborhood and city that surrounds it.**

WHERE'S GODEFRID?
OUR ECCLESIASTICAL BLIND SPOT

Cathedral historian Robert Barron acknowledges that in the study of cathedrals there is often too much focus on the building itself, and too little about the life and people around it. He says, "Too often, while recounting the histories of individual cathedrals and great churches, scholarly works mention in passing only the scantest details about the larger social, political, religious, and cultural contexts out of which the impetus to build each one grew."[14] Often we hear the stories of kings, priors, archbishops, master builders, or deans, but miss the stories of people who lived and worked in the shadow of the cathedral. We can fall prey to that same impulse when it comes to the way we think about our churches today. Our church buildings or activities can be so much in the foreground of our work and consciousness that we don't see the people and stories just outside our doors. Like the villagers of medieval Canterbury, who have been largely obscured from view by the distance of history, our neighbors today can be hidden by our limited perspective and narrow understanding of what constitutes "church."

I'm convinced that one of the major challenges for today's church leaders is a matter of perspective. For ministry leaders, the church, whether by that we mean the building or the institution, is often at the center of our time and focus. People in parish ministry spend most of our time there, along with much of our emotional, spiritual, and intellectual energy. This is a good and noble thing. However, we can become so focused on the interworking of our congregations that we miss what is going on down the block and across our communities. We miss the Inguelphs,

Eldriths, Feramins, and Godefrids—the Hungarian Pastry Shops—just beyond our doors. This myopia is especially dangerous in a time of institutional decline. Debates and worry over the fate of church institutions, while acknowledging the mortality of the institution, which seems a good and healthy thing, paradoxically reinforce the focus on the institution itself rather than pushing us to look beyond its boundaries. Even as the number of people present in our congregations dwindle, our fixation on the institution grows. We spend more and more time worrying over the internal operations of our institutions, even as fewer and fewer people attend and belong. Thus, we inhabit and concern ourselves with an ever-shrinking piece of cultural and spiritual real estate.

Moreover, we often operate with a totalizing view with the church at the center and everything else running out into the horizon. The church is so in the foreground of our experience that everything is interpreted in relationship to the church. We see Sunday morning sports as a threat rather than an opportunity to connect with people's daily lives. We tell a story about Nones turning their backs on the church, rather than appreciating the way in which they make meaning and practice their spirituality. We conceive of our faith communities too narrowly, not taking into account the broad expanse of community in lived Christian experience beyond our buildings. We curse the problems with church as institution, but, because we are so stuck in that frame, we propose institutional solutions, when the problem is institutionalism itself. For many leaders, this has created a kind of ecclesiastical blind spot, what Cynthia Baker has called an "anopticon"—a perspective that renders people and places invisible to our gaze.[15]

The Digital Cathedral is an invitation to shift this perspective. It is an invitation to see all of life as "in cathedral" and claim a much broader understanding of who belongs to our community, and where church and faith happen. The work begins by placing ourselves outside of our church buildings or ministry offices, both digitally or physically. When we do, as The Rev. Emily Mellott, national coordinator of Ashes to Go—a collection of congregations offering ashes outside their church buildings on Ash Wednesday—says, we are "practicing thinking differently" about place, the architecture of community and participation, as life more broadly "in cathedral."

WALKING THE CITY

In his masterful essay, "Walking the City," Michel de Certeau argues that if we only look at a city from a great height or distance, writing as he did in the late twentieth century from the World Trade Center in Manhattan, or the distance of history, a city remains a concept, a "read-only" computer file that can be viewed but not interacted with by the user. To understand the city, he writes, one must enter into the midst of it, walking the streets, taking in the sights, sounds, and smells, and absorbing its nuances and contradictions. Only then, he says, can we experience the complexity, creativity, and heart of the city—and, for that matter, the cathedral. He writes, "The ordinary practitioners of the city live 'down below,' below the thresholds at which visibility begins. They walk—an elementary form of this experience of the city; they are walkers . . . whose bodies follow the thicks and thins of an urban 'text' they write without being able to read it."[16] To understand the city, indeed, to create the city itself, one must walk the city and engage with others in "practices that invent spaces," just as I did that day in Morningside Heights.[17] To fully engage in our world today, we too must be willing to leave the safety and protection of our church buildings, our pulpits, our offices, and walk the streets, visit local and digital gathering places, in order to connect with those beyond our buildings, and to see what God is up to in the world.

HUMANS OF NEW YORK

If Certeau were alive today, I imagine he would have enjoyed the Tumblr blog called Humans of New York. Begun by Brandon Stanton in 2010, Humans of New York (HONY) is a collection of pictures, quotes, and short stories that offer "daily glimpses into the lives of strangers in New York City."[18] HONY has more than twelve million followers on social media and has spawned a series of best-selling books. Every day Stanton walks New York City streets taking pictures of strangers. He says, "It became more about picking a random person off the street no matter where they happen to be and celebrating them on a stage every night." With a photo and accompanying short text, he captures the humanity of the city that is missed from a distance. He says, "One of my favorite compliments is, 'Man, you take photographs of things people walk by every single day and don't notice and somehow you photograph them and make them beautiful.'"[19] It is a simple yet profound idea: tell the stories of people who often remain invisible. In the process, Stanton captures the beautiful and sometimes heartbreaking complexities of life, as in a picture of a man standing on the subway platform with the caption, "She got pregnant with another man, then asked me to be the godfather."[20] A single person's story can be deeper and higher than skyscrapers that surround him, and just as sacred as a great cathedral and its precincts. Storytellers like Stanton are leveraging new digital technologies to reconnect us to our neighborhoods and to each other. Perhaps it should be no surprise that Humans of New York has become such a phenomenon and captured the imagination of millions of readers and followers on social media. That is the invitation of the Digital Cathedral: to put ourselves in places to encounter others, to appreciate the depths of the everyday, and to name it holy.

IN CATHEDRAL

This larger understanding of both church and cathedral is essential for life and leadership in the Digital Cathedral. Rather than standing at the church door looking out, we need to be present in the places people work, live, and play, to enter into the sanctity of everyday life and understand the ways people make meaning there. We cannot define our culture, our community, or individuals from the literal or figurative perspective of the institutional church. We must put ourselves in the places where life happens, and recognize all of life as being "in cathedral." In the next chapter we will see how ministry leaders are embracing that perspective and how, through their ministries, they are making their neighborhoods their cathedrals.

2

MAKE YOUR NEiGHBORHOOD YOUR CATHEDRAL

"In a time of significant change, we cannot assume we will find religion in the predictable places or in the predictable forms."

—NANCY AMMERMAN

"Those who believe that in Christ God has brought life out of death, hope out of sorrow, and love out of cruelty are now called to see the world, the everyday and ordinary, with new eyes, the eyes of faith—and to live lives of hope and love directed to the neighbor in need. To be sure, this view undermines many of the safe distinctions that we have come to rely upon—particularly the distinction between the sacred and the secular; but it seeks to replace those dichotomous categories with integral notions like incarnation and sacrament. In so doing this view seeks to relocate the sacred not beyond but within our everyday experience."

—RONALD THIEMANN

LAST SUMMER, I TRADED THE GRANDEUR of the gothic cathedral for simpler, homespun worship in a public park in St. Paul, Minnesota. It was part of a pilgrimage I made to Humble Walk Lutheran Church, a new mission start congregation of the Evangelical Lutheran Church in America (ELCA).[1] I first learned about Humble Walk during my research for *Click2Save: The Digital Ministry Bible.* Humble Walk was using digital social media to extend and share their ministry in interesting ways, and so I interviewed the pastor, Jodi Houge, who gave one of the most memorable quotes of the entire book. She said,

> We recognized that most people don't come looking for a church, in our demographic. And so, we thought from the beginning, "We know this. The church is sinking." The facts are on the table for mainline denominations. So, we're not going to do these big glossy things that try and draw people to our cool, fancy, hip church. We're going to be where people already are and try to be the church where they are.[2]

For Humble Walk that means being deeply embedded in their local neighborhood, the West End of St. Paul. They have decided not to have a church building of their own. Instead, they meet in local gathering spaces in the West End. They hold Theology Pub nights, storytelling events, and Beer and Hymns gatherings at a local pub called The Shamrock. They host Bible studies at Claddagh Coffee House. On Sundays they worship in the common room of a local Jewish retirement community, and during the month of July they move worship outside to a local park.

That's where I caught up with them. We gathered on a beautiful Sunday afternoon in a local green space called Highland Park. Unlike the elegant noontime Eucharist at St. John the Divine, everything here was unadorned and ordinary. All of the supplies for the service were unloaded from the back of an old Volkswagen bus. People helped to unpack and set up, then took their places at picnic tables, on lawn chairs and picnic blankets. Things kicked off with a brief word of welcome from one of the lay leaders. We read the Gospel appointed for the day in the lectionary. In place of a sermon, we broke into groups to discuss it. There was a handout with some serious and fun promptings to get us talking. My favorite was about Matthew 7:7, "Ask, and it will be given you; search, and you will find; knock, and the door will be opened for you": "seek = find. knock = answer. ask = give. for realz?" After some conversation and prayers, communion was served on a small folding table with a handmade mosaic on top. There were

Summer altar at Humble Walk Lutheran Church, St. Paul, Minnesota. *Photo: Keith Anderson*

plastic IKEA cups—the kind my kids use at home—for wine and grape juice, and an old plate that looked like it had come from my grandmother's kitchen that held the bread. The service concluded with a Humble Walk tradition called "milestones," where people are invited to share significant moments that happened over the last week and place a small stone in a jar. Somehow the stones didn't make it into the van, so we placed sticks in the jar instead—milesticks, if you will. After worship we had a cookout of hot dogs with all the fixins. Then everything went back into the van.

Later that week, I went to the Shamrock Pub for dinner with friends so I could see where Humble Walk's popular Theology Pub, storytelling events, and Beer and Hymns take place. And there, while eating a Paul Molitor burger (which, by the way, I highly recommend),[3] I noted that, unlike some of the pilgrimages to great churches I had made before—to St. Peter's in Rome, St. Mark's in Venice, and Notre-Dame in Paris—to make pilgrimage to Humble Walk I had to visit multiple distinct locations. **I realized that, without a building, experiencing Humble Walk was, indeed, a walk. Embedded in the life of the West End, the people of the church had literally made their entire neighborhood their cathedral.** West Seventh Street, the main road in this part of town, is their nave. The side streets are the ambulatories. And the shrines, well, the shrines are everywhere—in parks and bus stops, coffee shops and pubs, churches and community gathering spaces, homes and apartments. They see the entire neighborhood as sacred space, holy ground. One of my favorite Humble Walk ministries is called *Operation Caffination*. On Friday mornings from 7:00–8:30, they hand out free coffee and donuts at the bus stop at the corner of West 7th Street and Randolph Avenue. On their website they explain, "Humble Walk doesn't have a church basement. This presents a problem when trying to have the standard Lutheran coffee hour. We decided to bring it outside." Here, the bus stop is sacred space, and, if you ascribe to the Lutheran joke that coffee hour is the third sacrament, you might even say it's sacramental.

These are not episodic forays into the neighborhood, or trendy ways of doing ministry. They reflect a deeply held understanding of sacred space with strong roots throughout the Christian tradition. As Belden Lane writes, "Religion isn't always a matter of otherworldly transcendence. It continually sets up camp in the ordinary."[4] Humble Walk's ministry practices are ways of naming the places where people already gather in the West End as holy. As Houge suggests in the quote above, this is not how most ministers in mainline churches are accustomed to thinking about how and where church happens. We certainly affirm that God is everywhere. We say that people are ministers in their daily lives. Yet in practice, we often limit our understanding of sacred space to our church buildings, and then we narrow it down further to specific scheduled times for worship and study. Humble Walk's distributed ministry presence and practice is a reminder that sacred space is everywhere, if we can remember to see and treat it that way.

SACRALIZING SPACE

In her book, *Sacred Power, Sacred Space,* Jeanne Halgren Kilde makes a helpful distinction between two approaches to sacred space, which she calls the "substantive" and the "situational." The substantive approach associates sacred space with designated religious spaces, like a church or a cathedral. They are religiously sanctioned centers for worship, prayer, religious study and formation, and community. They were built and exist for a particular purpose and are the sites for continual religious practice over many years. These places are deemed sacred and holy because a divine power is understood to dwell within them. This is where the vast majority of ministry leaders spend their time, and safe to say, feel most comfortable.

However, as Kilde points out, the setting aside of some particular spaces as sacred has some unintended consequences. It can imply that while one particular space may be sacred, others are not, or not to the same extent. Moreover, the substantive approach does not necessarily hold an appeal to those who are not already practicing believers. In contrast, the "situational" approach is more constructivist, expansive, and flexible in nature. In this approach, reflected in Humble Walk's ministry, sacred space isn't limited to a particular location, which has been designated by religious authorities or congregations, but can arise anywhere as needed. It is not dependent on religious imprimatur. Instead, Kilde writes,

> "How people organize themselves and behave within specific places imbue those places with sacred importance. . . . space is sacralized by human action and behavior, and certain spaces become sacred because people treat them differently

from ordinary spaces. . . . places are sacred because they are made so by human beings. . . . sacredness is situational. . . . Groups of believers create holy places by investing certain places or spaces with religious meanings and then acting upon those meanings."[5]

The ways in which Humble Walk sings hymns or studies the Bible at the Shamrock is a way, to use Kilde's terminology, of sacralizing that space. It is a way of constructing sacred space—not with the architecture of buildings, but with the structure of belonging and practice. It happens beyond our church buildings in local gathering spaces, when people pause to pray before a meal, give and receive love, serve their neighbors; when they find themselves at the intersection of life and faith.

People are, in fact, sacralizing space all the time. It doesn't just happen in fixed locations or times or because certain religious professionals show up. When ministry leaders and believers enter into these spaces, we are not somehow making them holy. Rather, we are acknowledging that these spaces are already sacred. It is an acknowledgement that life, faith, Sabbath, meaning-making, community, and religious practice are already happening. Sara Miles writes beautifully about this as she finds sacred amid the seemingly profane, locating Augustine's "City of God" within and among the "City of Man" in her hometown of San Francisco. She writes,

It's not just inside church buildings that you can find God: in the holy city, God is the temple and dwells among his people. The people cross themselves before lunch in a break room or a school, process down the street carrying pictures of the Virgin Mary, pray in the parks, light candles on their stoops to honor the dead, gather with crosses to sing hymns and protest immigration laws. Plenty of poor people in San Francisco like the homeless guys who build shrines in their encampment under the bridge, converse freely and intimately with God in public. And so do some rich, ostensibly modern people: they hold Bible study in the conference room of a downtown investment bank or send prayers via Twitter to their co-workers at a tech company. The city might be far less religious than most if measured by the number of people who attend churches, but in its streets it's the city of God.[6]

This is a situational approach to sacred space, in which sacred space is constructed by the way individuals treat a particular place or moment. Crossing one's self, reading Scripture, tweeting prayers are small yet meaningful ways of recognizing or encountering the holy in our midst.

WELCOME TO THE DIGITAL NEIGHBORHOOD

As Miles suggests, the discovery of God in daily life happens not only in local gathering spaces, but digital ones, like Twitter, Facebook, or Pinterest, as well. Indeed, any talk about our daily, lived experience now includes the internet and social media, which have become an integral part of our daily lives. Today 87 percent of Americans adults use the internet, 71 percent of those say they use it daily, with 68 percent of American adults connecting to the internet through mobile devices.[7] Seventy-one percent of online adults now use social networking sites of some kind and nearly all of them, 71 percent, (fully 56 percent of the U.S. adult population) are Facebook users. Fifty-two percent of online adults use multiple social networking sites, with 28 percent of online adults on LinkedIn, 28 percent on Pinterest, 26 percent on Instagram, and 23 percent on Twitter.[8] Furthermore, studies show that these social media play an important role in people's faith. Some 20 percent of online adults share their faith via social media and fully 46 percent of people have seen someone else share their faith.[9]

Social media are frequently dismissed by many as painfully mundane, but digital platforms can become the surprising locations for sacred space. Tim Snyder, a doctoral candidate at Boston University, has studied how social media are used in response to tragic events; he followed the social media response to the shootings at Sandy Hook Elementary School in Newtown, Connecticut in December 2012. Snyder describes how in the wake of this tragedy people turned to social media for comfort, compassion, and prayer. On Twitter, people used hashtags like #nowords to describe their speechlessness at what had happened. They posted pictures of candles or homespun tributes memorializing the victims. They interacted with complete strangers, offering words of hope and consolation. Snyder describes these as "improvised religious practices," which, to go back to Kilde's thinking, create "situational sacred space." Like the shrines that frequently pop up at the scene of a deadly car accident—where people place stuffed animals, candles, pictures, flowers, or whatever is at hand to memorialize that place—these social media locales become global digital makeshift shrines, where care, consolation, and compassion are expressed and shared. Snyder identifies these practices as a new phenomenon in the religious landscape. He writes, "These folk practices point to the durability of contemporary faith and suggest our shifting world may require new ways of understanding religious belief and commitment."[10] These practices are both improvised and provisional. The social media locations—hashtags, Facebook pages, Pinterest sites—remain sacred space insofar and for as long as the participants need it. As Snyder notes, #nowords had an altogether different meaning before the tragedy; it has, to some extent, reverted back since the shooting. Snyder writes of his study of religion in social media landscape,

> Our findings suggest that religious practices and faith may not be declining, but they are shifting in surprising and exciting ways. . . . When religious leaders and people of faith turn to social media to express their commitments to creative offerings of prayer, solidarity in the face of suffering, and love in the midst of violence, they demonstrate a positive use of religion in the American public square.[11]

In these times, social media function very much like a cathedral that, in response to a significant tragedy, may throw open their doors to mourners or host an ecumenical or interfaith service of remembrance. Cathedrals are natural places to hold such remembrances as they are often able to transcend religious affiliation, accommodate large numbers of people, and generally have the resources to offer excellent music and liturgy. Furthermore, cathedrals are places where many people, regardless of their religious identity, feel welcome to pray and to grieve. Today social media can provide a similar kind of space to express our grief and console one another in times of tragedy.

#SNEAKERSFORSARAH

We experience this in a more personal and immediate way when someone in our social network makes an announcement about a life change, whether a recent medical diagnosis, illness, death of a loved one, change in relationships status, or job loss. Immediately, comment threads on Facebook become places of prayer, blessing, and mutual consolation. Hashtags on Twitter become more than just handy ways to compile tweets; they become communities of compassion.

One of our good friends, Sarah, was recently diagnosed with advanced stomach cancer. It was a devastating diagnosis for Sarah, her family, and for our community of friends. In the face of such overwhelming news, it is hard to know what to do. Yet, a few of our friends hatched an idea that made the best of the sacredness new media practices can convey.

Back when Sarah was a teenager, she visited the hospital (for something unrelated) and was nervous. She happened to wear a pair of plaid Chuck Taylor All Stars shoes, also known as Chucks, which drew comments from all her doctors and nurses. It put her at ease, and since then she has associated Chucks with good, kind medical care. So, now every Tuesday when she goes to the hospital for her cancer treatment, she wears her Chucks. And every Tuesday our community of friends post pictures of themselves on social media wearing Chucks. So when Sarah checks Facebook, she knows that she is loved, supported, and held in prayer. My favorite picture is one of our mutual friends with Chucks on her hands, holding them together in a posture of prayer. Our friend and fellow pastor Jeff Stalley speaks for many of us when he writes, "I'm wearing Converse to let Sarah know that I'm thinking and praying for her when she is getting chemotherapy. And others are wearing Converse to let her know that, too. I'm not going to change the world. I'm not going to cure cancer.

Praying with Chuck Taylors for #sneakersforsarah.
Photo courtesy Janet Johnson and Stina Maksimowicz

But, hopefully, I'm going to help change Sarah's world."[12]

This example of "improvised religious practice," an ad hoc form of spiritual care, is highly visual, very public, and yet very personal. Every Tuesday my Facebook feed lights up with pictures of Chucks. Sometimes it drives me to tears. Often it drives me to prayer. Always it is holy ground.

JESUS HAS LEFT THE BUILDING (AND HE'S TAKING THE TRAIN)

It took some effort to remember I was in a sacred space as I stood outside in the freezing cold at the Ambler commuter rail station the morning of Ash Wednesday. I was participating in a growing practice called "Ashes to Go,"[13] in which congregations offer the

Imposition of Ashes—the historic Ash Wednesday ritual of making the sign of the cross in ashes on people's foreheads—at local transportation centers.

Begun in 2009 by a small ecumenical clergy group in the Tower Grove neighborhood of St. Louis, Ashes to Go has become increasingly popular with congregations, particularly within the Episcopal Church, in the last several years, with over three hundred congregations participating in at least thirty-five states, as well as Canada, Spain, and the United Kingdom. Emily Mellott is the national coordinator for Ashes to Go and rector of Calvary Episcopal Church in Lombard, Illinois. She began offering Ashes to Go in 2010, after asking why the 7:00 a.m. Ash Wednesday service at her church consistently drew only a handful of people. She asked, "Where are people at 7:00 in the morning because clearly they're not coming to this?" It turns out they were one block away waiting to catch the train to work at the commuter rail station.

Ashes to Go is a very public way of making your neighborhood your cathedral. When I joined members of the Upper Dublin community to distribute ashes on that cold morning in Ambler, we were outfitted in church vestments, displayed a sign indicating the opportunity to receive ashes, and had some literature about Lent and our congregation—no doubt an unusual sight on the morning commute. Some people just kept their heads down and kept walking in a "If I don't look at you, you can't see me either" sort of way. Some people came right over and received ashes. Even for those who chose not to receive, we were able to wish them a good morning and demonstrate being church in a different way, and that gesture seemed hugely important. One of our most memorable encounters came at the end of our time at the train station. We had just packed up our sign, ashes, and brochures and were heading back to our cars, when two women called out to us from the sidewalk near the train platform. "Wait!" they said, "We want ashes too!" They ran out across the parking lot to meet us. We put down our sign and brochures and gave them the imposition of ashes, saying "Remember that you are dust and to dust you shall return." They looked at each other and smiled. They seemed relieved to have caught up to us and blessed to receive the ashes. Just after that, a couple pulled up next to us in a car and asked for ashes. They put the car in park and we imposed the ashes on them while they were still in their seats.

Mellott points out that one of the reasons Ashes to Go works so well is that Ash Wednesday is a day when the church is already very public about its practice:

> It is this perfect thing: the liturgy is there; the symbol is there. It's a symbol that maybe gains more power outside the church because Ash Wednesday is one of the few times that Christians are visibly identified. We don't wear anything on our heads that expresses our faith. Our clothing is typically what everybody else is wearing. Ash Wednesday is one of the few times when you can tell practicing Christians by looking.

She continues:

> Theology pub, Ashes To Go, they're a gateway drug, it's just they're more healthier for you than some of the other things. . . . Trying on Ashes to Go really is practicing thinking differently about church and evangelism and that encounter with the world. It's practicing thinking differently. . . . Ashes to Go is a great leading edge, I think, because people hear about it, it sounds exciting, it sounds like it's easy enough to do, and then once you do it, you start to have to explain what you do and talk about it, and you begin to think about different ways to encounter people and be church.

Ministry leaders find themselves in a new religious landscape, one where the mainline church has lost the central and privileged place it once held in American culture and the number of religiously unaffiliated individuals continues to grow. We cannot simply wait for people to show up in our church buildings. Nor can we remain trapped in a narrow understanding of "substantive" sacred space. Rather, like Humble Walk, we must recognize, name, and engage the "situational" sacred spaces that are continually constructed beyond our buildings. Mellott puts it succinctly: "The question is, 'If people are not coming to the church, how does the church come to the people?' That's a fundamental question of Ashes to Go, the fundamental question of coffee shop office hours and the theology pub."

As we move into these local and digital gathering spaces, and help to construct, name, or participate in situational sacred spaces, we will begin to "relocate the sacred . . . within our everyday experience."[14] The best way I have found to do that is to relocate myself physically, moving from the church office to neighborhood locations and social media platforms. In the act of inhabiting a different space with a particular intention to be present, available, and prayerful, I am able to rediscover the sacred in everyday and unexpected places, and help others do the same. My own experience echoes what Sarah Miles writes in her own experience of Ashes to Go,

> The sheer unpredictability of the city encounters makes it possible to presume, as many churches do, that God's grace is sequential—measured out at regular intervals in baptism, confirmation, communion, marriage, burial—and will happen to everyone at the prescribed time, in the same way. In a city, grace just falls all over the place.[15]

This is an exciting, challenging, and perhaps frightening prospect for ministry leaders. In this environment, some approaches to ministry leadership are more helpful than others. In the coming chapters, I will describe a networked, relational, and incarnational model for ministry leadership that can help leaders meet the challenges and opportunities of this new time.

SHiFTiNG FROM NEWTON TO NETWORKS

"Life uses networks; we still rely on boxes. But even as we draw our boxes, people are ignoring them and organizing as life does, through networks of relationships. . . . To become effective at change, we must leave behind the imaginary organization we design and learn to work with the real organization, which will always be a dense network of interdependent relationships."

—MARGARET WHEATLEY

"Understanding how networks work is one of the key survival skills of the twenty-first century."

—HAROLD RHEINGOLD

LIFE IN THE BIKE LANE

On most days, you can find Laura Everett in the bike lane, riding her bike around her beloved Boston—across Jamaica Plain, up Beacon Hill, on her way to a church, mosque, synagogue, or perhaps the bike shop. Everett is a passionate city biker, urban homesteader, and the executive director of the Massachusetts Council of Churches. At the worship service where she was installed as the new director, among the items presented to her for use in her ministry were a bike helmet and an iPhone. Everett uses both these tools, her bike, and access to social media to build networks of understanding and collaboration across denominational and interfaith lines throughout Massachusetts, crisscrossing her city, the state, and the internet, for the sake of the unity of the Body of Christ. In the process, she is making her city, her state, and Twitter her cathedral. Echoing Certeau's description of walking the city, she reflects on biking her city,

> The parts of the city I formerly whizzed through on the T [the name for Boston's subway] were now visible to me, because the speed of a bike asks you to pay closer attention to what's around you. . . . I fell in love with Boston as a city once I really understood the geography and the people and the history and how it all connected.[1]

And not for nothing, her bike has a cool license plate that says "CLERGY" next to the seal of the United Church of Christ, the denomination in which she is ordained.

Everett's mission is to make visible the unity that exists among Christians of the seventeen member church bodies in the state. As she shared in *Click2Save*, the Council's understanding of that mission and the strategies it uses to carry it out have shifted in response to our new digitally integrated environment.[2] Everett still cultivates and builds ties among traditional denominational partners. She meets with cardinals, metropolitans, bishops, and their staffs. At the same time, with the help of digital social media, she has been able to create new networks among individual ministry leaders in Massachusetts and across the country. Additionally, she participates in other networks, including urban bicyclists, local crafters and foodies with her adventurous forays into cross-stitching, canning, and cooking.

Everett's position, by its nature, requires her to be a networked leader, but in a time of institutional changes and with the explosion of digital social media, that means something different today than it did a few short decades ago. Everett and the Mass Council have responded by cultivating multiple layers of networks, not just the historic relationships between synod and diocesan offices, but with pastors, priests, parishioners, and non-church-goers alike. Many of these networks converge on her

Twitter feed. As she says, "If you follow me for biking, you're also going to get a lot of Jesus." On Fridays you might find her at Hub Bicycle, a small bicycle repair shop across the river in Cambridge, which hosts #cannolifriday, a social gathering, with cannoli biked over from Boston's North End. In a sign of how interwoven her church and bicycling identities are, she told me, "Because most of the people there interacted with me on Twitter first, they usually call me by my Twitter handle." It's an ironic twist that thanks to her Twitter handle (@reveverett), her biking community calls her Rev. Everett, whereas the people at the Massachusetts Council of Churches just call her Laura.

This effective networked leadership was highlighted in *The Boston Globe*, but not where you might expect—not in the religion section, but rather in the DIY (do-it-yourself) Boston blog, in a post entitled, "Crafting to Build Community with Pastor, Lobbyist, and Bike-Community Yogi Reverend Laura Everett,"[3] which described her work in networking churches, urban bikers, and crafters as all part of a whole. In fact, the article itself came about because of social media. Everett had posted a picture of her needlepoint of the Boston subway system on Instagram and then Twitter, where it came to the attention of a *Globe* writer. The article described Everett's pursuits of yoga, urban biking, and church work as a holistic form of community building. It also featured several of the Instagram pictures, which had inspired the piece. Some months later I asked Everett how she felt about the article. She reflected,

> It's about church and bicycles and urban homesteading and intentional living and curiosity about the people and the city around me, in ways that feel really accurate. . . . But there's still a little bit of reticence about it because while we say that's what we want out of our church leaders, we don't have a ton of models for that.

Everett herself is such a model—and an exemplary one at that— but it took no small amount of courage for Everett or the Mass

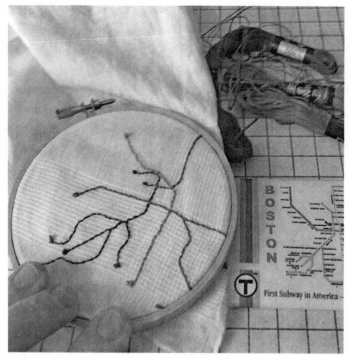

Cross-stitch of the Boston subway map by Laura Everett. *Photo courtesy: Laura Everett*

Council to agree to be profiled in this way. Often, ministry leaders, particularly those with greater levels of authority in church institutions, cultivate a very staid public persona that conveys that *the Lord's work is official business.* While that may be, that kind of affect feels inaccessible to many—and out of step in the less formal, more personal culture social media has helped to create. This contrast in approaches, Everett says, could not have been more clear to her than when, just following the article's publication, she was back in the bike lane in Boston when another prominent church leader passed her by—riding in the back seat of a large black SUV.

Everett exemplifies leadership that is networked, relational, and incarnational—three key characteristics of ministry in a digital age. We will explore each of these qualities in this section of the book.

FROM NEWTON TO NETWORKS

Many church leaders face challenges similar to Everett's in their own ministry context. They are responsible for the well-being and vitality of traditional institutional expressions of the church, which, often for reasons beyond their control, are faltering. Suddenly, many of the strategies used for decades no longer seem to work and they find themselves "mired in the habit of solutions that once worked yet now are totally inappropriate."[4] In a refreshingly honest interview with the Episcopal Story Project, the Rev. LeeAnne Watkins, rector at St. Mary's in St. Paul, Minnesota, shares how her congregation recently cancelled all its adult education and midweek services because people were simply not coming. She says, "We cancelled it all and I feel like a failure as a priest, but on the other hand it feels like the right thing to do because it logically just doesn't make sense. I think the world is changing."[5] Instead, she says, people are excited about participating in short-term service projects that the members themselves coordinate. Even as a traditional format for faith formation is waning, something new—a new kind of networked and experiential formation—is emerging in its place.

While Watkins and her congregation have embraced this shift, though certainly not without struggle, many ministry leaders lament and resist the ways the church seems to be changing. What appear as new opportunities to some seem to symbolize the entropy of church institutions to others. However, in recent years, commentators from Margaret Wheatley to Rob Bell have tried to reframe this shift using the language of quantum physics, suggesting that this new evolving networked reality reflects how the world and our churches are actually supposed to work.[6]

They point out that for centuries we have operated under a Newtonian understanding of the world, named after Sir Isaac Newton, the great physicist and mathematician of the seventeenth and eighteenth centuries. Newton postulated that the universe is like a grand machine. Therefore, the way to understand the world is to break everything down into its constituent parts. Once you have separated and classified those parts, you can understand the whole. In this framework, church organizations are viewed as the assemblage of interlocking parts, which church leaders, who function as ecclesiastical mechanics, maintain by replacing or repairing parts—be they people or programs—when needed, keeping everything in good working order. An unfortunate consequence of this approach is that church leaders often feel that letting one part or program die has implications not only for that one area, but also for the whole. It assumes that without that particular part the congregation itself will not be able function. Therefore, to some, a change like Watkins describes feels like the canary in the coalmine, the beginning of the end, a harbinger of the death of the church.

However, in recent years quantum physics has disproven this longstanding Newtonian view of the world. In quantum physics the world is understood not as a machine but as a network of complex relationships. Today scientists study the universe by observing the relationships between particles and how they react when they encounter one another. These particles can behave in a variety of different ways depending on proximity and conditions. These are not immutable parts, but elements that change depending on their environment. Nicholas Knisely, bishop of the Episcopal Diocese of Rhode Island and himself a trained quantum physicist, explains, "Quantum physics is spontaneous, its local, small effects dominate and not in ways you can easily understand. Your job is to be resilient, not be to controlling." In a quantum world, ministry leaders must be keen observers of their environment, tend to the relationships that comprise it, and be responsive when changes happen.

One way to visualize this shift from Newtonian to quantum, or, as Wheatley describes it, from boxes and networks, is to compare these two diagrams. The first diagram is an example of a very typical, if simplified, congregational organizational chart, with Jesus, the church council (or vestry), and clergy at the top and all the various ministries underneath. Immediately we can see how

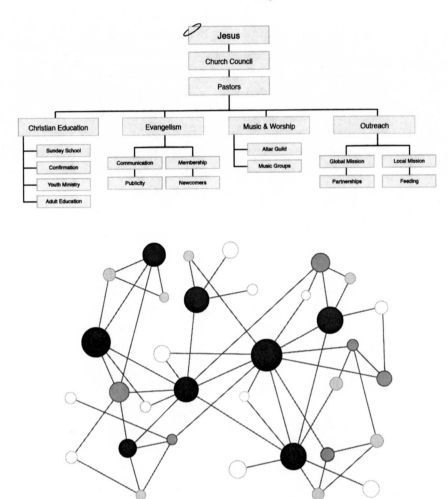

Simplified congregational organizational chart and network map illustrate two ways of understanding the same congregation

our institutional self-understanding is based on separating out the parts, with expectations of predictability, and the assumption that relationships and communication will flow in certain hierarchical, linear ways. It suggests a self-contained system. Below that is another way of picturing the same congregation as a network, with intersecting connections—what Wheatley calls a "dense network of interdependent relationships."[7] What we see here is a mapping of the dynamic relationships present in the congregation.

Each line represents a relationship between people. Those linked to the most lines denoted by the larger, darker circles are highly connected individuals. If we had more room, this network map would extend further, with congregational members connecting out into their personal networks, families, friends, neighbors, and colleagues. These diagrams are two ways of looking at the same congregations—but from very different perspectives.

These two lenses lead to two very different views about the health and vitality of the congregation. The Newtonian view breaks down the congregation into its constituent parts, gauging success by how many and which committees and groups there are, and how official lines of communication and authority are functioning. The other view, informed by the networked perspective, is about mapping the new and deepening, unexpected and surprising connections taking place between people and groups within the congregation. Although an institution may appear to be failing from a Newtonian perspective, it may be healthy and thriving using a quantum frame. These two perspectives often lead to ministry leaders feeling as though they are leading two different congregations, one in which the traditional programs are failing even as more networked activities take off. At the same time they are managing the Newtonian congregational machine, they are also nurturing the quantum relationships that allow new connections, ideas, and opportunities for ministry to emerge. They have come to recognize, as Dwight Friesen writes, "The size of a church is not that important within this networked paradigm; what's more important is its connectivity."[8]

And yet, the Newtonian view of the world, church, life, and faith is persistent and often reinforced by our traditions and even our church buildings. This is the floor plan of a church built in the late 1960s, the heyday of modernism and mainline growth. It is undeniably Newtonian. Each part of the building is separated out according to its function. There are two front doors across from one another: one for the sanctuary, and one for the offices. Each function of the building is compartmentalized from the others in

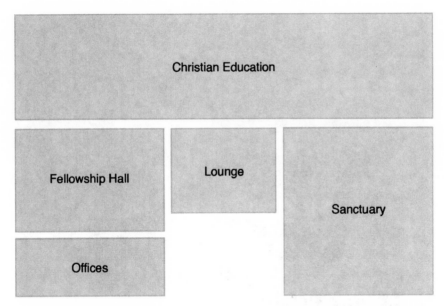

Church floor plans often reflect the ways we separate our common life into Newtonian categories or boxes.

very distinct spaces with heavy oak doors, sending a message that these are separate and distinct parts of the congregation and its life of faith. Worship is separate from administration, which is separate from Christian education, which is separate from fellowship. Is it any wonder we so easily fall prey to these Newtonian dichotomies and divisions when the very space in which we conduct our ministry is so shaped by these assumptions? Over time we have come to see our faith, community, and the Gospel itself through this Newtonian lens.

Taking this one step further, consider the way that we often categorize people. The following diagram is an example of how we sometimes classify the individuals associated with our congregations. We define them first, in relation to the church, then proximity to membership, and then levels of participation. They move from box to box, beginning as visitor until they reach the pinnacle of highly involved, highly giving members. But what about the people (including an ever-increasing group of religiously

visitors

repeat visitors

prospective members

new members

members

active members

The variety of categories we apply to people associated with our faith communities

unaffiliated) who do not fit in those boxes? They fall into our ecclesiastical blind spot. They don't exist until they become potential parts, or members, of the congregational machine.

We must conceive our organizations, our lives, and the world differently, shifting our focus from what or who is contained in each box, to the spaces in between those boxes, and to the connections and relationships that transcend and transgress the boundaries we draw. One of the most important challenges a networked world poses to ministry leaders, as LeeAnne Watkins and her congregation discovered, is that life and faith do not happen in predictable places, times, or relationships, or in ways that we might expect or wish. Instead, people have multiple levels of belonging and participation across a range of networks. We may define people in relation to the church, but that is not necessarily how they define themselves. As we will see, individuals increasingly define themselves by the networks they create and participate in using digital social media, be they religious, spiritual, political, social, or all of the above. If we want to speak and lead in ways that are culturally resonate, we must engage and relate, as life does, in networks—and at the outset of the twenty-first century, that means digital social media as well.

THESE ARE YOUR NETWORKS. THESE ARE YOUR NETWORKS ON THE INTERNET.

Although the digital networks like Facebook and Twitter are relatively new, networks themselves are not. They have always existed, whether we recognized or could name them as such. Everyone belongs to a network of some kind and usually to many at the same time: family, friends, classmates, professional colleagues, fellow weekend warriors, hobbyists, and more. I often joke that the most networked groups in the congregation I've served are not the youth group, but the altar guild, the group responsible for setting up for worship each Sunday. Not only are they tuned to the pulse of congregational life through worship and the rhythm of the liturgical year, they are connected and in conversation and relationship with many people throughout the congregation, and thus function as a hyper-connected networked nerve center within the congregation. If you want to know what's really happening in church, ask the altar guild.

If networks are at the heart of life, and perhaps even church, then today they find their great expression in digital social media, which reflect and amplify this networked reality. Digital social media make visible the networks of which we are a part. As we click around on Facebook, we can see our mutual friends and discover new connections. We can click from node to node of the network, seeing how broadly but also how closely interconnected we are. Being present and active in social media helps us to better understand and effectively engage with our networked world.

Lee Rainie and Barry Wellman have written that we are living through a "triple revolution"—the internet revolution, social media revolution, and mobile revolution.[9] In just the last twenty-five years with the birth of the world wide web, people have gained access to the world of information; with the rise of social media, they now have platforms to create, publish, share, and to publicly engage and shape that information with others; and with the ubiquity of mobile devices, they have it all in their pockets on cell phones. It is a dramatic change that has happened in an exceedingly short period of time. Understandably, many people feel disrupted and disoriented. Despite the discomfort this may cause and the challenge it may pose for ministry leaders and faith communities, it is essential that we engage these changes, as the combination of these three technologies has vital consequences for the practice of ministry and the future of our faith communities.

NETWORKED INDIVIDUALISM

One of Rainie and Wellman's central findings is that people are shifting away from groups and institutions in favor of networks. The combination of the internet, mobile devices, and digital social networks has formed a new emerging infrastructure for relationships and community that previously only localized groups and organizations, like churches, could provide. In the not very distant past, if you wanted to talk about faith, you went down the street to your local church building. Of course, many still do. However, now people can also find information, connect directly to others regardless of location, and build networks all on their own. People are no longer reliant on hierarchical institutions to supply either the physical location or the organizational structure to enable relationships, community, coordinated social action, or even religious practice to happen. Thus, there is less need or inclination to leverage existing seemingly antiquated institutions when people can create or participate in preexisting or newly constructed networks. Rainie and Wellman write, "Each person has become a communication and information switchboard connecting persons, networks, and institutions. At the same time, each person has become a portal to the rest of the world, providing bridges for their friends to other social circles."[10] This is "in contrast to the longstanding operating system formed around large hierarchical bureaucracies and small, densely knit groups such as households, communities, and workgroups."[11]

The recent Pew Research study *Millennials in Adulthood: Detached from Institutions, Networked with Friends* shows this trend accelerating among younger generations. Pew reports that Millennials, the generation between the ages of eighteen and thirty-four—the one most woefully underrepresented in most of our congregations—are not only less engaged with institutional religion, but many of the institutions that have shaped our civic life, including political parties and marriage. The authors write, "Adults of all ages have become less attached to political and religious institutions in the past decade, but Millennials are at the leading edge of this social phenomenon." At the same time, the report finds that Millennials have "taken the lead in seizing on the new platforms of the digital era—the internet, mobile technology, social media—to construct personalized networks of friends, colleagues, and affinity groups."[12] Rather than joining membership-based groups, they are turning to networks to meet their needs for news and information, as well as support and consolation. If we want to meet the needs of our current congregations and to continue to share the Gospel with younger generations, we must understand networks and the new technologies that fuel them.

In this networked reality, ministry happens in ways that are related to the variety of networks in which people participate. Rather than sitting atop the institutional flow chart, clergy must become meaningful nodes in the network. *Authority*, in this new social reality, is earned based on how you participate within the network and how you attend to the relationships therein. It's true that Millennials and others still value more traditional forms of authority associated with expertise and even position. But these are no longer certain, unquestioned markers of authoritative status. People still do defer to me a little when I'm in my clericals, but that often comes down to social politeness, rather than a real sense of attentiveness to what I say in particular, "just because" I am the pastor. This is leadership, "from somewhere off to the side . . . leaders lead from where they stand without the trappings of hierarchy and privilege, indeed any sort of authority at all. Instead, it's a type of lateral leadership."[13]

In my own Lutheran tradition, the authority of the pastor is understood as tied to the particular role played within the congregation—my "office," the office of Word and Sacrament: preaching, teaching, and administering the sacraments. It's a vital but narrow area of authority when you consider everything that happens in a church. Outside of that, my authority really lies in the relationships with people in my congregation, being present over time, at life's milestones, from birth to death and everything in between. You know you've become someone's pastor, not because you are allowed to preach from the pulpit, or preside at the Table, but when you are called (or texted, messaged, or tweeted) when they are in need. In large part, the same holds true for life online. We must be meaningfully present and consistently active in those networks in order to gain trust. In this way we demonstrate *authenticity*, that all-important descriptor of leadership in the digital age, which comes from knowing one's place in the network, trust earned through participation rather than automatically conferred by a title, and consistency and coherency of self-presentation across networks over time.

FROM GROUPS TO NETWORKS

Not only are people moving away from institutions, they are also less likely to be formal members of a group. This insight was popularized in Robert Putnam's book, *Bowling Alone*, in which he used bowling leagues to highlight a larger societal trend: although more Americans were bowling than ever before, fewer and fewer were bowling in leagues. They were less likely to organize themselves into formal, membership-based groups with sustained relationships. The challenge here is that we have tended to organize congregational life around groups (another box), with the idealized group, for many, being a weekly small group that meets over many years. We associate such groups with strong bonds of attachment, belonging, and intimacy—and by contrast, can view digitally mediated relationships as less substantial, durable, or real. (And yet it should be noted that even within long-term face-to-face groups, intimacy can be found lacking. While institutional groups use time spent as a proxy for intimacy, it can often be an illusion.) As Watkins found at St. Mary's, people are moving away from these kind of groups and toward more loosely connected networks. Rainie and Wellman contrast groups and networks in this way:

> A group is densely knit (most members know each other) and tightly bounded (there aren't many connections to people who don't know everyone else), whereas a network is sparsely knit (most members do not know most other members) and loosely bounded (plenty of those small-world-making distant connections to people outside the core).[14]

Although we have long favored groups in congregational life, networks are a valid and increasingly common way of connecting with others, living out faith, and engaging in ideas and experiences of consequence. These more loosely connected networks may be more *ad hoc*, but they are no less real for those who participate.

We experienced this in our family when my son Finn, then seven years old, broke his leg in a freak accident. When he was on the way to the hospital and we still did not yet know if his leg was indeed broken or the extent of the break, I asked for prayers on Facebook. Prayer flooded in from across my networks of friends and colleagues. As we updated his status through diagnosis, surgery, and recovery, that extended network was a source of strength and support. But we also relied on the tight-knit relationships and groups in my congregation when people brought us meals, took our kids for playdates, and sat with Finn as we tended to work and family. Both the networks and the established groups played an important role in Finn's recovery and that of his worried parents. While our digital network couldn't bring meals to our house, as church folk are wont to do in times of need, their emotional and spiritual support was just as important to us. We were especially touched by well wishes and words of encouragement from people we only knew online. We benefited from both groups and networks as Finn—and we—recovered and healed.

MY IPHONE IS A PLACE

Another important change is the shift from places to people. Just a few years ago, in order to contact someone you could make a call from one landline phone to another or, at the outset of the internet, send an email from a desktop computer in one's home or workplace. You had to be in a *particular physical place* to be reached. Now, with 90 percent of Americans walking around with cell phones and 58 percent with smartphones, we are close to fully mobile and can be reached almost anywhere.[15] A physical location is no longer required; contact can be immediate via call, text, email, messaging apps, or social media. Raine and Wellman write, "Mobile connections can become 'places.' In some circumstances, people can become more defined by their mobile phone numbers and internet aliases than by where they physically live and work."[16] It is becoming increasingly common that we find ourselves connected to people through social media, giving little thought to where they physically live, because we can always reach them in the same place online, and vice versa. In short, now my iPhone is a place. My cell phone number, email address, Facebook profile, and Twitter account are the digital places where I am always present, or at least accessible.

This creates new freedoms for ministry leaders. Since we no longer need to sit in a church office for someone to reach us by landline phone or desktop computer, we can be more present in local gathering spaces. Many clergy now hold "coffee shop office hours," encouraging people to drop by the local Starbucks or (better) independent java joint. Sometimes people do and sometimes they don't, so it's wise to bring a book or laptop just in case. In any case—whether you're chatting with congregants, meeting new neighbors, or working on your sermon—"the pastor is IN." The Digital Cathedral in your neighborhood is open for ministry.

As we are more available in digital gathering spaces, we are more able to be present in local gathering spaces. As we will see later in chapter five, the more digitally networked and accessible we are, the more incarnational our ministry can be.

A NETWORKED ECCLESIOLOGY

Like the networks through which people increasingly live their lives, the Digital Cathedral is distributed and situational, local and digital, non-geographic; it is networked, relational, and expansive, whether it be Canterbury, the West End of St. Paul, the streets of Boston, train stations, pubs, coffeehouses, neighborhoods, farming fields, or the internet. Whether visualized through the images of Prior Wilbur's Waterworks or experienced in the rhythm of life in a neighborhood like Morningside Heights, cathedrals themselves are extensive networks that reach beyond the stone and stained glass of the building itself. Cathedrals often have a more networked ecclesiology than local parishes, which are more likely to be collections of homogenous groups, maintained through high levels of volunteer engagement. "Cathedrals allow for a far looser connection," consciously tending a wide range of constituents from bishops, to tourists, and fostering ecclesiastical, artistic, and secular partnerships, which span the nation and in some cases, the globe.[17] Cathedrals also create openings for the increasing number of individuals in American culture who might never engage with the church otherwise. The historic mission of cathedrals lends itself to life in a networked digital age, and can exist in some measure alongside or within the parish model through social media, local gatherings, and engagement in networks beyond our congregations. Thanks to the triple revolution of the internet, social media, and mobile devices, the world is now our parish.

The Bishop of Norwich Cathedral, James Graham, illustrates this networked nature of cathedrals by describing a day in the life of his cathedral.

> Children playing in the cloisters; mothers chatting to each other; a couple eating sandwiches; visitors pushing prams; vergers rearranging chairs; people lighting candles, kneeling quietly; others simply gazing into space; one or two engaged in animated discussion with a guide; others curious about what was taking place in the nave; still others walking past the event [a service for a nearby university] down the side aisle seemingly oblivious to it. . . . *They did not make a community in themselves, but the cathedral was large enough to include them without asking them any questions or seeking from them any justification for being there. . . . Spaciousness in a cathedral does have a liberating quality in our present age. What was once regarded as likely to be forbidding is now a vehicle for "letting be."*[18]

What Graham describes happening in the cathedral, which is no doubt mirrored in the precincts and neighborhoods surrounding it, is exactly what I see on my Facebook news feed and Twitter stream: parents posting about the joys and challenges of family life, people sharing the latest news and ideas, pictures of meals, stolen moments of beauty and delight—almost but not quite in parallel to one another as people engage with each other in that space. In the quieter confines of a cathedral, it may be a nod, a smile, and pleasantries with staff, volunteers, and fellow pilgrims. Here in this cathedral space—and in digital social networks—there is a range of people gathered for a variety of purposes, who find connections in the shared experience of being in that space together. Just as the people in the tour groups I joined at St. John the Divine, we had come from different places, for different reasons, and were inspired by different things, we were nonetheless held together in the cathedral environment. Likewise, the Digital

Cathedral is broad enough to encompass not only a variety of places, but also a variety of people. There may be little expectation they will become members or join a group, but there is a sense that we all belong, that they and we can "let be."

This represents a shift from the way we have commonly thought about religious practice, identity, and belonging. Many of our assumptions and practices are reflected in Emile Durkheim's classic definition of religion as a form of social cohesion, ". . . a unified system of beliefs and practices relative to sacred things . . . beliefs and practices which unite into one single moral community called a Church by all those who adhere to them." Today, amidst the growing population of Nones, and Rainie and Wellman's networked individualism where "many Americans have moved to a flexible and individualized way of engaging with religion,"[19] we find our unity less in a specific belief, practice, or moral conviction—though it is debatable how much we ever did—and more in the networks themselves. It has always been the case that what people profess is often very different from what they practice (for instance, contraception in the Roman Catholic Church). What's different now is that people are more comfortable professing that they don't believe in a particular doctrine (for instance, the Virgin birth). Ultimately, as the British sociologist of religion, Abby Day, has demonstrated in her research, it is the *relationships* to which we belong that play a formative role in the expression, practice, and performance of belief. Of her longitudinal study of youth and belief, she writes that when a change in belief occurred for her subjects, "it was always mediated by changes in social relationships."[20] Further, she observes, "I did not find that young people were drifting through an a-moral universe or were unable to cope with life's challenges in the absence of grand meta-narratives. . . . They were informed and sustained by the social relationships and contexts where they felt they belonged."[21] These relationships are at the heart of our digital and face-to-face social networks, which themselves are valid expressions of faith and community—the kind of unity that Laura

Everett seeks—engaged networks and communities of people with diverse beliefs and practices.

Today, we can no longer assume a single system of belief or single community. Instead, we increasingly find belonging and spiritual meaning in the networks to which we belong and in which we participate. We are, as Heidi Campbell has said, "one in the network."[22]

THE NETWORKED MINISTRY LEADER

Today's ministry leaders must be networked leaders. We must be bilingual, speaking both the language of groups and the language of networks, and able to help our faith communities engage networks within and beyond our doors in both local and digital gathering spaces. People of faith have an important role to play in these networks. We should be a graceful presence in our attentiveness, kindness, and encouragement of others, offering prayer, celebrating milestones, and sharing the love of God in so many words or clicks.

As we do this, we must monitor and contribute to the health of the networks, those deeply intertwined webs of relationships, within our faith communities while actively engaging with networks beyond our churches. We should seek out local networks in which to participate according to our particular gifts and passions. For Laura Everett, it is biking and crafting; for others it may be music, volunteering, gardening, or a host of other interests. As nodes in each of these networks, we are connection points, networked switchboards, between those inside and those beyond the walls of our particular faith community.

PRACTiCiNG RELATiONAL MiNiSTRY

"The great digital continent does not only involve technology, but is made up of real men and women who bring with them what they carry inside, their hopes, their suffering, their concerns, their pursuit of truth, beauty, and good. We need to show and bring Christ to others, . . . we need to pass through the clouds of indifference without losing our way; we need to descend into the darkest night without being overcome and disorientated; we need to listen to the illusions of many, without being seduced; we need to share their disappointments, without becoming despondent; to sympathize with those whose lives are falling apart, without losing our own strength and identity. This is the walk. This is the challenge."

—POPE FRANCIS

"In the quantum world, relationship is the key determiner of everything."

—MARGARET WHEATLEY

IT WAS THE SELFIE HEARD 'ROUND THE WORLD—or at least 'round the Church. In August 2013, Pope Francis held a private audience in St. Peter's Basilica for approximately five hundred teenagers who had travelled to Rome from the Diocese of Piacenza and Bobbio, about fifty miles south of Milan. During the visit, a few of the teenagers asked the Pope to take a selfie with them (a selfie is picture you take of yourself or with others and then post on social media).[1] Pope Francis agreed and posed with three of

Pope Francis takes a selfie with youth from the Diocese of Piacenza and Bobbio, August 2013.

the teenagers; they then posted the photo on Instagram and Twitter. The image immediately went viral, being shared and re-shared millions of times across social media and traditional news outlets. This papal selfie garnered worldwide attention for several reasons. It shows Francis connecting with youth against the backdrop of the centuries-old basilica, symbolizing the continuity between the ancient and modern worlds. He is engaged with digital media and twenty-first-century culture—to his credit, it seems he knew what a selfie was. Or, perhaps he just embraced the invitation to connect with these youth. Importantly, it was not an official photo taken by a staff photographer. It was a grainy picture taken on one of the teenagers' own smartphones. Altogether it portrays the pope as approachable, friendly, and relatable.

Beyond the charm of the photo itself, this selfie has become symbolic of Francis' refreshingly relational leadership. Indeed,

Pope Francis is well suited to the digital age, not just because he tweets more than his predecessor or because he has a more sophisticated communications plan. Rather, his is the kind of personal leadership stance that lends itself to a social media world. His words and actions are simple and straightforward—especially his concern and advocacy for the poor—and are consistent across local and digital platforms, demonstrating authenticity. He has a deep humility, eschewing the trappings of his office like the red Prada papal shoes—and taking selfies with teenagers (and even more since[2]) and not just more formal photos with the rich and powerful. And crucially, he prioritizes remaining in relationship with others despite holding different theological commitments, famously saying, "Who am I to judge?" when asked about LGBTQ persons, inviting non-believers to join in a prayer for peace, and performing marriages for couples who have lived together or had children outside of wedlock.

In these and many other ways, Francis marks a profound shift from his predecessor, Pope Benedict XVI, a shift that goes beyond personal style or charisma. Contrast Francis' selfie with the scene of Benedict XVI sending out the first papal tweet, sitting at a large desk, typing on the papal iPad, surrounded by cardinals and courtiers, captured by a staff photographer. Hey, that wasn't bad for an eighty-five-year-old Pontiff. But it reveals something of Benedict's approach to social media, which resembled more broadcast media than social media, more one-to-many communication, rather than a many-to-many conversation—tweets as one-hundred-and-forty-character pronouncements from the pope, rather than a platform for relationality.[3] Pope Francis expresses through his words, actions, and, yes, selfies, a desire to be in relationship, to be connected.

As Francis demonstrates, clergy can no longer just hold audience from high above in a balcony—or the pulpit, or the church office. They must also be present and engaged in the digital places where people of all ages and traditions gather by the billions. As he wrote in his message for World Communications Day in 2014,

"Effective Christian witness is not about bombarding people with religious messages, but about our willingness to be available to others."[4] Pope Francis embodies the kind of ministry leadership that is resonant with today's world, not because he is a social media guru, but because of the quality of his networked, relational, and incarnational ministry. The seventy-seven-year-old pope shows that it isn't a requirement to be a so-called digital native[5] or an expert on every social media platform in order to be effective in ministry today. The quality and consistency of our presence and our willingness to engage broadly with others speaks volumes. In this chapter, we will explore this relational quality of ministry as it is practiced across local and digital gathering spaces.

Admittedly, the term "relational" may at first seem like an obvious quality for ministry leaders. After all, ministry is focused on relationships in pastoral care, faith formation, evangelism, outreach, and service. We relate to people, groups, and networks continually. And yet, the kind of relationality that we will consider in this chapter is more exceptional than we might first think. After all, if it were so common, Pope Francis may not seem like such a huge breath of fresh air in the global religious landscape. If anything, reflection on what it means to be "relational" should cause us to honestly examine our leadership practices and our assumptions about how we engage others within and beyond our congregations.

THE RELATIONAL MINISTRY LEADER

One of the powerful effects of digital social media is that they have changed people's expectations of their leaders and the institutions. People expect their public leaders, whether in government, business, non-profit, or religion, to be personally present and accessible in these digital spaces. Ministry leaders are most effective when they are authentic and tell a compelling story.

It is, in part, why Benedict seems so tone deaf and Francis is so celebrated. While Benedict led with the trappings, prestige, and authority of his office, Francis leads through being in relationship with those in and beyond the church. What is perhaps most striking of all is his simple humanity.

This contrast reflects the way in which communication technologies have, over time, shaped the role of ministry leaders and what makes for effective leadership. In his book *The Relational Pastor*, Andrew Root traces the relationship between technology and ministry leadership over time. He writes that in the hunter-gatherer period, where communication was primarily oral, spiritual leadership focused on cosmic storytelling—explaining the why, how, and what of life, "interpreting new phenomenon (wildlife, early winter, war) within the cosmic stories of the past."[6] As agriculture took root and writing emerged as a new means of communication, spiritual leaders became the authorized reader and interpreter of sacred texts, and the managers of sacred objects. During the industrial revolution, in the period of steam and coal power and mass printing, religion became associated with the nation-state, as a way of protecting a way of life that was moral and upstanding. In this period, ministry leaders served as moral exemplars and ideal citizens. The oil era, which was accompanied by the rise of radio and television, introduced increased competition among congregations. Since people were no longer limited to churches within walking distance, they could now drive to a church that better met their needs. In response, ministry leaders became visionary programmers. In this period, the period from which we are just emerging, "the ideal pastor became a creative, energy-bursting visionary that individuals could identify with and therefore would want to come to that church, bringing more and more individuals into participation with the offered programming."[7] As we enter into another shift toward alternative energies like wind and solar, and a new communications technology featuring the internet and social media, we must move toward another mode of leadership: relational ministry, which is focused on relationship with others and Christ. Relational ministry leads with and prioritizes staying connected over time. It is within the context of that relationship that meaning-making, theological and biblical reflection, sharing the Gospel, and love take root.

Of course, there are vestiges of these earlier elements in the pastoral role and ministry leadership writ large. We continue to function as cosmic storytellers, serving as repositories of the stories and histories of our faith communities. We are handlers of divine elements—sacraments and sacred texts. We are expected to be moral exemplars and to manage excellent programs and cast a compelling vision. Those all remain part of the work of ministry, and depending on the ministry context and the leader's personal giftedness, one may be more pronounced or desired than others. The current shift—and it is a dramatic shift—is from visionary programmer to relational leader. In the second half of the twentieth century, seminarians—myself included—and church leaders were told that we must cast a large vision for the congregation, for, as they say, "without vision the people perish" (derives from Proverbs 29:18) and to generate programming to support that vision. The ministry leader was out in front, envisioning a plan for the future for the congregation to follow. This understanding of the role of ministry leaders is persistent today. It is often one of the first questions asked of potential pastoral candidates. When I interviewed for my first call, the first question the Church Council asked was, "What is your vision for us?" More than one bishop I interviewed for this book said it's often one of the first questions asked of them when they travel around their territories.

In the end, this visionary-programmatic approach is a consumerist and perhaps even cynical model of ministry, in which people become consumers of programs, objects to be won and converted not necessarily to Christ, but to church membership. It also puts congregations and clergy in competition with each other for the biggest vision, the best programs, and the most members. This mentality has only become heightened in a time when Mainline churches are losing membership and money, and so are desperate for more human and financial cogs to help sustain the Newtonian congregational machine.

The problem with this approach, as Root writes, is that we often treat relationships and people as means to an end, rather than an end in themselves. We use relationships as a means to influence people to choose our congregation, and we use membership as a means to solicit giving dollars. Churches tend to take a similar approach to social media. We "friend" or "follow" and encourage people to like our Facebook pages, not for the sake of relationship, but for the sake of membership. This is the opposite of how the social media economy works, where people, ideally, are open and generous, giving away inspiration, ideas, sharing their stories, expecting little in return. Social media is not a place for churches to broadcast and sell. It is a place to establish and nurture relationships. As Heidi Campbell writes, "The internet has become the campfire around which people gather to tell their stories, meet people, and form relationships."[8] Several years ago, Campbell conducted a study of several early online religious communities, all pre-dating digital social media and fueled by what now seems like primitive technology: email lists and dial-up modems. She found that what people longed for and found valuable in these online, digitally mediated communities were relational connections. She writes,

> People look for relationships, to be connected and committed to others. They desire care, to be cared for by their community. They desire value, to be seen as valuable as an individual and part of a community of value. They seek consistent communication with members of their community. They long for intimate communication, where individuals share openly about their beliefs and spiritual lives. Finally, they gather around a shared faith that influences how they see others online and how they understand the interconnection between online and offline aspects of life. This presents a picture of community based on communication,

> commonality, cooperation, commitment, and care. *It portrays community as more concerned about how individuals are treated than about the structure or focus of the community.*[9]

Email lists allowed individuals in these groups to connect directly, providing them a platform for engagement outside traditional structures for gathering together a community. In a networked environment, relationships are the currency of community. They are, as Wheatley writes, "the key determiner of everything."[10] However, for far too long, our church structures have been the focus of our attention and concern. In a digitally integrated, networked, and relational environment, our focus on structures needs to recede into the background, and relationships need to come to the fore. Amidst the constant bombardment of advertising, information overload, and, at times, stifling institutional structures, what people really seek is relationship.

In my own experience I have found this to be true. I was recently reunited with David Crowley, founder and president of Social Capital, Inc., whom we interviewed for *Click2Save*, and who, after the writing of that book, joined my congregation with his family. I asked David why they joined the congregation. He said there were a number of reasons, but the first time he contemplated the possibility was when he saw a picture I posted on Facebook of a beautiful copy of the Qur'an that one of our members had brought back from a trip to Iran. We displayed that Qur'an one Sunday in response to the threats of Qur'an burnings made by Terry Jones, pastor of Dove World Outreach Center in Gainesville, Florida on the tenth anniversary of the terrorist attacks of 9/11. David said, "We were impressed that a church would do that. We could see ourselves being part of a church like that." I had known David as a leader in our community and we had been Facebook friends for some time. We both lived in Woburn, were identified leaders in the community, and shared a passion for social media. I enjoyed being connected to David, but had never even suggested joining my church. What I did was tell the story of our ministry consistently over time through social media. The picture of the Qur'an became an inflection point, which shifted our relationship into a different dynamic.

This kind of relational ministry takes time. Because activity on social media is so instantaneous, we oftentimes think that we will see the fruits or gain members just that quickly. That's not necessarily so. Relationships, online or offline, take time to develop. It takes time for connections and trust to be established and relationships to deepen. We often go right for the hard sell, and when that doesn't work, we give up and move on to the next viable potential member. David and I had a number of face-to-face and digital encounters over the course of a few years before he and his family eventually joined the congregation.

However, there can be exceptions to the rule. Recently, I was helping to host an event for Nadia Bolz-Weber's *Pastrix* book tour. I was monitoring the Facebook event page to see how many people had RSVP'd, when I noticed that someone I didn't know named Margi had written a post saying that Nadia's book had rekindled in her a sense of calling to ministry. I appreciated her comment, so I simply liked it, not expecting any response. As Margi would later say, "I saw that this Keith Anderson person liked my comment and I looked into who he was. I looked at his Facebook profile and his blog and saw that he was a local Lutheran pastor." Soon after, I received a direct Facebook message from Margi with more detail about her faith journey. I messaged her back and sent her a friend request. It turns out she lived nearby. Later that same week, unannounced, she came to our bi-monthly Coffee and Conversation gathering at a local coffee shop. She and her three children wound up joining our church within a couple months.

For all their differences, these two stories are very similar. Both started by being present in digital spaces, in this case, Facebook. I was connected to David because we lived in the same town and shared similar interests. We connected episodically around issues of shared concern on Facebook and Twitter, and we both blogged. Sharing that picture of the Qur'an was one of the ways I used social media to provide a window into our ministry, as I tried to dispel stereotypes of all Christians as xenophobic. I connected with Margi because I wanted people to hear Nadia's story and hear Lutheran theology communicated through a fresh and important voice. I wasn't fishing for new members. I was trying to tell a different story about church, faith, and Lutheranism that Nadia captured so well in her book. I was listening, attending, connecting, and engaging, not recruiting or selling my congregation.[11] I was genuinely surprised and delighted when both David and Margi joined. Of course, not everyone we engage with online or in person will join our church. But that is not the ultimate goal. The goal is to be in relationship, and in relationship we have an opportunity to share the Gospel, finding ourselves in relationship together with God. As Andrew Root writes, "the heart of ministry is not giving people objects to possess (either in programs or even doctrines) but spaces to be encountered, places to become persons one-to-another, to confess their need and to be known, to dwell in and with one another."[12] Those spaces can be online just as easily as they can be in person.

IN CATHEDRAL FIELDS

Robin Denney has employed relational ministry as an agriculturalist and missionary in South Sudan and Liberia, and more recently as the lay pastoral leader for Trinity Episcopal Church, in Gonzales, California. Gonzales is located in the Salinas Valley, the produce capital of the world—what we might think of as the fields of the cathedral. Her experience in Gonzales is instructive. She told me, "The first thing I started doing was walking around town, frequenting local establishments, getting to know the streets, and praying as I walked." Over time, she built connections with local community members, listening for the needs of the community and learning how to respond to those needs, a list that ran the gamut from computer lab to ESL classes, fellowship, and worship. Her experience of hosting a booth at the local farmers' market is particularly helpful in demonstrating the shift from marketing to relational ministry:

> I went down and talked with the manager of the [farmers'] market and he was really friendly and he let me set up a booth for free for the church. So, I put up my Bible study banner. I was really excited. I was going to have conversations with people. But people would pass on the other side of the market to avoid my booth. And it was a really cool banner too. It was really youthful and had electric colors and kids would be attracted to it. And they'd walk up and all I had was flyers on my table. They'd look at the flyer as if to say, "Is there anything for me here?" And they didn't see anything, so they just walked away, and I was like, "What's going on here?" And so I told Jesus, our congregational development canon for the diocese, and he said why don't you put out a sign that says, "May I pray for you?" in English and Spanish. And I thought if they don't want Bible study they're not going to want me to pray over them in public. But I said, "Sure, I'll try that. I'll roll with anything." It was just a handwritten sign. I took down the Bible study banner, and people started coming over. It wasn't like a line of people, but they definitely stopped avoiding the booth. Then we started giving away coffee, so that started bringing people over. I was having conversations with people and found that naturally I became kind of the chaplain of the market. Because the vendors would come over when it was kind of chilly and take a cup of coffee and I didn't take any money for it, so they'd bring me produce. They'd come over and say could you pray for my son, "He's having back trouble." . . . Sometimes people would ask me to pray for something for them at a different time. Once this guy bought his son over and said, "Pray with this lady." Then I brought coloring sheets and crayons for the kids. So it was just a great way to have conversations with the community and

build validity for the ministry. I did make several connections there with people who were really interested. People loved to talk about, "What is the Episcopal Church, and how is it different from the Catholic Church. You have women priests? That's weird."

This story illustrates well the shift from programmatic to relational leadership. In an earlier era, advertising a new ministry program was typical and effective. It assumed that people were already inclined to go to church. The only question was which one—and it was probably the church with the better program and nicer sign. Years ago Denny's fancy new sign might have worked quite well. However, now in a digital age, relationship is paramount. In a time, or in communities, where church is not culturally normative, we need to do the work of relating to build trust, deconstruct negative preconceptions, and create the occasion from which deeper connection and participation in our faith communities can take place. Denny did this by simply offering to pray for others using her homemade sign. It was an invitation into relationship, connecting with people using the only traditional church category that still highly resonates with the Nones.[13] It was only when Denny made this shift that she became the "chaplain of the farmers' market."

Across the country, Kristopher Lindh-Payne, co-rector at Epiphany Episcopal Church in Timonium, Maryland, tells the story of how he headed off to a local Panera café and restaurant on Sunday morning, not to replenish the church's coffee supply but to pray for people. Sitting outside on a cold January morning, he had a homemade cardboard sign with a message written in black marker, "May I offer prayers for healing for you or someone you love?" The idea grew out of the parish's experience of Ashes to Go, Emily Mellott's "gateway drug." He writes,

On Sundays we offer two services with communion, and even with strong lay leadership and a cadre of clergy, we could wait a long time before all the pews in our building are filled up for both liturgies (images of flying pigs come to mind). In a time when more and more people make the choice to not participate in a regular rhythm of worship, prayer, and faith formation in community, maybe God is calling us to take our faith to the streets in thoughtful, care-filled ways.[14]

Offering such prayer, or ashes for that matter, is a relational gesture. It isn't marketing—though these can garner local press coverage, and it may lead to greater awareness of our ministry—as much as it is an offering of love and grace with no expectation of return. It is an expression of loving our neighbor and sharing the Gospel. The same invitation can be extended in social media. I occasionally write a Facebook post asking, "For what shall we pray today?" People, many of whom do not go to church, respond with prayer concerns for themselves, family, friends, or global issues. Often, they wind up praying for one another. Once it seems that everyone who wants to convert has, I offer a closing prayer.

However, that relational gesture isn't always as straightforward as an invitation to pray. As we will see in the coming chapters, any form of presence in community can invite connection and relationship for the sake of relationship. These gestures create the conditions for encounter and connection with others and with God. In all of these examples, showing up and being present where people are gathered—the farmers' market, Panera, or Facebook—is most significant. If we want to be in relationship, we need to be where people are. Many people at the farmers' market or Panera may not have asked for prayers, just as many don't receive ashes during Ashes to Go, but making the first move, as it were, in indicating a desire to be in relationship is a crucial step. It is that same desire to be in relationship that we express when we are present online, not just on organizational social media platforms, but personally, interacting with people on Twitter, Facebook, Instagram. Sharing our story and listening to the stories of others becomes the soil where relationships can take root.

IT'S A NUN'S LIFE

Sister Julie Vieira of the Catholic religious order of the Immaculate Heart of Mary in Monroe, Michigan started *A Nun's Life* online ministry in 2006 as a way of dispelling many of the misconceptions about nuns and educating people about religious life. However, early on this ministry took an unexpected relational turn. She told me,

> One of the transformative moments of blogging and interacting with people through comments was that people were startled that they could be in direct contact with an actual Catholic sister. They cared about what it was like for us to be nuns, but what they really cared about was that they could talk to us about their cares and concerns because they somehow trusted in the tradition of religious life. . . . So our ministry just totally turned at that point and for me it was like this inner conversion and I think it was that growing realization that this isn't just a place to put stuff out. This is a place of human encounter. That was back in 2006 and the ministry built on that fundamental insight about personal encounter. These are authentic relationships that we're dealing with here online.

This inner conversion Vieria describes echoes the experiences described throughout this book in which ministry leaders start by focusing on what they want to say, what they have to offer, and then, through encounters with others, are invited to listen, respond, and be in relationship. As Vieira told me, it invites us into a deeper encounter with others and a deeper understanding of God. She says,

> Every encounter online makes me think about how deep God's reach is. We know this theoretically. We have all these teachings in our tradition and in Scripture that affirm that, but when you see that kind of interconnectedness and how God can work in such marvelous ways. To me, that is always very amazing in the true sense of the word. Amazing.

RELATIONSHIPS WITH A SIDE OF MINISTRY

Upper Dublin Lutheran Church in Ambler, Pennsylvania, my congregation, places a high value on relational ministry. It is a central part of the congregation's work and worship. During two of the three worship services each Sunday, there is an open "sharing time" where people can share joys, concerns, and God moments with those gathered. Ushers pass around the wireless microphones and people share stories that are often moving and compelling—stories of spiritual insight, difficult medical diagnoses, thanksgiving, or concerns for friends and family members. Once everyone who wishes has spoken, we gather those joys and concerns into a concluding prayer. This culture of relationality extends beyond worship into the week. Meetings and study groups begin with "woes and wows," sharing how God has been at work in their lives. New member classes are primarily focused on relationship building among newcomers, staff, and church council. This goes for our digital life together too. I jokingly say that our congregation has its own social network called "Reply All" because members and staff frequently "reply all" to emails in order to help problem solve, plan, offer support, or just check-in. In all of these settings, our relationships with one another, the wider world, and with God become the context in which we conduct the church's business, plan ministries, learn, and grow in faith.

Lead pastor Dyan Lawlor, who has served Upper Dublin for more than eleven years, helps to cultivate this highly relational environment. I interviewed her in her office, in which hangs a framed quote from Joseph Sittler, "It is the task of the pastor to draw people into a deeper relationship with the living God, not into a deeper relationship with the pastor." Lawlor reflected about how her early life experience shaped her approach to relational ministry:

> Being raised in my family at the time I was a teenager when my dad was governor [of Minnesota] kind of parallels my own sense of then being a pastor, where you're set apart as some big

wig. I spent my adolescence in high school and college trying to prove that I was just like everybody else. And then they'd say, "Oh, Levander [her maiden name], isn't your dad the governor?" And then I'd always feel like I'd been highjacked. Now I can't just be accepted. They're going to watch me to see how I act. And the assumption is you'll be snooty and stuck up and think you're better than everybody. . . . Then I went into ministry and it was the same feeling, that, "Oh, you're the pastor," and they're going to look at you with these lenses to see if your behavior is somehow holier than thou. . . . I fought that sort of thing. I never wanted to be considered set apart. I want to be accessible to people.

That impulse to connect as a real person has evolved into a ministry that places a high value on developing relationships. Lawlor is willing to take an extended time to listen and engage. She says the moments of connection and conversation "are my reconversion":

So I guess I let the meter run sometimes on these chats with people because there's some sort of gold dust that arises from the pile that you wouldn't have gotten if you were only a taskmaster. When I go to Appalachia and I sit with the people on the front porch and they're coal miners and they've got black lung and they haven't finished high school, I think there's just gems—all kinds of stories that make me feel God is really there and alive and well. I suspect that at the core I need constant reconversion. . . . I'm feeding off the faith of the members and reconverting myself so I can then recapitulate it back to them.

It can be messy and time consuming, and seemingly inefficient. And yet, the value on relationality does not hinder the work of the congregation. It creates high levels of trust and, therefore, flexibility and openness, which allow the congregation to act quickly and take on big challenges. Upper Dublin, of course, has many of the typical congregational structures and we follow them as well as we can, but the relationships are at the forefront. The congregation has discovered, as technologist David Weinberger writes, "authority and expertise are losing some of their gravity. It's not whom you report to and who reports to you or how you filter someone else's experience. *It's how messily you are connected and how thick with meaning are the links.*"[15] As we are connected more directly and personally to others than ever before, relationships are at the heart of it all. As Lawlor reflects,

> I think the goal of relational ministry is what God had in mind—being connected heart to heart and soul to soul and then it's no effort to care, it's not a job to care, it's a natural outpouring of concern for each other. It's only when hearts touch that you're making a connection that I think God can applaud.

EXERCiSiNG INCARNATiONAL IMAGiNATiON

"The incarnational logic of Christianity resists a simple separation of divine and human, spirit and flesh, sacred and secular by focusing on the deep interpenetration of those apparent opposites."

—RONALD THIEMANN

"The Incarnation tells us that if we want to be like God, then we must be courageous enough to fully and unreservedly embrace our humanity."

—PETER ROLLINS

"In Christian thought, the one great practical truth of the incarnation is that the ordinary is no longer at all what it appears. Common things, common actions, common relationships are all granted new definition because the holy has once and for all become ordinary in Jesus Christ."

—BELDEN LANE

TALK AND TEXT

"OK, EVERYBODY, TAKE OUT YOUR CELL PHONES." The newly consecrated bishop of the New England Synod of the ELCA, Jim Hazelwood, had been on the job for only a few days and was now standing before a group of five hundred teenagers at the annual synod-wide youth gathering at Hammonasset State Park in Connecticut. A group of adolescents that size can strike terror into even the most seasoned speakers. Under the circumstances, the newly consecrated Hazelwood could have been forgiven for taking his allotted fifteen minutes to introduce himself and talk about his hopes and plans for the synod. Instead, Hazelwood flipped the traditional script and invited the youth gathered there to *Talk and Text* with him. He posted his personal cell phone number on a screen and invited the youth to text him their questions and he would respond. He told them, "You can text me any question you want from the silly to the significant." And they did. He says, "Within two minutes my phone was just on fire. I had 369 text messages. I totally overshot my monthly texting plan."

He received silly texts from the teens, asking him to say their names, share his favorite color, and daring him to dance, but they also posed serious questions like why suffering exists, why prayer seems to go unanswered, what the Holy Spirit is, and "Do you think God sends unbelievers to hell?" He had far more questions than he expected, more than he could answer in such a short time. So, the next day he recorded a video of himself reading questions from his cell phone and offering some answers and posted it on YouTube.[1] It was so well received that *Talk and Text* has now become an annual tradition at the Hammonasset event. Reflecting on why this approach works so well, he writes,

> I'm not telling them to deny the reality of the world they live in by condemning social media or text messaging. Actually, I'm embracing it. They appreciate it. I may be having fun with them, even a little silly, but I remain the adult in the room. In other words, when I answer their questions honestly, they appreciate and respect me. It's interactive. We no longer live in a world of presentations; we live in a world of engagement. I'm completely vulnerable, and they appreciate the risk I am taking. They see me goof up, struggle, and when I don't know, well, they like that I don't know.[2]

In this, Hazelwood demonstrates networked and relational, accessible and authentic leadership. He allows himself to be put on the spot, responding in real time to the needs, questions, and concerns of those gathered. It is conversational, responsive, and social, rather than the all-too-common synodical or diocesan info-mercial with "now a word from our bishop." He may not have been using social media, per se, but he did find a relational and digitally integrated way of engaging with the youth and adult leaders present there. He let the teens set the agenda with their questions, and he responded. In what has become a hallmark of his tenure as bishop, Hazelwood demonstrated his ability, and the potential for other ministers, to weave together digital and face-to-face engagement for the building up of the church and the sake of the Gospel.

BISHOP ON A BIKE

Hazelwood easily ranks as one of the more social media savvy bishops in the country. Soon after being elected bishop, he launched a website and blog called "Bishop on a Bike"[3] (the bike is his motorcycle), where he posts writing and videos about church leadership, Nones, missional church, and creative ministry ideas and practices. He has continued to use the same Facebook profile he had before being elected bishop, and has added a Twitter account, a YouTube channel, and most recently, an Instagram account.[4] With all of these platforms at his disposal and his social media acumen, Hazelwood could have easily over-relied on these media to connect with his geographically disperse synod of one hundred and eighty-five congregations flung far across all five New England states and upper New York, but Hazelwood has dedicated himself to being physically present across the synod.

When he was first elected as bishop, Hazelwood set an audacious goal: to visit all the congregations of the New England Synod in his first year. That would be one congregation every other day in a territory of over seventy thousand square miles. Hazelwood explains that this came from a pastoral impulse to know the synod, and a piece of wisdom from Edwin Friedman's family systems theory, "You cannot impact a system you are not connected to." When I spoke to Hazelwood via Skype, he had visited all but three congregations in his first eighteen months in office—not quite his original goal, but still a remarkable feat, visiting at a rate of ten congregations per month. Some days he had breakfast, lunch, and dinner with three different congregations. After a while, he said, it can be hard to remember where you are. "It was kind of like for a lot of bands when they go out on tour. They get lost to where they are, so there's that big sign before they go on stage, 'You are in Pittsburgh.' So they come on stage and go 'Pittsburgh! How are you?' and don't say a city name again, because they don't remember." His dizzying efforts have been greatly appreciated by those he visits and those who follow his travels on social media.

On these jaunts, Hazelwood again blends the digital and face-to-face. When he visits a congregation, he takes pictures—at the very least, of the outside of the building, the sanctuary, and some of the people—and posts them on Facebook. In so doing, Hazelwood helps to tell the story of these congregations and ministries, giving others a window into the life of these faith communities. All his videos, tweets, pictures, blog posts, check-ins, and status updates tell the story of the synod as composed of people, churches, and communities, and not just the Office of the Bishop. At times, he documents his visits in greater detail, such as blogging about celebrating the Chinese New Year at a new Lutheran Chinese congregation in Boston, leading the synod men's retreat at Camp Calumet in northern New Hampshire, and even patching a pothole outside the synod office. He says that social media is,

> really key because I could be doing this prior to the web, prior to social media, and maybe I would write a newsletter at the end of the month. Even if it was the early 1990s you could photocopy a picture of one or maybe two places you had been, but the delay on that would be a month later . . . But this way the instant aspect of it is really giving people a sense in

almost real time of what I'm doing. And ninety percent of it is done with a smartphone.

In an ironic twist, when things are shared online, they can actually become more real for people. (I often tell people that if something isn't online, it's like it didn't happen.) Just sharing a few pictures and checking-in on social media has a huge impact: immediately you've expanded your audience from the thirty people at the local church to hundreds, perhaps even thousands, and those pictures and experiences are captured and preserved as a kind of digital archive. It creates a deeper connection not only to the bishop, but to brothers and sisters in Christ in other neighborhoods and communities. Hazelwood says that he picks up new Facebook friends and Twitter followers with each visit, so the connections he makes during his in-person visits continue to grow and deepen online well beyond New England. As one colleague observed, through social media Hazelwood has become a bishop to many people beyond his own synod.

DIGITAL OR FACE-TO-FACE: A FALSE CHOICE

Hazelwood's work provides a counterbalance to one of the most frequent complaints about digital social media and cell phones—that they interrupt or substitute for face-to-face engagement. This critique is nearly as old as the internet itself, and has been reinforced with unfortunate early descriptions of the web such as "virtual reality" or "cyberspace"—as if it were distinct and separate from the "real" physical world.[5] To be sure, our digital devices can distract us from a great many things, but they also bring us together not only digitally, but also face-to-face. Increasingly, with advances in mobile devices like smartphones and tablets, the ubiquity of high-speed internet connections, and wearable technology like the Apple Watch, the line between the digital and face-to-face is becoming blurred.

As Ronald Thiemann writes, this critique is symptomatic of a culture that often divides the world in a binary way, as "a series of dichotomies—sacred/secular, believer/non-believer, spiritual/mundane"—to which we can add digital/physical—"that distort our reading of our contemporary situation."[6] Life in the Digital Cathedral begins by deconstructing these false dichotomies and approaching the world in a holistic way by finding sacred space embedded in the secular, acknowledging the blurred line between believers and Nones, and recognizing that the mundane is infused with the spiritually sublime. The choice between digital and face-to-face is ultimately a false one in part, because as with all these categories, it defies people's lived experience. Our daily lives are often far more integrated—and digitally integrated—than religious leaders and institutions perceive. People pray on their commute to work, find spiritual renewal in running, and enact holy hospitality when they host family and friends. They pray on Facebook and read the Bible on their iPad. They move between phones and faces, check-ins and conversation, often with great fluidity. Digital devices and the web are an integral part of people's lived experience. Pew Research reports that 81 percent of cell phone users send or receive text messages; 60 percent access the internet on their phones; 50 percent download apps; 49 percent get navigational directions, recommendations, or other location-based information; 48 percent listen to music; 41 percent watch video; and 40 percent record video.[7] These digital devices and their applications are woven into the fabric of our daily life and work. What might these realities mean for the practice of faith and for ministry?

Part of the challenge to transcending these binaries is that we too easily glorify earlier technologies from allegedly simpler times. A popular internet meme shows a black-and-white picture of people riding the train with their newspapers opened. No one is engaging with each other. They can't even see each other because their view is completely blocked by the broadsheet. Overlaid on the image are the words, "All this technology is making us anti-social." When I posted it on Facebook, my childhood pastor now in his 70s and active on social media, commented, "Ah,

A popular internet meme applying a common critique of social media to a pillar of broadcast era communications, the newspaper.

yes. We really were social in the 'good old days.' I can remember commuting in NYC on the subway, the ferry, and the NY Central with scenes just like this . . . and they weren't reading on Facebook about how their sick friends were doing or where the church picnic was being held." The same critique might also be extended to television and radio, the other pillars of broadcast media, in which we are passive receivers of information, rather than actively engaged with others. These technologies are not better just because they are more familiar to us. In some cases they are far less social.

Rather than making us anti-social, social media, by connecting us with ever more people, can actually create *more, not fewer,* opportunities for face-to-face encounters. But it must be done with intentionality. It requires *incarnational imagination.* Like Jim Hazelwood, we cannot be content to leave connections and relationships on the screen. Social media can't carry our relationships completely. We must identify and create opportunities for face-to-face encounters. As Hazelwood's story shows, used together, social media and the face-to-face can mutually reinforce one another, strengthening and deepening relationships over time and distance.

WORDS MADE FLESH

The incarnation—the belief that God took on human form in Jesus Christ—is central to the Christian faith. Christianity claims that Jesus became incarnate as a baby born to humble parents in a manger in Bethlehem. As the Gospel of John puts it, "the Word became flesh and lived among us" (John 1:14). He was fully God and fully human. He lived, suffered and died, and rose again in bodily form. Even after his resurrection, the disciple Thomas insisted on touching the nail scars and putting his hand in the wounds on Jesus' hands and side (John 20:24–29). Jesus' incarnation was God's presence among us, engaged with the breadth of humanity, confronting the powerful, and liberating the oppressed. Jesus himself walked the city as well as the countryside. Throughout Galilee, Samaria, and Judea, he visited villages and towns, sat in boats, ate in people's homes, strolled along beaches, conversed at wells, fed and taught people on hillsides and deserted places, and encountered people in the streets. He entered Jerusalem on Palm Sunday, walked the streets, cleansed the Temple, ate dinner with his disciples in the Upper Room, prayed in the Garden of Gethsemane, appeared before the chief priest, was tried in Pilates' quarters, and finally marched to Golgotha, and then three days later, emerged from a tomb.

In this human, physical form, Jesus entered the mundane places of his time—places forgotten or dismissed by the religious elite—and infused them with his divinity and the presence of God. Because of Jesus, Christians claim all the world—including these everyday places—is hallowed not only because God created it, but also because Jesus walked upon it. These were the places he healed, taught, fed, and forgave. Furthermore, many Christian traditions understand the Eucharist to be the real presence in wine and bread, Jesus' body and blood, truly present for us. Christianity, from the birth of Christ to this Sunday's Eucharist, is an embodied faith.

In a time where screens seem to threaten to disembody and digitize our relationships, it is ever more important to exercise Christianity's "incarnational logic"[8] as a safeguard against reliance on digital devices alone. Matthew Nickoloff, pastor of the South Wedge Mission, a mission start congregation of the ELCA in Rochester, New York,[9] sees this as a central facet of his ministry. Nickoloff, a Millennial himself, says that some of the young adults in his community have become so accustomed to communicating through their digital devices, that his role, in some ways, is to teach them to engage face-to-face as a way of practicing the incarnational character of Christianity. He told me,

> Whereas social media has trained them to be momentarily inspired and superficially interested in a wide variety of events and lives, Christianity is about seeking a commitment to a concrete life and to a spirit of inspiration that is not our own. Just as Jesus coming near to us in the flesh meant that he had to meet us face-to-face, and risk the harm, the disappointment, and the limitations of the commitment he had to God's relationship with us, so too moving away from the safety net of social media and into the messiness of lives lived together— where people can hurt you, disappoint you, and ultimately, make demands on you. But I think nothing is more necessary in a world that increasingly confuses a tech-gnosticism for the Gospel of the communion of flesh and blood bodies with a flesh and blood God.

Neither living a completely digitally mediated life through our devices nor living in utter denial that these actually technologies exist is sufficient for navigating life and faith today.

"WHERE DID YOU GUYS MEET?" "ON TWITTER."

I first met Bethany Stolle on Twitter. We were both following the tweets from the annual Princeton Forum on Youth Ministry at Princeton Theological Seminary. Bethany, then based in St. Paul, Minnesota, was working as a curriculum designer for sparkhouse, and I was newly located at Upper Dublin Lutheran Church outside Philadelphia. When she noticed through our tweets that we shared common interests in technology and changing church, Bethany suggested that we have a Skype conversation as a kind of digital introduction. Some months later that connection led to Bethany and her colleague Jim Kast-Keat coming to interview the staff, parents, and youth of Upper Dublin Lutheran Church as part of research for a new confirmation curriculum (more in chapter ten). Later that fall, I, in turn, interviewed Bethany via Skype about technology and faith formation for a seminary class I was co-teaching on the catechism in the digital age. We continued to be connected on Twitter, Facebook, and Instagram. Then the following summer, I was in St. Paul, Minnesota for a conference, and we met again, this time along with *Click2Save* bestie Adam J. Copeland, whom I had never met in person, and with friends from Connecticut and Hawaii. My connection with Bethany has evolved over the course of two years, primarily online, but we seized those incarnational moments, which have helped to strengthen and deepen our connection, because we were intentional about meeting in person when possible. All of this, quite unexpectedly, led to collaborating on this book. In a moment of panic just days away from my deadline when I needed graphics to help depict the shift from Newtonian to networked ways of imagining our faith communities for chapter three, I reached out to Bethany and she stepped in to design those graphics.

That impulse to connect, in this case on Twitter, Skype, in person, and then back again, and to do meaningful work on behalf of the church, is crucial to life and ministry today. While any given moment might not be significant in and of itself, the cumulative connections over time, across digital platforms, and face-to-face can lead to a genuine friendship, fruitful partnerships, and an ever-widening circle of collaborators and friends.

GOING DEEP IN THIS PLACE

Grace Episcopal Church, located in Medford, a suburb just north of Boston, has been revitalized by exercising incarnational ministry. The rector, Noah Evans, says, "We use all of our social networking, Facebook, Twitter to be connected with our parish but . . . *the center of our life and mission is going deep in this place, at 160 High Street, and radiating out from there.*" Grace Church takes seriously its presence in the community. Over the last few years they have created a movement called Green Up/ Clean Up, which helps to organize the Medford community to care for its local parks. They hosted an interfaith vigil after the Boston Marathon bombings in 2013, and helped with a health and fitness fair inspired by Michelle Obama's Let's Move campaign to encourage people to live healthier lives by eating well and exercising. They also engage in one-on-one conversations in their community in Medford, constantly looking for ways to partner with local groups and individuals. Evans shares,

> One of the things that Grace does that is really beautiful is that we see it as very important to be blurring the lines between who's sitting in the pew and who's outside in the community. It comes out of a vision that we are a neighborhood church, or a town church, and it harkens back to the old understanding of the geographical parish. . . . It's really out of the belief that the parish is all our community and not just what's inside the doors of the church.

In that historic parish model the neighborhood immediately surrounding the church building falls within the spiritual care of the congregation, whether the individuals who live there are officially members of the church or not. "The congregation," then, is not just those who attend worship on Sunday morning, but anyone who lives within their part of town.

The challenge that many churches face is that, while the neighborhoods around our churches have changed, dramatically in some cases, our congregations have not. This is one of the consequences of the oil-era commuter churches described in the previous chapter. Many churches are comprised of people who *used* to live in the neighborhood—and many who have never stepped foot in it—but now live elsewhere and commute to church on Sunday morning. Thus, our churches often operate with an understanding of their neighborhood that existed fifty or a hundred years ago, rather than as they are now in their current social, ethnic, or economic composition. The whole idea of going to the local coffee shop or pub, walking the streets of our towns and neighborhoods, should not be so novel, yet it is because we have taken to commuting to church in our cars, rather than walking the streets. We drive *past* neighborhoods—perhaps several—and the very neighborhood in which our congregation is located, on the way to church. As Grace, Medford and other ministries profiled in this book demonstrate, a deeper connection to our local communities can lead to congregational health, vitality, and growth. Congregations need to find creative and authentic ways to be more connected, and as Lutheran pastor Paul Hoffman has said, to "exegete our neighborhoods" to better understand our local context and partner with our neighbors—not just through purchased demographic studies and surveys, but with our feet.

Like the newly popular movements of locally sourced and sustainable agriculture in farmers' markets and CSAs (community supported agricultures), we need locally sourced and sustained ministries. This was a great challenge at my former congregation where perhaps only 25 percent of our congregation lived in the same town as the church, and most of those were older members, who represented and remembered a much different time and town. We tried a number of different ideas to reconnect with our neighborhood. For a time, our Church Council held its meetings at local community agencies like the Boys and Girls Club, the YMCA, and a social service agency called the Woburn Council of Social Concern. We met the directors, toured the facilities, learned about the work, and then held our meeting in one of their meeting rooms. At the same time, we followed them on Facebook and Twitter, and kept tabs on local news on Twitter with the commonly used hashtag for local news, #woburn. In addition, as a way of honoring the other neighborhoods our members called home, we hosted gatherings in living rooms, pubs, and cafés in their towns as well.

These practices flowed from an incarnational impulse to be present where people are, the same drive that motivates Grace Church. Noah Evans says,

> I think of church as a place where we practice doing a lot of things. We practice loving people. We practice forgiveness. We have these sacraments, which are a way to rehearse having a very deep interaction with others and with God. The Eucharist is a great example of that. And then we're meant to live that in the world. It's not something that's meant to live within the doors of the church. As we finish worship every Sunday we say, "The worship has ended. The service begins."

During Advent, Evans and members of Grace set up a blessing station at a local commuter rail station, displaying a sign: *"Blessing Station. Come and experience a moment of Advent peace in the midst of life's busyness."* They offer it on the winter solstice, the shortest day of the year, offering the light of Christ in the midst of winter's darkness. In 2012, that fell exactly one week after the shootings at Sandy Hook Elementary in Newtown, Connecticut. Evans reflects on that experience,

> When we did the blessing station after the shootings in Newtown, and to have parents standing there at the train station and looking at us like, "What the hell are you doing?" and then suddenly having it click and coming up, and having a laying on of hands and prayer, which is incredibly personal, even more than putting ashes on someone's forehead, was amazing. It was amazing to me that people were willing to enter such a vulnerable

space at a train station, but it happened again and again. There were a lot of parents praying for the safety of their children. It told me that there's a way to do the street liturgical ministry also in concert with what's going on in the wider community. There was deep fear and anxiety among parents with kids of that age and we were able to respond to that right where they were. It is an important way of sharing what we do in church every week all the time.

When we physically relocate ourselves in the community, in the park, train station, or town hall, it transforms the way our community sees us, but just as importantly, it transforms the way we see ourselves and imagine what our ministry is and could be. When we enter into these places, we create the conditions for encounter and mutual transformation with our neighbors. Evans says, "We get it wrong when the church becomes a place to go, and not a people to be, and a people to be happens all over the place."

Ministry leaders like Evans and Hazelwood understand that *local is also a social and multi-media platform*—that is, a site of the social that connects to other platforms, both locally and digitally. Your neighborhood is a networked social media platform right alongside Facebook, Twitter, and Instagram. As we will see in the coming chapters, local and digital gathering spaces are similar in a number of important ways. They require a ministry stance that is consistently and meaningfully present, open to being in relationship over time, and engaged with people beyond our membership rolls. Any *digital* social media strategy ought to be connected to a *local* strategy, and vice versa. As a colleague once shared with me, one of his church's outreach strategies was searching Twitter for local tweets where people where requesting prayers.[10] They would find these prayer requests and tweet back a short message and pray for them. He told me, "What we've learned is: before we can love our neighbors, we need to know who our neighbors are."

LAUNDRY LOVE

"For some reason, washing machines and dryers really bring people together," says Jimmy Bartz, founding pastor of Thad's, a mission station and experimental community of the Episcopal Diocese of Los Angeles, named for one of the oft-forgotten disciples, Thaddeus.[11] Like Humble Walk Church, Thad's has gathered in all manner of places for worship, from a living room, to a Denny's, a Jewish Community Center, and a writer's workshop. One of their ministries, which embodies the spirit of incarnational community and is part of a growing faith-based movement, is called "Laundry Love."[12] On the last Monday of the month, they invite anyone—the homeless, those in need, or those in transition—to come to a Venice-area laundromat and do their laundry for free. Thad's supplies the quarters, soap, and dryer sheets. They do as many as 600 loads of laundry each month. As anyone who has shoveled clothes into a washer and dryer knows, doing the laundry is a highly incarnational activity. There just isn't an app for that. Bartz describes Laundry Love as "a modern-day footwashing."[13] As people do their wash, volunteers and members of Thad's visit with the guests, get to know them. It's relational ministry, with a side of laundry. It is not an end in itself. He says, "The program exists so that it would be an incubator for more personal love-spreading, difference-making mission in our own individual lives."[14]

ORDAINED TO THE LAUNDROMAT AND THE WORLD

Scott Clausen, a member of the Thad's leadership team, chose to be ordained a deacon in the Episcopal Church, not in a great cathedral, but in the laundromat during a Laundry Love event. The suggested attire was appropriately diaconal, "Casual attire appropriate for washing clothes and serving food." In the middle of the laundromat, amidst cycling washing machines, tumbling dryers, and laundry carts, members, friends, and those doing their laundry, the bishop laid hands on Clausen, as everyone gathered extending their arms out to bless him. Claussen explains the choice of being ordained in the laundry saying,

> We chose not to use microphones, lecterns, or a grandiose altar. We responded to the space in a way that respected the work that was going on all around the ordination service. In that way, we hoped that the ordination service would reflect the orientation of the diaconate toward serving those in need. The result was a service in which we all stood on equal footing, and all who gathered participated in the service if they chose to do so.[15]

Claussen's ordination is a vivid reminder of how we are all called to be an incarnational presence in our local communities. Our calling, whether lay or ordained, is not just to the parish or a specialized ministry, but to the community and to the world. Incarnational ministry leaders blend, find, and name the holy in local and digital gathering spaces. They even treat dryer sheets as sacramental—outward and visible signs of an inward and spiritual grace.

EPILOGUE: LESSONS FROM A VERY HUMAN ALIEN TIME LORD

Networked. Relational. Incarnational. These are not new qualities of ministry. They date from well before the digital age or even the age of cathedrals. They go back to the very beginnings of the church. And yet, we have been so shaped by the broadcast media era, which has been overly focused on messaging, marketing, and transactional relationships, that we have lost something deeply important along with way—perhaps, as Peter Rollins suggests in the epigraph, we have lost and need to reclaim some of our very humanity.[16]

Ironically, it has taken an alien time lord named Doctor Who, the lead character in the long-running British television show of the same name, to remind me of that. The Doctor is a 900-year-old time lord, the last of his kind, and he travels through space and time on his TARDIS, short for Time and Relative Dimension in Space, which looks like an old British police phone booth. (It's bigger on the inside.) The Doctor jumps through time and space, here and there, across "wibbly wobbly . . . timey wimey . . . stuff," solving problems and holding at bay those of ill intent. In our own terrestrial way, we also move between time and space. We jump back and forth between our mobile devices and face-to-face conversations, between physical and digital social networks, often at the same time. We are, in a sense, leaping through space and time when we are catching up on old Facebook posts after time away from the screen, looking for tomorrow's news today on Twitter, or transported via Instagram pictures to a friend's pilgrimage to the Holy Land.

Doctor Who, therefore, can be seen as a valuable model for digitally integrated ministry. He manages these moves and the people he encounters with great care and kindness, following an ethic that is appropriately Hippocratic: defend the vulnerable; seek to do no harm. The Doctor bears three crucial marks of ministry leadership in a digital age that we have discussed in the section: networked, relational, and incarnational. Through his prolific travels, the Doctor encounters a vast array of races and species: Silurians, Judoons, Sontarans, to name just a few. He stays connected to and nurtures a vast network of relationships and brings people and groups together when circumstances dictate. Ministry leaders must be networked as well with a broad range of individuals and groups locally and digitally, far beyond the bounds of professional or denominational association. We must nurture connections with sometimes disparate individuals and groups, and find ways, when authentic and appropriate, to connect them.

For all his futuristic technology, Doctor Who's focus is ultimately on relationships. He always travels with a companion, and collaborates with all sorts of different characters to solve problems and subdue threats. Ministry leaders know about relationships. They are the heart of ministry: to engage in relationships for their own sake, not as means to an end, but as ends in themselves, for it is in such relationships that we encounter Christ.

Thanks to the TARDIS, the Doctor pops up in person all over the universe. We may not have a TARDIS, but we do have Twitter—and a range of other social media, through which we are able to engage with one another in real time as never before. Along with that online engagement, as ministry leaders, as people with incarnational imagination, we ought to look for opportunities to meet face-to-face whenever possible—not to somehow make those relationships "real," but to acknowledge their reality. Those face-to-face encounters reinforce our relationships when we are apart and only able to connect online.

Ministers today must enter into today's digital cathedral as networked, relational, and incarnational leaders. In the next section, we will explore further practices and theological implications of this incarnational ministry. As we locate the sacred in our daily lives, in the flesh, our daily work, in the seemingly mundane. And so, as the good Doctor would say, "Geronimo!"

6

EVERYDAY SACRED

Locating God in Daily Life

> "What cathedrals provide is the opportunity for people to explore and perhaps to cross the awkward boundary between the secular and the sacred and to handle the insecurities of liminality."
>
> —CHRISTOPHER LEWIS

> "I have come to believe that the true mystics of the quotidian are not those who contemplate holiness in isolation, reading godlike illumination in serene silence, but those who manage to find God in a life filled with noise, the demands of other people and the relentless daily duties that can consume the self."
>
> —KATHLEEN NORRIS

AN ULTRASOUND, A BEER, AND A NEW JOURNEY

I was working from home that day. My wife Jenny had gone for a doctor's appointment and I was watching our two kids, ages three and five. We were expecting our third child and Jenny had gone in for an early check-up. I was sitting at the dining room table working on my laptop when she arrived back home. When I called into the kitchen asking how it went, she walked over and handed me a picture of the ultrasound . . . and a beer. It was only 3:00 in the afternoon. I looked at the ultrasound, and feeling like a veteran parent with two kids already, I pointed to the little peanut in the picture and I said, "Hey, there's the baby." Then Jenny then pointed to the other little peanut I had missed, and

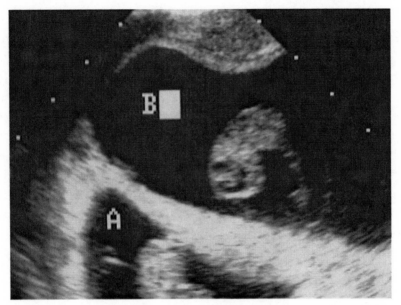

An early ultrasound of the Anderson twins sparked a search for God in daily life.

said, "No, there are the *babies*." We were having twins. And that's when I understood why she brought me the beer.

I also understood that this little 3x5 black-and-white picture was about to change our lives forever. In short order, we would double the number of kids and triple the size of our family. I think it's safe to say we were a little freaked out. It also became clear to me that my spiritual life was going to change as well. Up until that point, my spirituality had been anchored by regular silent retreats, many taken at the Society of Saint John the Evangelist (SSJE), an Episcopal monastery in Cambridge, Massachusetts. I realized that those getaways would not be possible for some years to come and I would have to find spiritual nourishment outside the monastery. My spiritual life would have to become much more *incarnational* than it had ever been before. Rather than getting away from the world to find God, I would have to go more deeply *into* the world, into my everyday existence, to find that spiritual connection. I would have to find God in the midst of what Dr. Jon Kabat-Zinn has called "full catastrophe living."[1]

I also knew my upcoming summer sabbatical would take on a different character. There would be no big trips to the Holy Land, ancient biblical sites, or the great cathedrals. I would have to stay close to home, helping my very pregnant spouse and caring for our two young kids. I would need to find the sublime amidst the seemingly mundane. So, my congregation and I crafted a sabbatical plan to do just that. We called it *Everyday Sacred*, inspired by Sue Bender's book of the same name.[2] I put together a reading list and signed on to a personal spiritual deepening program with the Shalem Institute for Spiritual Formation.[3] Fortunately, I was able to stay connected to the SSJE and the spiritual wisdom of the brothers there through their robust social media presence, which includes sermons, blog posts, and videos. Finally, I hoped to mine my own Lutheran tradition, and more broadly, Reformation theologies, for a theological underpinning for this project—all the while washing dishes, cleaning the house, and tending my family more intentionally and mindfully than ever before.

AFFIRMING THE ORDINARY

In fact, Reformation traditions have a rich, if underappreciated, heritage concerning what Charles Taylor has called the "affirmation of ordinary life."[4] Prior to the Reformation, monasticism, with its life devoted to worship, study, and contemplation, was considered the highest and most holy station in life, with the priesthood right behind it—both ranking high above every other kind of social or professional status. This perspective had a long history in Western culture, dating as far back as the days of the Greek philosophers Plato and Aristotle, who maintained that the life of the mind and philosophical contemplation were much higher pursuits than the humdrum of everyday living. Much later, as Christianity came into sway in the West, this life of the mind came to be expressed in religious or spiritual contemplation, most especially the rise of monasticism, so much so that at the dawn of the Reformation, family life and secular work were treated as "zones of spiritual underdevelopment."[5]

One of the consequences of the Reformers' understanding that salvation comes by God's grace alone, received through faith, apart from works, was that no particular station or calling in life was higher than another. No one could earn salvation or higher status in God's eyes. It was a free gift; no one could achieve greater sanctity through cloistering themselves away from the world or through taking vows of poverty, chastity, and obedience. This placed everyone—the monk, priest, housewife, barber, and student—all on level ground. Eventually, in light of this understanding, the Reformers insisted on closing monasteries and convents. In so doing, Taylor argues, they relocated the sacred to everyday life and redefined what it meant to have a holy calling. He writes,

> By denying any special form of life as a privileged locus of the sacred, they were denying the very distinction between sacred and profane and hence affirming their interpenetration. The denial of a special status to the monk was also an affirmation of ordinary life as more than profane, as itself hallowed and in no way second class. . . . *The repudiation of monasticism was a reaffirmation of lay life as a central locus for the fulfillment of God's purpose.*[6]

Closing the monasteries was a physical symbol of the Reformers' understanding that the sacred could not be confined or best apprehended within a cloister, but was available anywhere to anyone, each in their own station of life. In doing so, they named all ground as holy and helped to, if not collapse, then mitigate the traditional dichotomies between the sacred and the secular, and the spiritual and the mundane, described in the previous chapter.

Martin Luther, who had been an Augustinian monk himself, left the monastery, married a former nun, and had several children. He was the first great theologian in hundreds of years to be (legitimately) married with children. This no doubt put flesh and experience to his theological convictions. Perhaps inspired by his own encounter with parenthood and child rearing, he writes about the spiritual calling of changing diapers,

> When our natural reason . . . takes a look at married life, she
> turns up her nose and says, "Alas, I must rock the baby, wash
> the diapers, make its bed, smell its stench, stay up nights with it,
> take care of it when it cries . . . and on top of that care for my
> wife, provide for her, labor at my trade." . . . What then does
> the Christian faith say to this? It opens its eyes, looks upon all
> these insignificant, distasteful, and despised duties in the Spirit,
> and is aware that they are all adorned with divine approval as
> with the costliest gold and jewels.[7]

Admittedly, this *is* hard to remember when you are a sleep-
deprived new parent, changing diapers, washing onesies, cleaning
spit-ups, and warming up bottles. It's hard to believe that changing an exploding diaper could be the highest form of spiritual
practice, and I'm sure that more than once Luther wished for the
peace and quiet of the monastery when his kids got too loud.
Nonetheless, for Luther, the domestic life, once considered a
second-class station—once considered profane, the very opposite of sacred—was now the highest. For Luther, this extended
beyond care of the family and the running of the household into
one's daily labor. He writes,

> Every person surely has a calling. While attending to it he [*sic*]
> serves God. A king serves God when he is at pains to look after and
> govern his people. So do the mother of a household when she tends
> her baby, the father of a household when he gains a livelihood by
> working, and a pupil when he applies himself diligently to his stud-
> ies. . . . Therefore, it is great wisdom when a human being does
> what God commands and earnestly devotes himself to his vocation.[8]

Despite the traditional gender roles here, Luther is actually rather
progressive for his time. He lists a range of people here all in a
single breath, both men and women, from the all-powerful king
to the lowly student. He says that no matter your job, whenever
you do your work well and faithfully, you are fulfilling your holy
calling in the world. For Luther, this was just as holy, if not more
so, than worshipping in the monastery several times a day. From

this perspective, each person's tools become a means of loving your neighbor. Luther wrote,

> If you are a craftsman . . . only look at your tools, your needle, your thimble, your beer barrel, your articles of trade, your scales, your measures, and you will find this saying written on them . . . "My dear, use me toward your neighbor, as you would want him to act toward you with that which is his."[9]

With the eyes of faith, each tool of the trade—from diamonds to diapers—is a means by which we can love and serve our neighbor. In this way, each person is a priest in her or his daily work. Only now the sacred objects extend beyond Scripture and the sacraments to beer barrels, thimbles, and measures. Today, we might even include social media and smartphones in that list. For, five hundred years later, our calling remains the same: to live out as best we can our particular calling in life, to use all the tools and resources, including digital ones, at our disposal to proclaim the Gospel, and to love and serve our neighbor.

THE NONE ZONE

Despite this rich inheritance, this understanding of vocation can be conspicuously absent in our congregations. Homiletics professor David Lose has noted that sermons often fail to address the realities of our daily lives. They address what he calls the *congregational zone*—sermons that relate to congregational life and experiences; and the *global zone*—issues of war, poverty, and health; but they neglect what he calls the *middle zone*—our daily experience.[10] He writes,

> Jobs, looking for a job, relationships, parenting, managing too many things at once, money, family, school, hobbies, volunteering, the media, local current events—that is, the stuff that constitutes our daily lives—often seems to be painfully absent from much of our preaching.

Echoing a common theme in this book, Lose encourages preachers to get out of the building and visit people where they work and live. But it's not just in preaching that this talk of vocation is absent. It happens in other programming as well. We learn *about* being Lutheran or Episcopalian or United Methodist, *about* the church, *about* the Bible, but less often do we connect to people's lived experience. How are we helping people to connect the story of their lives with the larger narrative of God and God's people? How do we help people see their daily work, their entire lives, as suffused with the holy?

In my own Lutheran tradition, when we speak of our ministry in daily life, our vocation, we often use the catch phrase "the priesthood of all believers," a handy way to refer to the understanding that everyone has a calling and is a minister in their daily life. However, we frequently reduce the meaning of this phrase to doing the things the priest, pastor, or rector doesn't have time to do. The priesthood of all believers becomes narrowed to supplementing the work of the priest or pastor and keeping the gears of the congregational machine turning. Indeed, ministry leaders frequently send subtle messages that the highest calling is not our daily work and family life, but our involvement in the church.

We intimate that the best and most faithful Christians are the ones who are at worship every Sunday and attend committee meetings three nights a week. And God bless those people! But their parenting and jobs are holy callings, too. We complain when families miss church because of a Sunday morning soccer game, but how do we honor families for being present for their children and name that as part of their holy calling as well? People often experience great tension between their commitments at church and their daily life. They feel torn between what they have intuited is the highest calling, serving at church, and their calling to tend to the home and do their job well. In many ways, we treat church work as a new monasticism, as the highest and most holy calling, though it is rarely contemplative and often much more functional.

The fullness of the reformers' understanding of vocation can help unlock this tension and help see people, their parenting, jobs, vocations, and avocations as part of God's work in the world. It offers a much broader understanding of what constitutes ministry and a more integrated way of understanding our lives. That's not to say time apart isn't important. Retreats can help us to see God at work more clearly in our daily lives. Church activities are important ways for people to live out their faith and can be critical to a congregation's life together, but they are not the higher calling that we often make them out to be. In fact, when it comes to "vocation," the reformers' understanding is much more akin to the notion of being "in cathedral." Living out our vocation doesn't just happen in the church building or at church events. It is about being fully present to our daily lives. Today that includes local and digital gathering spaces, from the home to the cubicle, from the soccer pitch to Twitter, to the local coffee shop and beyond.

WHO CARES WHAT YOU HAD FOR BREAKFAST?

A common complaint about social media is that it can be painfully pedestrian. People use social media to post what they had for breakfast, check-in at the local gym, give updates on hobbies, issue proud parent reports about their kids' successes, post pictures of nature and selfies, lament a rough day at work, and post totally random stuff like pictures of cats and quizzes like "which Lord of the Rings character are you?" This sharing is often quickly dismissed as a waste of time and sometimes is used to argue against the religious value and use of social media. However, in light of the reformers' understanding of vocation, these too can be seen as holy things—pictures of food, homemade music videos, selfies with their dog—because they are part of and reflect each individual's holy calling. There is a depth beneath them. They open up onto a larger story. When we look at them through the eyes of faith, as Luther did those dirty diapers, we see that they too are sacred. When we respond to these stories and images on social media through likes, favorites, retweets, comments, or replys, we are affirming the ordinary in people's lives, and pointing to the sacred which is, to use Luther's phrase for the real presence of God in the sacraments, "in, with, and under" all of these experiences. One of my parishioners with a real knack for capturing the travails of parenthood once posted on Facebook, "So first the E coli and now a transformer explodes outside our house and the telephone pole has a flame on top and a live wire. Awesome. How can I sleep now? Pastor Keith we could use that house blessing sooner than later! ☺" It's moments like this, when seen through the lens of faith, as Wendy Wright has written, that "are at once terribly mundane and so transparently sacred—ordinary moments that, for an instant, connect us to the depth, width, height, and length of love."[11] We must take everyday life seriously, whether that life is in Canterbury in the twelfth century, New York in the twentieth century, or Facebook and Twitter in the twenty-first.

THE SACRAMENT OF THE DISHES

I certainly found this to be true on my sabbatical, where the mundane, particularly housework and parenting, was a central component. In fact, a surprising number of spiritual writers talk about housework as a spiritual practice. Kathleen Norris, who urges us to be "mystics of the quotidian"—quotidian meaning the everyday— tells the story of going back to church after many years. Watching the Catholic priest clean up the altar after communion, it occurred to her that he was basically doing the dishes. She writes, "I found it enormously comforting to see the priest as a kind of daft housewife, overdressed for the kitchen, in bulky robes, puttering around the altar, washing up after having served so great a meal to so many people."[12] I had never before thought of my washing the dishes for my family and what I do at the altar on Sunday morning as so deeply connected. For me, it blurs the line between the sacred and the mundane, and challenges my assumptions about which is which. I now think of this passage every time I reset the altar after communion. Fellow contemplative and Buddhist monk Thich Nhat Hanh writes that the point of doing dishes is simply to be present while doing the dishes. He says that when we do the dishes mindfully, "no boundary exists between the sacred and the profane." He says, "I must confess it takes me a bit longer to do the dishes, but I live fully in every moment, and I am happy."[13] For Luther, that washcloth is the means by which we love our neighbors, in this case those who happen to live in our own home or guests who come to dine. The most mundane, repetitive activities—even dish-washing—can be a sacred practice, a holy calling, part of the liturgy of our lives. As spiritual writers across religious and spiritual traditions remind us, life itself is our spiritual practice.

The Everyday Sacred sabbatical experience made an enormous difference in my ministry and our life together in that parish. While I was away on sabbatical plumbing the depths of my daily life, dishes and diapers included, the congregation explored these same themes by discussing spirituality and gardening, golf, baking, serving, and reading books on finding God in everyday life. We looked at our lives, our hobbies, our daily commitments and responsibilities, and asked, "Where is God here?" "What about this is holy ground for you?" "How do these seeming opposites fit together?" When we came back together, and in the years following, we had a much greater awareness of God in daily life. My preaching changed as I began addressing what Lose describes as the middle zone, that area that concerns itself with the everyday aspects of our individual and communal lives. We gathered for lunch where clusters of members worked downtown as a way to affirm their daily work. We introduced programming about spirituality and daily life. Members shared how the arts and crafts they created connected to their faith. One of our members, a personal trainer, talked about the spirituality of the body, breath, and being grounded. By delving into the realities of our daily existence, we discovered and came to a deeper understanding of how God is at work in our lives. We saw our daily work with new eyes. The tension that many parishioners felt between their work in the church and their work at home dissipated. They began to understand it as all part of a whole. Church became a place to gain renewed perspective on how God was at work in their lives, not a source of guilt for not doing more. And people were engaged in a different, more holistic way. They didn't suddenly quit all their church responsibilities because of these changes. Instead, those responsibilities were more integrated to the rest of their lives, providing opportunities to share gifts in new ways their daily work might not allow.

CATHEDRALS AT THE CROSSROADS

Cathedrals were conceived well before the Reformation, when clear distinctions between clergy and laity and the sacred and profane were very clearly at work. Cathedrals are "socially constructed spaces,"[14] and designed with hierarchies of vocation and sacred space in mind. In fact, cathedrals, both old and new, are designed to invite visitors into increasingly sacred space from the western portal (the front door) eastwardly to the high altar, which is considered the most sacred place in the cathedral. This is expressed in the cathedral's architecture: for instance, as you move from west to east in Canterbury Cathedral, you travel up a total of 38 steps and 25 feet of elevation, from nave to transept, choir, high altar, Archbishop's seat, to Trinity Chapel and the shrine of Thomas Becket at the easternmost end.[15] The steps between each section of the cathedral indicate a movement closer to the divine. In medieval cathedrals the high altar area, now open to laity and tourists in most cathedrals, was a space often reserved for clergy and separated from the nave using a wooden or stone screen. The average visitor to the cathedral could circulate *around* the choir and altar along the ambulatories, but the inner precincts were reserved for the clergy. This created a kind of duality, just as the presence of monasteries once did prior to the Reformation. Robert Scott writes,

> Embracing the concept of the sacred and believing that it is uniquely present in a particular place automatically sets up another, opposing type of place and realm of existence—one

that is not sacred. Just as "up" implies "down," the sacred implies the profane or secular.[16]

And yet these cathedrals, as we have seen, were built and sustained and shaped by the laity and those lower on the social and religious hierarchy. Stonemasons, carpenters, artists, and laborers built the cathedrals, and townspeople, cooks, brewers, weavers, and seamstresses helped to keep it running.[17] Much of the art in cathedrals reflects and tells the story of everyday life in their location. The architecture speaks of sacred mysteries, as well as everyday stories of local residents. In the cathedral of Laon, for instance, carvings of sixteen oxen pay homage to the animals that carried in building materials.[18] The nave of Grace Episcopal Cathedral in San Francisco is lined by life-sized murals depicting local history. On the Sunday morning I worshipped at Grace, I sat next to the mural depicting the 1906 earthquake and subsequent fire that shook San Francisco and burned the cathedral. The mural shows a young family with a mother clutching her baby, looking on as firemen respond to the blaze. The nave of the Cathedral of St. John the Divine in Manhattan is surrounded by fourteen prayer bays that are each dedicated to a different calling, including medicine, law, sports, the arts, communications, and education. Stained glass windows in the clerestory—the highest row of stained glass—at Washington National Cathedral weave together stories of the formation of Israel from the Pentateuch with images and stories about the founding of the United States. The sacred and the secular are purposefully and beautifully interwoven in these cathedral spaces.

In this way, cathedrals reflect but also subvert the distinction between the sacred and secular, between the holy and the ordinary, between a priestly and peasant class. Christopher Lewis, dean of Christ Church in Oxford, England, describes cathedrals as a commons, a sacred and public space where boundaries can be explored. They are places people can come "to explore and perhaps to cross the awkward boundary between the secular and the sacred and to handle the insecurities of liminality."[19] Bishop Nicholas Knisely of the Diocese of Rhode Island, who previously served as dean of Trinity Episcopal Cathedral in Phoenix, Arizona, describes cathedral ministry as "a crossroads ministry":

> Cathedral ministry is a crossroads ministry. Cathedrals tend to live with one foot in the secular and one foot in the sacred. I was very intentional when I was the dean of the cathedral in Phoenix, Arizona that that's what we would do. We had an art gallery that was secular but it was placed in sacred space. We had a secular choir that performed in sacred space. We had a sacred choir that performed in secular space. We were always looking for that way to cross the boundary. And I think that's true about cathedrals: at their very best they become the places where the boundaries are broken. And that scares people and empowers people all at the same time.

This extends beyond music, liturgy, and art, the historic staples of cathedral life. Each year St. John the Divine hosts a Blessing of the Bicycles, inviting bicyclists to bring their bikes into the massive nave of the cathedral to have them blessed. A few hundred bikers file into the space. The church bells that ring that day are the ones on the bikes themselves; the blessed saints are those who have died biking in the city over the last year. Blurring the delineation of sacred space, bikers are invited to process with their bikes up through the choir and in front of the high altar. Rev. Canon Julia Whitworth says they gather, "To pray, for those of us who are people of prayer, pray for safety, and joy, and fun, and appreciation for being in God's creation."[20] Whether they bike commuting to work or for pleasure, it is a part of their daily life and here it is seen, known, blessed, and connected to the story of Scripture. Similarly, St. Philip's Cathedral in Atlanta and their dean, Sam Candler, have been blessing runners at the Peachtree Road Race since 1999. Candler flings water on the 55,000 runners going by, which is an undoubtedly welcome refreshment in the heat of Atlanta in July. As he flings the water, he says, "Blessings to you! Blessings to you! We've got 55,000 visitors at the church today." In this way, Candler connects with what many runners find to be a passion, an avocation, and for some an obsession, and a part of their spiritual lives. St. Philip also hosts the local Peachtree Road Farmers Market. Candler reflects,

> We're trying to replicate what a cathedral was in the Middle Ages. They were the center of activity back then. Not just spiritual activity, but economic and commercial activity as well. Our farmers' market is . . . a good meeting place for God's humanity. You don't have to be a member of the church, live in the neighborhood, or even be religious.[21]

These practices point to a deeper understanding of incarnational ministry, which goes beyond being physically present in the neighborhood as an outreach or evangelism strategy. It is far more than that. It is about locating the sacred, affirming the holy in our daily lives, in the flesh, in the seemingly mundane. Offering Ashes to Go at the train station is not just about extending the liturgy to a public space, it is about hallowing the commute people make as part of their daily work. Grace Episcopal Church in Medford's Green Up/Clean Up initiative is an affirmation of the leisure and spiritual renewal people find in nature. Humble Walk hallows the life of its neighborhood by doing Bible study at the coffee shop, Beer and Hymns at the Shamrock, giving out coffee at the bus stop, and worshipping in the park. Thad's Laundry Love consecrates the humble act of doing the laundry. When we engage with friends and followers on social media, we are affirming the ordinary and pointing to the God at the heart of our daily lives and our relationships. When we exercise incarnational leadership and imagination, we help people to see their entire lives as "in cathedral," with its continual mash-up of the humble and sublime and we invite them to experience the mundane routines of their daily lives as a divine liturgy.

In all of this, we are helping people to see their lives—their whole lives—as God does: holy, sacred, and precious. This stance and practice of ministry leadership is essential for the church to reclaim for the sake of our people, and, as we will see in the next chapter, engaging with those beyond our faith communities.

7

NAMiNG IT HOLY

Common Ground for Nones and the Affiliated

"To listen for the presence of spirituality in everyday life is to listen for the variety of ways in which people reach beyond the mundane surface of their existence."

—NANCY AMMERMAN

"To understand religious practice in any society, including the building of magnificent and sacred spaces, we need to know something about people's everyday lives"

—ROBERT SCOTT

"A cathedral can be a spiritual home for those with little faith or even no faith at all."

—THE RT. REV. GRAHAM JAMES, BISHOP OF NORWICH

COMPLINE BY THE GLOW OF SMARTPHONES

"The Lord Almighty grant us a peaceful night and a perfect end. Amen." Amidst the darkened cathedral, smartphone displays emit a haze of ambient light. As the plainsong chant of Compline echoes through the cathedral, hundreds of people gather, sitting in the pews, laying on the floor, or mindfully pacing the aisles. Some listen with eyes closed in quiet contemplation, some gaze around at the modestly adorned sanctuary, while others are checking-in on their phones. This is Compline at St. Mark's

Episcopal Cathedral in Seattle, Washington, held every Sunday night since 1954. Compline is the traditional worship service for the close of day. It is quiet, contemplative, and designed to help those who attend enter into a night of peaceful and blessed rest. This service at St. Mark's frequently draws over five hundred people, mostly in their teens, twenties, and thirties—a remarkable feat given how vastly underrepresented this age group is across mainline churches.

It is also remarkable because Seattle, and the Pacific Northwest more generally, has long been leading the national trend in rates of religious disaffiliation, earning it in the early 2000s the moniker of "the None Zone."[1] While the demographics of the region have shifted in the decade or so since, Pacific coast states, along with Rocky Mountain states and New England, still have among the lowest rates of religious affiliation in the country.[2] Steve Thomason has served as dean of St. Mark's Cathedral since 2012. He told me, "When I was in the call process here, one of the people on the committee said, 'Now, when people here talk about coming out they're not talking about their sexuality. That's a non-issue here. They're talking about whether they tell their friends they go to church.'" Despite the fact that people affiliate with religious traditions at much lower rates than the national average, Thomason cautions, "the 'None zone' is really an overstated theory." He says, "It isn't to suggest that people are flocking to churches here, but they are deeply desirous of an experience with the divine. They are not people without faith. They may be people without faith communities that are named as such." In what continues a theme that has run throughout this book, the binary boundaries we draw between the sacred and secular, the digital and face-to-face—and, here, between the religiously affiliated and the Nones—defies a more complex reality. As we will see, lack of affiliation with an organized religious tradition does not equate to lack of belief, the absence of meaning making, theological savvy, experiences of transcendence, or encounters with the divine, nor does religious affiliation guarantee them.

One of the reasons Compline appeals to those who are not religiously affiliated, Thomason says, is that it creates a sacred space within which individuals can just "be." "The thing about Compline is that it has this incredible rich ancient tradition . . . and yet it's really a seeker service. The people who attend are not expected to do anything other than experience and enjoy." The nature of the Compline service as it's observed at St Mark's reflects the nature of cathedrals as open spaces and "houses of prayer for all people," including Nones. Thomason says, "Not everyone who is worshipping subscribes to a doctrinal set of teachings of the church and its tradition, and we hold that space for this to be a welcoming place." Though ancient, Compline is right in tune with Seattle's hip local culture. Thomason observes that what happens during Compline at St Mark's is:

> exactly parallel to what happens in coffee shops on every corner here in the northwest. . . . You go in on a Saturday morning or a weeknight and folks are just sitting there. They may be on their cell phone, they may be on their computer, they may be talking to a friend, but there's this kind of communal sense of presence in the place.

At Compline, people are free to come and be present, to interpret the music, the service, the prayers, the architecture for themselves, and just to *be* in that space. No commitment is expected or required of those attending, and yet it has become an entry point for many people into the cathedral community. The cathedral creates the conditions for ongoing connection and relationship without insisting on formal membership as a prerequisite or a necessary outcome.

Long before the rise of the Nones, but also before the post-WWII boom period for mainline denominations, William Lawrence, then bishop of the Episcopal Diocese of Massachusetts, extolled the role that cathedrals like St. Mark's play in providing

a welcoming space for people with a range of beliefs, or none at
all. In his 1919 book *The American Cathedral,* he wrote, "[I]n a
great and noble church the worshipper feels a sense of freedom:
he, though an unchurched pagan [today we might say None], can
quietly enter, and without committing himself to any form of religious faith, feel the sense of the eternities."[3] Therefore, he says,
"beneath the great arches of the cathedral may be kneeling side
by side men and women of many faiths and creeds, and the temple may become through worship a church of reconciliation."[4]
In what seems like a progressive idea for the early years of the
twentieth century, and perhaps still progressive at the outset of
the twenty-first, Lawrence writes that the work of a cathedral is
not necessarily *conversion,* but *reconciliation.* This is an important distinction and corrective for ministry leaders and church
institutions, which often quickly jump to trying to convert newcomers into avowed members of our churches, denominations,
and the Christian faith—and who are finding rapidly dimin-
ishing returns. Nearly one hundred years on from Lawrence's
comments, we need to reclaim an approach to ministry in which
reconciliation precedes conversion. Before seeking to change or
convert others, we must first listen, understand, reconcile, and,
at times, repent. In the Digital Cathedral, a spirit of reconciliation is paramount. Rather than rushing to convert the other, we
should instead create safe space and common ground to engage,
and to "let be." It is within this setting that durable relationships
develop, over time allowing the work of reconciliation and perhaps, then, conversion to occur.

NONES, THEY WALK AMONG US

Recent research shows that 20 percent of Americans and 30
percent of people under thirty are Nones, and the percentage is
increasing by 20 percent year over year.[5] This phenomenon, the
so-called rise of the Nones, has struck fear in the hearts of many
church leaders. "The Nones" has become a kind of code for the

cultural shift away from organized religion and church decline. These religiously unaffiliated are typically regarded as kind of a foreign group, "out there" somewhere, a distant blank screen onto which we project our fears. Much of the conversation about Nones, reflected in the popular literature on the subject, has focused on creating a new ministry product (or the appearance of one) that Nones will find palatable.[6] This only reinforces a conversion-first approach and, sadly, is bound to miss the mark. Instead, as Elizabeth Drescher recommends, we need to shift our focus from broadcasting *our* message (conversion) to *listening* to and appreciating how the unaffiliated themselves describe "their own approaches to meaning-making, self-realization, or self-transcendence"[7] (reconciliation).

Drescher also reminds us that Nones are not a single unified group. They are not all hipster Millennials who hang out in coffee shops on Sunday mornings while the faithful are at worship. Rather, they represent a wide range of beliefs, practices, backgrounds, and ages. As Thomason observed, just because they may not belong to a church doesn't mean they are without faith or community. There are some Nones who are deeply spiritual and even religious. Conversely, there are people in our own congregations who struggle—and some who are well acquainted—with doubt and disbelief. When we get beyond statistics and our own prejudices and preconceptions about Nones, we begin to see that the affiliated and unaffiliated have more in common than we might at first expect. I have seen this in my own parish experience. It seems that each time I have set out to plan a new ministry for that imagined proto-typical Millennial None, current members of my congregation inevitably come flooding in. Having experienced this several times in two different parishes, I have come to understand that, though they may not be full-on Nones, many of my members share the same interests and deep spiritual longings. In my attempts to reach out to those beyond my congregations, I have wound up meeting an important need of those within them.

NAMING IT HOLY

It turns out that attentiveness to everyday spirituality described in the previous chapter is vitally important when it comes to engaging with Nones. I learned this from a young man named John at the very first theology pub night I hosted several years ago. The conversation among those gathered that night was free and wide-ranging. We talked about life, baptism, spirituality, the problems with organized religion, and the challenge of inviting friends to church. As the night wore on, I was drawn into conversation with John, the young adult son of one of my most active members. John rarely went to church, and he shared with me that he had misgivings about the whole concept of organized religion. And then he said something I've never forgotten. At one point in our conversation, John was trying to put his finger on what he saw as some of the power that clergy have for the good today. He couldn't quite articulate it, but I knew where he was going. It popped into my head and then out of my mouth. I said, "It's naming it holy." He said, "That's it!" The powerful role he, as a None, saw clergy and ministry leaders still possessing is to name the things in people's everyday lives as holy. This includes not just what happens at church, but the activities and relationships of work, service, family life, or simply connecting with friends over a beer. As I understood John's point, ministry leaders of all sorts—especially ordained leaders who can become so consumed with the interworkings of the church—must be able and willing to look out from the cathedral, or the church building, and see the rest of the town, its people, and their lives, as holy ground.

John was absolutely right. The naming of the holy, for many of the reasons outlined in the previous chapter, is one of the key roles of ministry leaders today. It is something we can do whether we are scrolling through Instagram, Facebook, or Twitter, or having conversations in the neighborhood. We can name people's actions and conversations as the holy callings, activities, and moments they are. This not only helps parishioners see their lives more holistically, but it can help us connect beyond our congregations in digital and online gathering places with Nones.

A survey conducted amongst Nones by Elizabeth Drescher in 2012 found that it was precisely these everyday activities and practices that Nones considered most spiritually meaningful. The most spiritually significant were enjoying friends (32 percent), enjoying family (24 percent), enjoying pets (23 percent), enjoying and sharing food (21 percent), prayer (19 percent), enjoying nature (18 percent), enjoying and creating music (17 percent), enjoying and creating art (11 percent), and enjoying physical activity (8 percent).[8]

Some things immediately jump out from this data. First, as we saw in chapter four, the most durable traditional religious category of meaning-making among Nones is prayer. This is one of the reasons that offering to pray with others at the farmers' market, Panera, the train station, and through social media is consistently so well received.

Second, it is clear that this meaning-making is rooted in everyday experiences: enjoying family and friends, pets, food, nature, music, art, and physical activity. These are not just diversions, hobbies, or the humdrum of everyday life. They aren't things people do while they bide their time between visits to church. These are the activities and practices Nones themselves identify as spiritually important experiences. And so, if we are to engage the Nones who are present inside and beyond our congregations, online and in person, we must understand these as spiritually meaningful practices. We must acknowledge their spiritual significance and recognize them as holy.

In this context, sharing pictures of meals on Instagram is not just an annoyance, not just "food porn," it is part of a meaning-making process. When someone is at their kids' soccer game instead of at church on Sunday morning, they are enjoying family and friends. Just because it's not happening within the church walls at the appointed hour doesn't mean that the experience is devoid of spiritual content. Even for people who seem to be overly attached to their pets, there is something deeper at play in that experience of companionship and unconditional love. These everyday experiences are all charged with meaning. All of these practices are, at least in some measure, lived out across digital and physical spaces as people share photos of children, friends, and pets on Facebook; pin favorite recipes or scenes from nature on Pinterest; and share musical moods through YouTube videos or Pandora tracks. The life of prayer is often a very digitally integrated affair—often even more so for Nones—as people post prayer requests and respond to them all over the internet.

Lest we rush to judgment that more of these things should be happening under the auspices of the church, Drescher points out that the religiously affiliated make meaning in much the same way as Nones, only in a slightly different order. Only a couple categories are reversed and the percentages are very nearly the same.[9] Even for the religiously affiliated, worship appears far down on the list of monthly spiritually significant practices. And so, even for people who go to church with some regularity, the primary way they make meaning is through these other everyday activities. How, then, shall we respond? Shall we advocate for those explicitly religious activities to be higher up on the list? Perhaps. A more constructive approach may be to first engage with people where they already make meaning. Rather than proclaiming church or worship as the solution to every problem, the answer to every question, the holiest of callings, the only way to *really* encounter God, we need first to understand how people already make meaning in their daily lives and participate with them in that. Only then will we have earned the trust and gained the opportunity to relate those experiences to our story of faith and our faith communities. As this data demonstrates, we already have those experiences in our own lives to draw upon. We don't need a clever marketing strategy for reaching the Nones. We need an approach for engaging with people that transcends the arbitrary lines we draw and the dichotomous categories we create. For, the better we understand Nones, the better we understand the people in our pews, and the more resonant our ministry will be both within and beyond our church walls.

SPIRITUAL FOODIES

St. Lydia's Dinner Church in Brooklyn is connecting worship and liturgy with the practice of preparing and sharing food in remarkable ways. St. Lydia's worship is inspired by the early church agape meal (see 1 Corinthians 11:17–34), in which a community meal and Eucharistic worship were blended together. When people arrive at Lydia's, they put on an apron and help prepare dinner, which is then served family style at several tables. Worship takes place over dinner. The bread of the Eucharist is broken at the beginning of meal. The wine is blessed at the end. And so, the entire meal *is* the Eucharist. Over the course of dinner Scripture is read, a sermon is given, songs are sung, and prayers are lifted. St. Lydia's pastor, Emily Scott, says, "The fact that we're getting together and eating sets an understanding that we're first and foremost a community. . . . It takes the emphasis off the dogma and rules of religion, and it starts with something basic, which is what Jesus did, which was share meals with people."[10]

Like St. Mark's Cathedral, St. Lydia's has reached deep into the ancient Christian tradition and found something that is deeply resonant for both Nones and the affiliated alike. They name this meaningful practice of preparing and enjoying food as holy by incorporating it into the central act of the faith community, worship itself. The effect is reminiscent of Michael Pollan's reflection on his own experience of sitting at a meal with a group of friends who had helped gather the ingredients and prepare the food. As dinner begins, he looks around the table at his friends and the food, and recognizes it is a holy moment. He writes,

> [T]here's a sense in which the meal had become . . . a thanks-giving or a secular seder, for every item on our plates pointed somewhere else, almost sacramentally, telling a little story about nature or community or even the sacred, for mystery was very often the theme. Such storied food can feed us both body and soul, the threads of narrative knitting us together as

a group, and knitting the group into the larger fabric of the given world. I don't want to make too much of it; it was just a meal after all.[11]

Of course, it isn't just a meal. It's never *just* a meal. As Christians, who keep the Eucharist as the central act of worship and community life know, sharing a meal together is a holy thing. The conversations around the table, whether it is an altar, pub table, or coffee bar are holy conversations. The food is "storied food." The narrative of how this meal or any meal comes to be and the stories we tell over that food at the table intersect with the narratives of our lives, and, as Pollan writes, the world. This kind of meaning-making is not merely self-referential. It is experienced and shared with others in local and digital spaces, and points beyond that one meal, one place, or one gathering, out into the world.

BLESSING OF THE PETS

Pets also rank high on the list of spiritually meaningful activities for both Nones and the affiliated, and there is a growing trend among churches to offer a blessing of the animals. My own church holds its annual pet blessing during regularly scheduled worship in its outdoor chapel. We've blessed turtles, ducks, dogs, cats, and countless numbers of hermit crabs. People introduce their pets at the beginning of the service and later bring them forward to have them blessed. In these moments, this important aspect of people's lives—interwoven into their everyday routines, meals, walks, and a source of love and companionship—is seen, known, and blessed. It's an incredibly powerful message to communicate God's blessing on this vital part of their lives.

Emily Mellot, the coordinator of Ashes to Go, whom we met in chapter two, takes it a step further. She holds her annual service of pet blessings at a local veterinarian's office. The event started as a memorial service for pets that had died, and grew into a service of both remembrance and blessing. She explains,

Pastors Dyan Lawlor and Keith Anderson bless pets at Upper Dublin Lutheran Church's annual Blessing of the Pets. *Photo courtesy: Diane McGrath*

We do a very short service where we acknowledge the emotional relationship that we have with our pets. We acknowledge that this is an important relationship with God's creation. We pray for pets and for the people who are with our pets. We pray for veterinarians. I make sure that we acknowledge the loss [at the death of a pet] because most of the pet people there, even if they haven't recently lost a pet, have lost a pet at one time or another in their lives, and that's a very spiritual experience. . . . You know, it is the first loss most kids sustain. And we wind up by offering individual prayers. We bless live pets. I've prayed with folks who have brought ashes of their pet, photos of deceased pets, so that we tie that personal relationship in. And, of course, there are pet treats.

As we conduct these services and offer these blessings, we aren't just blessing the dog or cat. We are blessing a closely held and deeply valued part of people's lives. We are naming that ground in their lives as holy. Inspired by Mellott's example, our congregation hosted a pet memorial and blessing service at our local veterinary hospital where one of our church members is a vet. It was clear to me during that experience that we weren't only blessing the pets and their owners, we were also blessing the hospital staff in their daily vocation—in their passion and calling for rescuing, companioning, and healing animals. Now, when I take our dog, Charlie, into the vet's office, the staff and I are more connected and have a greater appreciation for each other's vocations.

SACRED STORIES, SPIRITUAL TRIBES

As we seek to understand and engage with people in their various ways of meaning-making, it is essential to understand the language people use to describe those activities. In her book *Sacred Stories, Spiritual Tribes*, which recounts her research with a range of individuals from the religiously devout to the religiously unaffiliated, Nancy Ammerman identifies two different modes of speech people use to describe religious experience: "theistic" and "extra-theistic."

- Theistic spirituality is overt language about God and how God is at work in the world or my life. This is a more traditional language of faith. It regularly employs specific terminology like "God," "Lord," and "Savior." Not surprisingly, the religiously affiliated tend to employ this language in describing their spiritual life and lived experience.

- Extra-theistic language is language about the something "more" in life, for identifying transcendent within the mundane, but not explicit God-language. Extra-theistic expressions of faith include words like "awe," "grounded," and "connected." Both the affiliated and Nones use this mode of speech.

Importantly, the two categories are not mutually exclusive. At any given time, the religiously affiliated and the religiously unaffiliated alike use these modes of speech to describe their experience.

However, when we are only attuned to the *theistic* ways people share their faith, we miss the ordinary ways the sacred is woven into their daily lives. We miss the other registers in which people express their faith using non-traditional language and practices. We also reduce witnessing and evangelism to telling people about our faith or our church. We look for broadcasts of propositional beliefs—"Jesus is Lord"—or a kind of Yelp! recommendation for a church—"Awesome sermon from Rev. Sally today at St. Whatsits!"—rather than an expression of living out the free and unconditional love of God in relationships with others, whatever we name it, or not. Widening the ways in which we understand how people express their faith, rather than narrowing them, creates, according to Ammerman, "a fertile boundary zone where spiritualities meet."[12]

Perhaps this overlap in these modes of speech should not be so surprising given that Nones and the affiliated share similar forms of making meaning.[13] Fully, 70 percent of Nones grew up in or have had some experience in Christian churches. Whether or not they are still active in a faith community, there is some remnant of that experience they are able to access and draw upon. The good news here is that Nones and the affiliated have common ground both in the categories above, and in the way they describe them. Those of us who wish to engage with Nones need to hear and recognize, as Ammerman writes in the epigraph, how people are "reaching beyond the mundane surface of their existence."[14] We need to be aware of our own language, consciously modulating it to employ extra-theistic language when appropriate. It is a way of speaking that tends to start with lived experience and moves into the *more*. Rather than quickly slapping doctrinal labels or applying theological categories onto people's experience, it asks that we dwell patiently in the realm of experience and feeling. It is an ongoing work of listening and translation. Ammerman describes extra-theistic language in this way,

> The extra-theistic landscape, then, echoes with talk about seeking—seeking transcendence in nature and beauty, seeking a sense

of unity and connection, seeking meaning to guide life's journey, and seeking the mystical truth that lies within. This is a language about spirituality that can be spoken by people who do not claim religious affiliation. . . . [P]eople who think of themselves as non-religious, if they have a spiritual vocabulary at all, are likely to speak of it as meaning, awe, connection, and inner wisdom.[15]

It's important to note that this is *not* non-theistic language. It is not a denial of the divine. Some feel that we start down a slippery slope when we move away from specific God-language and therefore the particularity of the Christ event and Christian tradition. Some have gone so far as to call it "dumbing down." This is not at all to suggest we jettison theistic, traditional, or specifically Christian ways of describing God's activity in the world. Rather, it is a matter of hearing with new ears and utilizing a mode of language, which, in fact, has a long history in the Christian spirituality. Our ability to recognize and employ these two modes of language can help us to engage in ways that lead with reconciliation rather than conversion. It can be a starting point and common ground for conversation.

Getting outside our church buildings is particularly helpful in becoming fluent in these two modes of speech. In my ministry, I notice a significant difference in the way people talk about God in the church building and the way they do at the coffee shop, brewpub, or home. The very same people who tend to use theistic language in a more traditional church setting often employ extra-theistic language in more relaxed local gathering spaces. If most of our conversations about God happen in church settings (and are led by ministry professionals), we are very likely primarily utilizing a theistic way of describing our faith or experience. Inviting those conversations in other contexts helps us to become more comfortable with using extra-theistic language.

In her earlier research Ammerman also identified another mode of belief and language she called "Golden Rule Christianity." Golden Rule Christianity draws on Jesus' instruction in the Sermon on the Mount to "do unto others as you would have them do unto you" (Luke 6:31, Matthew 7:12). Here, people talk about their spirituality as a way of acting ethically in their work and relationships. People ask, "Am I living a good life? And I doing unto others as I would want them to do unto me? Am I acting ethically?"[16] This mode of speech, she finds, is employed extensively in white, suburban congregations and plays out across the ideological continuum.

People often move with great fluidity between "golden rule," "theistic," and "extra-theistic" language. At a recent theology pub gathering, we talked about finding God in our daily work. Many people from my largely white suburban congregation used the Golden Rule approach and talked about how an awareness of God in their lives moves them to act ethically, to treat people as they would want to be treated. Those who employed theistic language talked about how they saw faith taking an active role in their day-to-day work. They told stories about particular situations where they saw God at work, and unexpected encounters or moments of serendipity. Others used extra-theistic language to speak about how they felt when they were using their gifts, with a feeling of being connected to something larger than themselves. They felt fulfilled and gratified by a deeper sense of the *more* in life.

CREATING SANCTUARY

Sanctuary Church in Marshfield, Massachusetts and its pastor, Mark Huber, know well the rise of the Nones and the cultural shift away from organized religion. Located in None-heavy New England, Sanctuary was founded in 2010 and is a joint mission congregation of the United Methodist Church and the ELCA. In the first several months of the mission start, well before Sanctuary had a building or even a name, Huber became a regular at local gathering places in Marshfield, particularly Starbucks, in part because he had nowhere else to go. Some months later, Sanctuary held its first worship services on a parishioner's back deck and is now housed in the building of a former United Methodist congregation that closed. They completely renovated the sanctuary, creating a multi-purpose space that can accommodate worship, fellowship events, and social ministry activities. They converted the balcony that once held the organ into a "coffee loft" with, in a poetic turn of events, old furniture donated by Starbucks.

Sanctuary lives up to its name in the way, like St. Mark's and Bishop Lawrence's prototypical cathedral, it creates safe and sacred space for Nones and the affiliated. Huber says this does not mean "one size fits all," but rather "one size fits many." Huber notes that the members of the Sanctuary community hold a range of beliefs and practices, including "a lot of people who are functional agnostics." He told me,

> Today, in this day and age, people hold a lot of conflicting belief systems. People are really comfortable holding all sorts of paradox and tension together. One parishioner shared with me that the space that Sanctuary has created has never made her feel the pressure to convert. She never feels that the belief system that she brings into this place is somehow silly or inferior.

Huber and Sanctuary Church have created a spiritual space large enough to hold a range of beliefs among its members, without a secret agenda to convert people or have them ultimately ascribe to a series of doctrinal beliefs. Rather, it seeks to be a place of sanctuary and healing for people who have been hurt in some way by organized religion, a place that makes space for people to doubt, and does not require them to identify as Lutheran, Methodist, or even Christian. It embodies a spirit of reconciliation rather than conversion. Huber wonders aloud,

> How do you stay in relationship with someone if you tell them at every party and playdate, "I'm right, you're wrong, and eventually you'll see." It's not a great way to sustain a friendship or a long-term relationship. There is this eternal balance. Part of it is being really respectful of the place they are in—and making that relationship and sustaining that relationship a huge priority.

ON THE FENCE

Huber's approach is inspired by a method of biblical interpretation called "polyvalence within parameters."[17] In biblical interpretation it means that there can be a range of interpretations about any given text within certain general limits. For example, people can and do interpret the story of the Exodus many ways, and yet those interpretations ought to fall within a larger understanding of God's faithfulness and redemptive work in the world. At Sanctuary polyvalence within parameters is about providing space for multiple meanings, identities, and beliefs within a broadly defined area, welcoming a wide range of beliefs and practices within broad limits. This is expressed at Sanctuary by what they call The Fence, their way of defining sacred space. On the beliefs and values section of their website, rather than official denominational statements of belief or creeds, are found images of fence staves with the following beliefs written on them:

- Err on the Side of Love
- We Know True Love Through Jesus
- We Know Jesus Through Scripture
- God's Spirit Is Still Active in the World
- Grace Is Overwhelming and Complete
- Openness and Diversity Draws Us Closer to God
- We Exist for the Work of God in the World[18]

Below each one of these statements is an expanded explanation and a biblical reference. These are sufficiently broad, non-doctrinal statements, incorporating theistic and extra-theistic language, which describe the kind of community they aspire to be. Huber explains,

> The whole point of The Fence was to say that this is the boundary that we're setting up. We're a Christian congregation. We bring in our God-centered grace focus lens as Lutherans; we

also bring in our holiness lens from the Methodists—things that help define the safe area we're creating. So if someone comes in and tries to shift our community focus . . . we have this fence to say, "No that's not really in line within the faith parameters boundaries that we're creating together." And people get that. That keeps us from getting lost down the rabbit hole that being such a diverse community could drag us down into.

Here, Sanctuary demonstrates a way to live into this more cathedral-inspired expansive view of incorporation and identity in community. As Huber reflects, "Being that safe center has enabled people both to engage in the very specific theologically centered Christ-focused community that we are, but it's open enough that they don't have to check their agnosticism at the door."

The safe and open cathedral-like spaces that Sanctuary and other ministries offer, either within or beyond their church buildings, create opportunities for engagement around spiritually meaningful practices and indicate openness to the various ways people describe them. Our ability to recognize and name those practices as well as everyday experiences as holy can help place us in relationship with those beyond our faith communities and foster the work of reconciliation. As we will see in the next chapter, this understanding and approach better equip us to host and participate in conversations in local and digital spaces—conversations that happen at the intersection of life and faith.

GOD ON TAP

At the Intersection of Life and Faith

"[T]he vibrant freewheeling spirit of the coffeehouse has re-emerged in recent years and now animates the Internet's discussion forums and social media platforms. Like coffeehouses before them, they provide a free and open space for debate and discussion."

—TOM STANDAGE

"There is clearly something about a cathedral . . . which breathes an unconditional welcome, allowing people to use its sacred space as they wish."

—THE RT. REV. GRAHAM JAMES, BISHOP OF NORWICH

"In the [sixteenth-century] Flemish countryside interested villagers and sometimes also clerics met after mass at local taverns to discuss biblical texts. It is not surprising that in this context a certain conviviality developed."

—CARTER LINDBERG

AT THE INTERSECTION

"What we had in mind was a colonial tavern," explains Dan Endicott, co-owner of Forest & Main Brewing Company. Forest & Main is a small pub and restaurant housed in a restored nineteenth-century Victorian house at the corner of Forest Avenue and North Main Street (thus the name) in Ambler, Pennsylvania. Dan and I are sitting in the bar area, which used to be the living room of the house. The interior is decidedly vintage, hipster, and a little quirky—kind of like Dan, as he will happily admit. The walls hold a collection of eclectic items—including a small picture of a cathedral. There is nothing commercial inside: no neon beer signs or television sets. The most notable technology is the record player near the bar, for B.Y.O.V. (bring your own vinyl) nights. The beer list is scratched on chalkboards in each room. As we sip a Belgian-inspired Saison, one of the most popular brews in their slate of craft beers, Dan explains that they chose this old house, instead of the larger building just next door, in order to create a smaller, more intimate environment for people to gather. They hoped, like a colonial tavern, it would become a crossroads for conversation and community. And it has. Forest & Main has quickly become celebrated for both its brewing[1] and as a neighborhood gathering place with good food, good beer, and good conversation. Dan, who was not raised in a religious tradition but remains curious and appreciative, likens both beer and Forest & Main itself to a religious icon. He says, "Once you get beyond the first look or the first sip, you discover there is something deeper, more complex going on." Dan knows of what he speaks. In addition to being a brewer who understands the complexities of a good beer, Dan is also an artist and has studied Byzantine iconography—something I discovered when one of the illustrations he created for Forest & Main bore the uncanny resemblance to Jesus blessing the cup at the Last Supper. Dan, here, was referring to the way religious icons draw the observer through the detail of the artwork, into the story of Scripture and ultimately into an encounter with the divine.

Like an icon, there is much more going both sociologically and spiritually beneath the surface of local gathering places like Forest & Main. These gathering places are all around us. They play a vital role in our local communities—and increasingly in ministry today.[2] In this chapter, we will look in more detail at pubs and coffee shops and their place within the expanse of the Digital Cathedral.

Forest & Main and local gathering places like it typify what sociologist Ray Oldenburg has called the "third places" in American culture, which he defines as "the great variety of public places that host the regular, voluntary, informal, and happily anticipated gatherings of individuals beyond the realms of home and work."[3] These include pubs, coffeehouses, as well as shops, bookstores, and barber shops, among others. While home, the "first place," and work, "the second place," usually have prescribed roles and responsibilities, third places are more flexible and open. Like Forest & Main, they have a unique character and function in the community. They are local, conversational, welcoming, rooted in the neighborhood, and valued as much for the community they cultivate as the cuisine they serve. Unlike some of the other local places we have seen throughout this book, these relational, networked, and incarnational hubs are not only places of *encounter*, but also places of deepening *engagement* through *conversation*, places where people can take the time to linger over a coffee, beer, or meal, and get to know one another. They are vital places of conversation and community, relationality and repose.

Ministry leaders are increasingly using these third places as venues for connecting with people beyond their church buildings, affirming the ordinary, and engaging in meaningful encounters and conversations. They are hosting gatherings at pubs and coffee shops to discuss theological topics, Scripture, current events, and everyday life. Practices like "theology pubs," "beer and hymns," and "coffee shop office hours" are something of standard operating procedure for emerging churches—done both out of necessity, since they do not have or may not want a church building, and of out a desire to connect with people in their communities and share the Gospel in new ways. It is a practice some traditional congregations are exploring as well.

THIRD PLACE AS SACRED SPACE

These locales can provide not just a *cultural* third place, but can function as a *religious* third place as well—that is, a place between the faith practiced privately in the home and that practiced corporately in local congregations. Bryan Berghoef, a pastor in the Christian Reform Church of North America who has been leading theology pubs for several years, suggests that a pub may be just the right setting to engage friends and strangers, believers and Nones in conversations about life and faith. He told me,

> People are longing for relationships, for meaningful dialogue about issues and a safe place to do that, where there aren't expectations of a certain belief or perspective. I think all those things come together at the pub in a unique way, or the coffee shop for that matter. But I think there is something about a pub setting that really allows people to feel at home and lower their guard and feel like. "Hey, this is low key. I can just pull up a chair like I might do on any other night and order a pint and something to eat and listen in and hear what people are saying and offer something and be heard."

Pub and coffee shop ministry gatherings are effective in large part because of the role these third places already play in the local community, and the relaxed and open atmosphere they provide. As Berghoef observes, they can become entry points for those not connected to a faith community and who may be wary of entering a church building. They also create a more relaxed environment for church members and ministry leaders. While moving beyond the church building onto someone else's turf may be initially unsettling there is a freedom—and, as Carter Lindberg writes, "a certain conviviality"[4]—that quickly develops in these spaces. Many of the formalities of church are absent. People don't feel that they have to somehow provide the right answers or behave in a certain way, and thus the conversation can be much more free flowing, relational, honest, and fun. These settings also relieve clergy of some of their traditional and sometimes constrictive roles as preacher, presenter, and teacher, and invite them to become listeners, facilitators, conveners, and guides. Church members feel the freedom to describe their spiritual experiences and questions in broader ways, and, as we have seen in the previous chapter, this provides an important way of engaging with newcomers and Nones.

As connections are made and conversations take shape, these third places can become profoundly sacred spaces. Like an icon, we can be drawn into an encounter with the divine, and find ourselves standing (or sitting) on holy ground. According to Berghoef, in these moments the pub,

> becomes sacred in a more accessible everyday way, and the dualism between sacred and profane whether we are thinking in those terms or not sort of dissipates, and we see that unity and sacredness of all of life and if I can have a conversation with a stranger . . . we can have this human engagement and I can hear their story and I can see their authenticity in it and I can see God in it. And that's a holy, sacred moment.

I've witnessed many of these moments during our own theology pub gatherings: when a middle school math teacher chokes up while talking about her job as a calling from God, when someone talks about the way certain music moves their soul, when a person offers words of consolation and reassurance to another, when a parent and her young adult daughter publicly express gratitude for each other, and when a newcomer shares something of their spiritual struggle. In these moments, a sociological third place becomes spiritually sacred space and "we glimpse what seems most familiar to us with wholly new eyes."[5]

These moments undoubtedly happen within the context of congregational life as well. However, while local congregations are, broadly speaking, a third place insofar as they are not the workplace (for most people) or home, they often do not function as third places in the way Oldenburg describes. He has identified eight common characteristics of these third places:

- *Neutral Ground*—People can come and go as they please, no one is required to play host. The space doesn't belong to any one person or group.
- *Leveling*—It is an inclusive place with no criteria for membership or participation. Rank and class are left behind at the door.
- *Conversation*—This is the main activity in third spaces.
- *Accessibility and Accommodation*—These places are open and available at convenient times, creating the conditions for "unplanned, unscheduled, unorganized, and unstructured"[6] gatherings and encounters.
- *Regulars*—The regular group of attendees help set the tone of the place "whose mood and matter provide the infectious and contagious style of interaction and whose acceptance of new faces is crucial."[7]
- *Low Profile*—The physical setting is rather plain, not flashy, and certainly non-pretentious. It creates a comfortable spot for regulars rather than a novelty for strangers or transient customers.
- *Playful Mood*—Third places are punctuated by laughter. "Here joy and acceptance reign over anxiety and alienation."[8]
- *Home Away from Home*—People are able to relax and be themselves, without the expectations of work or home, and where "Warmth emerges out of a friendliness, support, and mutual concern."[9]

Although we may think of our congregations as warm and welcoming to newcomers, the experience is rarely *neutral* or *level*. Our buildings are open at certain times around scheduled worship or programming, which tends to be more presentation and less *conversation*, more serious than it is *playful*. There is a range of unspoken expectations about participation, involvement, and membership. In contrast to Bishop Lawrence's ministry of *reconciliation*, the focus inside our buildings tends to be on *conversion*, which from the outset can create tensions for visitors already uncertain about church. In fact, according to Oldenberg's criteria, cathedrals tend to function as more of a classic third place. Their doors are typically open throughout the day to visitors and pilgrims. People come and go as they wish, remaining anonymous if they choose. They are welcome to admire the architecture, art, or music; participate in worship; or just sit and be present in the space. The experience is not prescribed, and there are lower expectations regarding participation and affiliation. As Graham James, Bishop of Norwich, writes, "There is clearly something about a cathedral . . . which breathes an unconditional welcome, allowing people to use its sacred space as they wish."[10]

CREATING CATHEDRAL SPACE

While we may not be able to keep our doors open all hours of the day and night, we can approximate that "unconditionally welcome" environment in local and digital gathering spaces, as well as our church buildings. Sanctuary Church in Marshfield hosts a variety of public events in their multi-purpose worship space, from open microphone music nights, to large meal-packaging events which include hundreds of local volunteers. In so doing, they encourage a variety of people with a whole range of beliefs and practices to be present in that space and connect around common interests, without the hard sell of joining the church. St. Gregory of Nyssa Episcopal Church in San Francisco opens the doors of its beautiful sanctuary, filled with stunning icons, to provide space for people to work or meet up with friends. They say,

> We're going to throw open the doors of our church to whoever wants to use it as a study space, work space, meeting space, social space. Use our wi-fi for free. Have some coffee. Meet your neighbors, or just work quietly by yourself.

St. Gregory also hosts a food pantry in its sanctuary space, where food for the hungry is given away in the same space where the Eucharist is celebrated on Sunday mornings.[11] In Philadelphia,

Calvary United Methodist Church hosts a "Community Contemplative Space" once a month, offering their community "a safe and quiet drop-in space for community members to engage in spiritual or contemplative practices they find meaningful."[12] Calvary's minister, John Pritchard, says,

> "We are not in any way doctrinal or demanding any kind of interpretation or content to that experience. So, people can come and be still as atheists, they can come and be still as Buddhists. . . . We have people come as Jews, people who come as Methodists, etcetera." It attracts, he says, "folks who would not come to an organized religious, traditional religious experience, who would not come to worship on a Sunday morning, who would come to an experience like that."[13]

In these ways, Calvary, Sanctuary, St. Gregory, and other churches are offering a cathedral-like "third place" in the context of their congregational buildings and ministry. However, some have also recognized the need—indeed, the imperative—to move outside the church building to "third places" like pubs, coffeehouses, farmers' markets, and parks, to create a broader welcome. For while we should seek to craft a welcoming and open experience for visitors to our churches, the fact remains that fewer and fewer people are stepping into our church buildings at all.

PRAYING AT THE PUB

In its work of making its neighborhood its cathedral, Humble Walk Lutheran Church hosts three regular events at its neighborhood pub, The Shamrock, theology pubs, storytelling events, and Beer and Hymns (which is just like it sounds: people gather together at the pub and belt out hymns while enjoying their favorite beverage). These are a large and vital part of their congregational life. Beer and Hymns, for example, regularly draws more people than worship on Sunday mornings. For many people, one or more of these events *is* their church. That's just fine for Humble Walk's pastor Jodi Houge. Echoing Bishop Lawrence's spirit of reconciliation, she says,

> I feel like it is a *healing* thing that we are doing. . . . The fact
> that we would be in a bar and having a beer and doing this thing
> and being so fluid on our edges, that opens up something for
> people that walking into a Sunday morning worship or coming
> to your Vacation Bible School doesn't. It's meeting people where
> they are, but where they *really* are, not just saying that. It's meet-
> ing them where they are and then not doing any sort of bait and
> switch, or looking to convert them. If you only come to our bar
> events, then we applaud that and claim it. We will never try to
> hoodwink you into a pew, but the invitation is always there.

Humble Walk's presence at the pub and coffee shop puts them in
ongoing relationship with people who would likely never come to
worship on a Sunday morning, who may have reservations about
joining a church or identifying themselves as Christian, and yet are
still a part of the Humble Walk community. They sing hymns, they
pray, they encounter Scripture, they build relationships, just not in
the context of Sunday morning worship. These ongoing connections create the opportunities for sacred moments to emerge.

Houge tells a remarkable story of ministering to the staff at
The Shamrock. Humble Walk had been meeting at the Shamrock
for about a year and had come to know the staff there pretty well.
One night during Beer and Hymns, she noticed that the servers
seemed down.

> Our regular server said afterward, as I was packing up my
> stuff and talking to the last few people. "Would it be possible
> if I brought the staff in and you could pray with us tonight,
> because one of the bouncers died this morning and the staff is
> here hanging out because they don't know what to do? They're
> broken up about it." And I said, "Sure." . . . They all came
> in. And they're all young twenty-somethings, a typical bar staff.
> Maybe twenty-five people altogether, and the manager, and
> the bartenders, and the bouncers—burley twenty-something

young men weeping and leaning on one another. And then I asked, "Tell me about your friend." And then out come the stories, both good and bad. . . . A very real picture of their friend came out. . . . And then we prayed in a circle and then they all went back to work. . . . The next day Humble Walk brought a memorial bouquet for the staff at the bar.

This moment happened because of Humble Walk's consistent, meaningful presence over time at The Shamrock. The members of the congregation became known and trusted, and so when this moment of extraordinary sadness and grief struck the staff, they felt they could ask Jodi to pray. This story highlights one of the overlooked parts of cultivating a meaningful presence in these local spaces. While we often focus on how to minister to our members and reach out to the Nones, the fact is that the most consistent interaction with people beyond our churches is usually with the staff, whether it's the server, the bartender, barista, or owner. Our consistent presence in these public spaces, whether local or digital, creates opportunities for care and connection— for what most everyone can recognize as real ministry.

FILL MY CUP

Along with pubs, coffeehouses have emerged as another key "third place" in our culture. Starbucks, along with a great variety of locally owned coffee shops, has fueled the resurgence of coffeehouse culture over the last thirty years. However, it isn't simply about grande mocha frappuccinos (though they are delicious), but about social connections—with baristas, friends, neighbors, and strangers, and a "communal sense of presence" described by Dean Steve Thomason in the previous chapter. Clergy have begun to utilize coffeehouses for off-site office hours, sermon writing, or intentional gatherings for conversation, leading some to refer to the ubiquitous coffee chain as *St. Arbuck's*. While this beatification of Starbuck's is done in jest, it points to the ways these places function as situational sacred space through conversation, theological reflection, and Bible study. In these and many other ways, it offers a heightened awareness of God's presence in everyday life beyond the church building.

Haley Vay Beaman, the pastor for children, youth, and family ministry at Zion Lutheran Church in York, Pennsylvania, hosts a regular coffee shop Bible study for teenagers called Fill My Cup. Fill My Cup meets once a month at a Starbucks near the church. She says that the move to Starbucks was spurred by the sense that the teenagers in her church were ready for a different venue than the church's senior high youth room. When they gather, they spend the first part of a two-hour session sharing their highs and lows, followed by Bible study, and then they close with prayer. (Notably, Beaman helps make it affordable for the youth. She asks each person for a $2 offering and the church covers the remainder of the cost of the drinks.) She says that this change in venue has generated new energy among her youth and created new connection with people beyond the congregation. She says,

> It's not a big coffee shop, so we sort of take over. We have to gather chairs from the entire place to fit our group. We're on the couches in the corner and we're right by the front door, so people pass by. We're doing Bible study so they see our Bibles on the tables. They see us pray together. They overhear our conversations. In a coffee shop there is a lot of white noise but there's also time to hone in on someone's conversation. People have stopped by the group, and two young adult guys have joined our congregation at different times.

Beaman here highlights another important aspect of third place ministries—and social media, for that matter—the power of allowing people to overhear our conversations. Discussing the Bible and praying in public is a way of being church without being in people's face about it. People can observe or listen, making the choice to connect and join in the conversation or not. This is a similar dynamic to social media. While we may only engage with a handful of people in a series of tweets or Facebook comments, many more people are overhearing (or reading) that engagement. And that overhearing works in both directions. When we place ourselves in these local or digital spaces, we may overhear things that move us to connect with others, or to prayer. I remember one day when I was sermon writing at my favorite local coffee shop. A woman and her frail elderly mother were sitting at the table next to me. I inferred that the daughter had brought her mother to the coffee shop for a little outing. As they sat, quietly sipping their tea, I was moved by the tenderness of the relationship, and the challenge I sensed for the daughter in caring for her aging mother. It moved me to pray. I posted on Facebook, as I am wont to do on occasion, "For what shall we pray today?" and included a prayer for caregivers. Several people then responded with a series of prayer requests and concerns. That unspoken encounter in the local coffee shop led to a digitally mediated prayer meeting.

Like Houge, Beaman reports that the connection with the staff has also been a remarkable part of the Fill My Cup experience.

> The relationships that have been forged in that time have been really incredible. The baristas have been open to our group participating in the life of their store. There are other times when I just come in when I have a day off and they're just, "Hey, Haley, what's up?" They know that the relationship there is real and they can be themselves, to the point where they know we're coming and they prep the place for us and they're like, "We're so glad you're here," and they know the kids by names. And they started to do special things, like if someone got a latte—you know how they can make the foam look like a heart—they were making it look like crosses. There's something about the comfort level that has been formed there that's really amazing. *It's almost like I have become their pastor too. Even if they don't believe in organized religion, they are able to participate in a new way.*

This profound statement reflects both Beaman's understanding of her role as pastor to people within and beyond the traditional bounds of her congregation. She sees and treats both the church and the coffee shop, both members and baristas as part of an extended cathedral community.

It may be that Nones never join the group, the conversation, or the church but our presence creates opportunities to be connected, meaningfully engaged, to minister and share the grace of God in ways that just waiting around for people to show up to our church does not. Most of the people who attend our God on Tap theology pub nights are church members, though we do regularly welcome newcomers. Some people find us online or through word of mouth. Church members often invite friends or family members whom they would never ask to church on Sunday morning but think would be comfortable at the pub. Parents frequently bring their young adult children, who tend not be involved in church in other traditional ways. Some of these guests (and perhaps some of our members) may be considered Nones and we are glad to welcome them into that space, but most of our interactions with Nones happen outside that designated ninety-minute gathering time. They happen beforehand as people mingle when they get their drinks at the bar. They happen afterward when we return to the bar to hang out and share some of the conversation with interested patrons or staff, and engage their experiences and stories. The connections extend from there. There was the former waitress at Forest & Main who told me about growing up in a conservative Christian context; when I run into her in town or at the YMCA, she greets me, "Hey PK!" (short for Pastor Keith). One evening I went to the pub on my own for dinner and a drink, and a person at the bar I didn't know turned to me and asked, "So, how did that God on Tap thing get started?" When carrying extra folding chairs into the pub for God on Tap, I overheard one person, a Forest & Main regular who has never joined our conversation, explaining to a friend sitting on the porch what we do. Or the newspaper reporter, who sat in on the conversation for a story in the local paper and commented afterward how moved he was as people described what they were grateful for.[14] Our presence in these spaces opens up occasions and opportunities to connect, and to share a different way of being church and a Christian than what is customarily portrayed in the media. It may also present opportunities for collaboration, as when we partnered with Forest & Main, to host a beer tasting event to raise money for our neighborhood community food pantry.

URBAN ABBEY

Urban Abbey, a coffee shop, bookstore, and worship center in Omaha, Nebraska, grew out of a series of theology pub gatherings called Wesley Pub, begun in 2008 by Debra McKnight. Three years later, supported by the local United Methodist conference and First United Methodist Church in Omaha, they moved into their current storefront in the Old Market district of Omaha, at first sharing the space with a local bookstore, and then assuming the space entirely. The storefront space has a coffee bar, a small bookstore specializing in spirituality, and lots of tables, chairs, and couches. In the center of it all is an understated, yet beautiful glass font—a quiet statement that all the life and activity of the abbey happens around the promise of new life in Christ. I asked McKnight about what they had in mind when they started the abbey. She explained,

> An abbey was a place where people worked, lived, studied, worshiped and ate food—things that drew them together, even though they might have had different roles and different ways of living [in] that community with a kind of deep hope that it would matter in the world.

In the four years since its inception, Urban Abbey is living up to its name. It engages a wide range of people and has partnered with several local non-profits, to which they have donated over $35,000. McKnight describes how this hope of an urban abbey has become a reality:

> I'll go down to the abbey on a Saturday morning during the Farmers' Market and there are families and teenagers and a

homeless youth that's volunteering behind the counter and our manager knows everybody's name. . . . We really are offering a presence of hospitality and deep care into the world. We're not doing that with an expectation of anyone coming to worship or giving a gift. We are just trying to be present in a way that is totally natural and normal in their lives.

This includes a warm embrace of Nones. In fact, one of McKnight's friends, "a great outspoken atheist" designed the whole storefront space. McKnight says,

We have some committed atheists who love coming in and who are part of us, and help with things like technology and photography. They're not going to come to church, but I can tell that the space matters and means something to them. And I think if they felt like it was in danger of not existing, they would want to stand up and be counted in making it possible to continue.

The abbey has opened what we might call a cathedral space for people of different faiths and practices to engage in community, relationship, and meaningful work. Like a cathedral, the abbey has a variety of ways for people to feel connected and engaged—from social service initiatives, involvement with the local community, theological reflection, the arts, and worship. Though a relatively small storefront, Urban Abbey is spiritually broad and diverse enough to allow for many different ways of belonging and belief without expecting people to sign on the bottom line to the Apostles' Creed. One community member notes how Wesley Pub, now under the umbrella of Urban Abbey, "helps me as an agnostic to feel welcome and accepted into the community. I wouldn't describe myself as spiritualistic. I don't believe in a god. But I'm not against seeking him out in the company of others, and this is a group I feel very comfortable doing that with."[15]

Theology pubs and coffeehouse ministries, when they embody the characteristics of third-places-come-sacred-space like Humble Walk, Fill My Cup, or Urban Abbey, create fresh opportunities and experiences for fellowship, formation, and evangelism. They put people at ease and invite new connections among people with a variety of beliefs and practices, and none at all. Like the brewery and bakery in the Canterbury precincts, they and the people who frequent them all fall *in cathedral*. In the next chapter, we will explore in greater detail the conversations that attend these gatherings and how they shape the work of theology.

SOME PRACTICAL ADVICE AS YOU GET STARTED

One of the reasons the third place ministries described in this chapter work so well is that individuals like Houge, Beaman, and McKnight have done the hard work of understanding their community, their mission, and their particular context. Although the location, personal styles, and group dynamics will differ according to each group and setting, there are some key common elements that help to shape these groups that bear consideration should you chose to organize one: *location, content, atmosphere,* and *digital presence.*

Location—As we have seen, location is crucial. As much as possible, the venue should already function as a "third place" in the local community, a place already known and enjoyed by people in and beyond the congregation. Whenever possible, support locally owned businesses. Those owners are often around day-to-day, and they are typically networked to the neighborhood, which facilitates making even more connections to the community. Most places are open to groups and are happy to have the business on a slow night of the week. Depending on your context, you might also consider non-food-or-drink-related settings.

Make sure the overall feeling in the space matches the ethos you are trying to achieve. We have our version of theology pub called God on Tap at Forest & Main. It works in large part because of the physical space as well as the ethos that the owners and staff have taken great care to create. It's important to visit local pubs and coffeehouses to get a feel for the environment. Presbyterian minister Adam Walker Cleaveland, who has hosted theology pubs for several years, described to me his approach to finding a location for his theology pub gathering. He recounts, "I spent an evening doing research, driving around to five or six places on the evening I knew I wanted to do theology pub. I visited around the time of the night I knew I wanted to do it, just to get the feel of the place."

It generally works best to have a space set apart within your location but not entirely closed off from the rest of the place. Pay attention to the noise level and make sure people can actually hear one another from across the room or table. If you are in a separate room, leave time at the beginning and the end for people to mix in public areas. My favorite part of God on Tap is after we've

Continued

Some Practical Advice as You Get Started *Continued*

---

adjourned from our room upstairs and flowed back down to the bar. Conversations continue, new connections are made, and staff and locals are engaged in the conversation.

Format and Content—The content of these gatherings can vary greatly depending on the interests of the group and the leaders. Typically, each gathering has a particular topic or theme. Some gatherings focus on current events, while some groups work their way through key theological categories. Some emphasize storytelling, while others focus on people's lived experience. Some groups have a handout for each session, while others do not. Some choose to have guest speakers or facilitators. Whatever the format, the common denominator seems to be taking something in our lived experience and ask faith questions about it, inviting people into conversations at the intersection of life and faith. At God on Tap, we usually choose topics that key off Elizabeth Drescher's categories of meaning-making from the previous chapter. We start with something like music, or the outdoors, or varieties of ways we spend time enjoying families, friends, pets, or food, and ask faith questions about them, in order to draw out their importance in our lives and to wonder how God is at work in those as well. We've talked about our daily routines as a form of liturgy and debated whether God cares who wins the Stanley Cup. We've invited people to share their image of God and what they are grateful for.[16] The advantage of being grounded in everyday experience is that everyone has something to share. This sets the bar to participation fairly low. Importantly, it also recognizes that people are experts in their own lives. As the facilitator, I'm not there to tell them how to understand their experience. I'm there to help us reflect individually and collectively and to see our everyday experience with new eyes, to discover the sublime amidst the mundane. By contrast, our "Coffee and Conversation" has no particular topic. We just talk about whatever happens to be on people's minds and hearts that day. Through the mundane, we find commonality, support, and encouragement, and from there, inevitably, it seems, religious or spiritual insights emerge. Because these discussions are so open-ended, some facilitators find it helpful to have a set of ground

Continued

Some Practical Advice as You Get Started Continued

rules for the conversation. At the beginning of his theology pubs, Cleaveland shares these rules of the road:

- Everyone's voice has the right to be heard.
- If your voice is causing others NOT to be heard . . . take a break and listen.
- There won't be any "wrap up" in the end, no sense of "this is what you should believe."
- We gather here together as seekers, all on our own spiritual journeys. Let's respect that.[17]

He adds, "I tell folks that I hope that they feel more confused than when they entered and leave with more questions than answers."

Atmosphere—Creating a good atmosphere is more art than science. Much of it depends on your location and the setting within it. The vibe of the place will permeate your experience. Group regulars are crucially important to help hold the space and to help the group manage itself, responding to awkward moments or inappropriate comments. Regulars know when to tell a story to help keep the conversation going, or when tension needs to be broken with a good laugh. When you are just starting out, it may be helpful to identify some people who will form that core group or you may just want to see who keeps coming back. Although we want God on Tap to be an outreach, that core group of regulars from our church helps to sustain the group and provide a welcoming environment; a critical mass of people puts new people at ease because they aren't put on the spot, they can listen for a while before they decide, if they decide, to speak. Like much of this work, you figure it out as you go. It is important to recognize and affirm the variety of ways people will describe their experiences. Cultivate an environment that is comfortable with both theistic, non-theistic, and golden rule spirituality. There's no need to correct or translate into church-speak. Just let people speak for themselves.

Digital Presence—It is important to have a digital presence for your group as well. As I was in the planning for God on Tap, I realized that if we wanted to create a physical outpost beyond the church campus, where we could connect with people beyond our

Continued

Some Practical Advice as You Get Started *Continued*

congregation, we should also have a digital outpost to match. We created a website, *godontap.net*, separate from our church website to give it its own identity. The heart of the website is the God on Tap blog. Each month, about a week before our gathering, I write a blog post about our upcoming topic. Posting in advance allows people to think about the topic, so they are primed when we arrive and we can jump right in. Everyone who comes to God on Tap and is willing to share his or her email address is automatically added to our email list and gets the blog post when it is published. We also share those blog posts on Twitter and Facebook. We started out with a Facebook page, but after meeting for almost a year the group said that a Facebook group would serve the purposes better, to promote interactivity and conversation, so we shuttered the Page and switched to the Group. We also created a Twitter account @godontap and encourage people to use the hashtag #godontap if they tweet during our gatherings. This digital presence not only makes us discoverable to potential new participants, it allows us to keep the connections and conversation going between our monthly face-to-face gatherings.

9

THEOLOGY WiTHOUT A NET

Conversation at the Core

"Neither poetry nor theology is an esoteric enterprise; both are
efforts to discern the incarnate within the ordinary discourse of
everyday speech."

—RONALD THIEMANN

"Today, the leaders who influence our faith and action are
those who convene (or moderate or enable) the conversations
that change our life—or the activities that transform our
understanding of ourselves, our world, and our God."

—PHILIP CLAYTON

"The best image I know for conceiving what theology ought to
be is . . . free-flowing, open, and unfettered conversation."

—GORDON KAUFMAN

THE SNOW HAD JUST STARTED TO FALL when I pulled into
the campus of Muhlenberg College in Allentown, Pennsylvania. I
had come to preach at the weekly Sunday evening worship service
at Enger Memorial Chapel, a beautiful Gothic chapel—a kind of
cathedral in miniature, with a long narrow nave, a choir of carved
wooden stalls, and a beautiful high altar. The Sunday evening services at the chapel are set between the stalls of the choir. Chairs
are arranged to face a small table, which serves as the altar for
the night. Lighted prayer candles and piano music create an intimate gathering within the grand Gothic space. I was there at the
invitation of Callista Isabelle, who has served as the chaplain at

Muhlenberg since 2012. After the service, she shared with me the ways she is making the campus her cathedral. She told me, "only a fraction of the campus community might spend time regularly in the chapel, but a much higher percentage is going to be in the dining hall, on the sidewalks, in the classrooms, and on the theatre stage. I strive to be a presence in those places in various ways, digitally and in person." In addition to the chapel and the chaplain's office, Isabelle identifies the student center, administration building, as well as the campus theatre and sports fields as places where her ministry extends. She also points to the ribbon of sidewalk that connects the small campus as a crucial part of campus life and her ministry. She told me,

> In many ways the sidewalk that runs from the chapel on the east end of campus to the student center on the central west end of campus is a short little one-block sidewalk, but it's where everybody walks at some point in the day. So if I'm just walking down that sidewalk, I'm likely to have several conversations or a least many points of quick contact with people. That is often where moments of pastoral care happen in fleeting ways. You see somebody looking exhausted or you saw that somebody posted on Facebook that they were sick and then you have the chance to quickly check-in about how they're doing. Often they're just very quick "Hi"s because they are rushing off to class or a meeting and you're going the other way, but very often I'll find myself just walking next to somebody so we can have a quick conversation. Those sidewalk moments can be really important.

This practice of walking the sidewalk embodies Isabelle's approach to ministry as a form of *accompaniment*[1]—quite literally walking the way with the students, faculty, and staff of the college.

Isabelle's description of the campus sidewalk echoes Certeau's walking the city, Robin Dennett's walking prayerfully through the streets of Gonzales, and evokes Abbot Wilbur's cathedral Waterworks. Just as the Canterbury Waterworks invited us to pay attention to the networked, relational connections between the cathedral, its precincts, and the town, the Muhlenberg sidewalk redirects our focus from the buildings that we typically think of as constituting a college campus to the networked paths that connect them. Both invite us into a networked perspective that is essential to ministry in a digitally integrated world, one in which we must constantly be on the lookout for these kinds of connections and links. Yet, just as the newly fallen snow that Sunday night hid the Muhlenberg sidewalk from my view, these networked pathways within our local communities and new digital neighborhoods are often hidden in plain sight. We can become so focused on what's happening inside our church buildings and faith communities that we miss out on the ways people are connecting with one another, living their lives, practicing their faith, and talking about God just down the street—or, in this case, the sidewalk.

These sidewalk encounters, with their constant flow of interactions and conversations, echo the digital exchanges of Facebook, Twitter, and other social media. In these spaces "quick 'Hi's," take the form of Snapchats, likes, favorites, mentions, retweets, Instagram posts, and comments, which often lead to more in-depth communication. For this reason, social media have rightly been described as constituting a giant global conversation made up of billions if not trillions of smaller ones. Coffeehouses, pubs, and even sidewalks are a form of social media themselves—local gathering places, where news and information are shared, where new connections are forged and relationships are reinforced. Of course, these days, as we sip an espresso, lift a pint, or rush off to class, we are also simultaneously connecting on our mobile devices, checking-in, posting, texting, Instagramming, and thus engaging with an even more expansive network of followers and friends. For many, like Isabelle, these digital and face-to-face encounters have become a vital part of pastoral practice. They also powerfully shape the way we talk about life, faith, and God.

A STATE OF ACTIVE INTERPLAY

Philosopher of communication theory, Marshall McLuhan, anticipated many of the changes and shifts we are experiencing in today's networked world in his classic work, *The Media Is the Massage*. He writes,

> Information pours upon us, instantaneously and continuously. As soon as information is acquired it is very rapidly replaced with still newer information. Our electrically configured world has forced us to move from the habit of data classification to the mode of pattern recognition. We can no longer build serially, block-by-block, step-by-step because instant communication insures that all factors of the environment and of experience co-exist in a state of active interplay.[2]

This was written in 1967 in response to the then cutting-edge technology of television, early computers, and what now seem primitive electronic communication technologies. McLuhan's point, all the more true and relevant for us today, is that the way we have processed, classified, and organized information is no longer sufficient for the volume, breadth, and pace of information that confronts us. In a remarkably short time, we have gone from getting our information from a relatively small number of trusted sources like the morning paper and the nightly news, to a second-by-second torrent of information, media, and voices delivered directly to our digital devices. We simply cannot process or organize information fast enough to keep up. This is, in part, because of the sheer volume of information generated in the world today. In 2010 former Google CEO Eric Schmidt said, "Every two days now we create as much information as we did from the dawn of civilization up until 2003."[3] Let that sink in. Every two days we generate as much information as existed in the entirety of human history up until just over a decade ago. It's no wonder people often describe a sense of "information overload." However, the amount of information is only one part of the challenge we face. An equally important element is our expectation, forged in the era of broadcast media that this information will

come to us as *one topic* in *one place* at *one time*, in *one direction*—
as if it were being read to us by Walter Cronkite on the 6:00 CBS
Evening News. This presumption is no longer sufficient in our new
digital reality, in which authority is distributed and information is
multi-directional. As McLuhan suggested nearly fifty years ago, we
need new and better ways of engaging the world of ideas. Rather
than taking a Newtonian approach of classifying and categorizing
information into hopelessly overflowing files and inboxes, we need
a quantum approach that continually maps the relationships, connects the dots, and recognizes the links between people and information, as these new digital technologies are "breaking things out
of their old organizational structures, and enabling individuals to
sort and order them on the fly."[4]

In the face of this constant flow of information, people have
come to rely on their friends to help find quality, relevant, and
trustworthy content. Pew Research reports that 30 percent of
American adults get news on Facebook,[5] 10 percent on YouTube,
and 8 percent on Twitter.[6] And far more than that rely on their
friends for recommendations on blog posts, articles, pictures, videos, movies, and books. In this way, news and information are
filtered or curated by the people we friend and follow on social
media. We have come to rely on our Facebook friends and Twitter
contacts for relevant news and information because none of us
have time to scour the internet and discover them all ourselves,
as if we could. In this sense, ideas and information have become
relational. News consumption, reading,[7] engaging with other television viewers by using hashtags like #orangeisthenewblack (no
spoilers, please!), and learning have become—or, in some cases,
returned to being—social activities.[8] Just as the now common act
of searching the internet once revolutionized the way we discover
and access information, social media have revolutionized the way
we discover, engage, shape, and share that information with others. This is beginning to change the ways we think about ideas
and information themselves. Whereas ideas and information were
once presumed to be singular and static, residing in one place like

a book on a shelf, the daily paper, a single webpage, or even one category in a theological system, ideas are now understood as *relational* in the sense that they are organized less in terms of fixed categories and places, and more as they function in relationship to other ideas and people. We are moving toward a quantum way of engaging information by paying attention to the relationships between ideas—the digital sidewalks, as it were—observing what happens and what new possibilities arise when ideas and people encounter one another online and in person.

THEOLOGY GOES SOCIAL (AGAIN)

These changes and this new environment have profound implications for the practice of theology in local ministry settings. The word "theology" comes from the combination of the Greek words *theo* and *logia*, meaning, "speaking about God." The very root of the word indicates theology's social nature—as conversing with others regarding ideas, concepts, and experiences of God. However, we often think of theology in either of two very specific (and less than social) ways—as a certain *set of beliefs* handed down— "this is our Lutheran theology," or as a particular *methodology*. To McLuhan's point, these narrow definitions and related practices are, on their own, insufficient for our electronically configured and digitally integrated reality. Today, theology must once again be social. Theologian Philip Clayton describes how our understanding of theology is changing as we shift from a print to digital culture, or, as he calls it, from the Age of Gutenberg to Google,

> In the Age of Gutenberg, you read theology in a book; you heard it preached in sermons; and you were taught it by Bible teachers. In the Age of Google, theology is what you do when you're responding to blogs, contributing to a wiki doc or Google doc online (or on your own computer), participating in worship, inventing new forms of ministry, or talking about God with your friends in a pub.[9]

The theological practice Clayton describes as happening in these local and digital gathering places is continual and conversational.

On any given day on social media, a childhood friend might message you about having lost his faith. A parishioner might post about a "God moment" or "mountaintop experience." You may happen upon a comment thread or Twitter conversation about the problems and gifts of organized religion. Someone posts a spiritual quote. Another reports the death of a loved one. Each day, and perhaps even within the same hour or minute, a range of questions, ideas, and theological points arise, moving with great fluidity between pastoral care, theological reflection, community building, and more. At theology pubs and coffeehouse conversations, the designated topic may be money, the Bible, music, or work, but the questions and comments bounce around like a pinball, probing the connections, going off on tangents, transgressing theological categories of vocation, theodicy, Christology, soteriology, and then circling back to the topic at hand. Theology is a social activity, and yet in a broadcast media world had become systematized, categorized, and seen as the provenance of highly trained experts.

Take, for instance, that congregational staple of adult Christian education, the adult forum, which is often far more Gutenberg than Google. It is usually composed of a forty-five-minute presentation, followed by a short question-and-answer period. It is expert oriented, with the presenter imparting knowledge to a frequently homogenous *audience*—a term I use here intentionally, as passive receivers of information. There is one speaker, one audience, one topic, and information flows in one direction, making for a very controlled theological environment. Another pillar of adult formation, the sermon, often follows a similar pattern. The preacher may hold forth anywhere from ten to twenty minutes in a monologue, no doubt informed by encounters and conversations during the week, but a monologue nonetheless with perhaps some polite comments—"Nice sermon, pastor"—and limited conversation afterward during the coffee hour.

These models of theological and homiletical practice reflect the way many ministry leaders, myself included, were trained. That training happened in rather controlled theological environments:

in classroom amphitheaters, around seminar tables, and in study sections with professional subject matter experts. We were trained and formed to be the next wave of those experts. Some traditions even refer to ordained ministry leaders as "theologians in residence." But being the "theologian in residence" means something much different now. It's not imparting information to people one theological category at a time, it is bringing people together in conversation to think theologically and make meaning between their personal experience, their world, and their God.

There is certainly an important place for these more traditional models of preaching and Christian formation, however we ought to recognize that this one-directional expert-to-audience pattern is becoming increasingly the exception in people's digitally integrated lives. Thanks to social media, people are accustomed to having a greater voice, whether in protest movements like #Occupy or #blacklivesmatter, in debates about local community issues, or in matters of faith. They are affirmed and encouraged in that voice by members of their social media communities through likes, comments, retweets, shares, and other forms of engagement. People have something to say, and today, like never before, they have the tools and platform to say it. Today, expertise and authority are derived less from a certain *gnosis*—a special understanding or secret knowledge gained in seminary or divinity school—and more from lived experience. People increasingly recognize that they too are experts—experts in their own lives. The idea that they would sit and listen to one voice for a forty-five-minute forum or a fifteen-minute sermon suddenly feels out of step with how they live their lives. No doubt, for many that time is a welcome refuge from our always-on culture and its constant flow of information. For others, it just feels out of touch. More and more, we need to offer people ways to gather, to have voice, and to engage, process, and make meaning of their lives and the world. By convening conversations in our churches as well as local and digital third places, we help people take the time to reflect on their stories and look at life theologically and through the lens of faith.

THEOLOGY AS CONVERSATION

Well before the explosion of internet technologies, theologian Gordon Kaufman called theologians and ministry leaders alike to an understanding of theology *as conversation*. He writes,

> It has been a mistake in the Christian churches to think of theology as basically *ideology* rather than conversation, that is, to suppose that theology is essentially a body of truths which can be defined clearly and can be passed on from generation to generation, instead of an *activity* requiring continuous adjustment of the thinking of each of us to all the others with whom we are *ipso facto* thinking together.[10]

Kaufman's constructivist approach to theology seems particularly well suited to our current situation. It recognizes that we live in an increasingly secular world, where faith can no longer be assumed and cannot be a prerequisite for wrestling with questions of meaning. It does not allow for quick appeals to traditional sources of authority. It takes mystery as its starting point and it is emerging and evolving. Most of all, it happens through conversation—it *is* conversation—with a wide range of voices. He writes,

> Since theology is principally concerned with what is ultimately mystery—mystery about which no one can be an authority, with true or certain answers to the major questions—I suggest that the proper model for conceiving it is not a lecture (monologue); nor is it the text (for example, a book): it is, rather, conversation. We are all in this mystery together; and we need to question one another, criticize one another, make suggestions to one another, help one another.[11]

For Kaufman, truth is only discovered, created, and apprehended through a conversation with many voices and viewpoints. This is a kind of theological version of McLuhan's famous observation that "the medium is the message"—that technologies communicate something themselves.[12] If theology is only a specific set of beliefs or a certain method, it only belongs to experts and insiders—to the already initiated. When theology is open conversation, it allows for a variety of voices. It belongs to and includes everyone. This is one of the correctives social media brings to the church. Equipped with Facebook and Twitter accounts, people can engage in conversations about God, faith, life, and meaning without waiting to be credentialed or receiving permission. In these spaces, people can explore their images of God, share stories of death and resurrection, and describe hidden graces found in difficult times. Today, as Clayton writes, *"Theology is not something you consume, but something you produce."*[13]

CONVERSATION AT THE CORE

Both Kaufman's and Clayton's approaches dovetail with what Oldenburg describes as the central activity of third places— *conversation.* Whether it's a tweet, comment, blog post, or video, be it online or face-to-face, whether people are manipulating keyboards, touch screens, or lifting a pint, these actions and activities are all about initiating or sustaining conversation across local and digital platforms. You know, my favorite local coffee shop may not have the best coffee in town and the wi-fi is a little spotty, but that's not what I go for. I go because it has a room full of well-worn wooden tables of all shapes, sizes, and finishes. Around those tables and mismatched chairs, conversations buzz and communities are formed. The coffee shop is not so much about the coffee as the space it creates for conversation. And so it is with social media. And theology. **Today, theology, like social *media*, is less about the media and much, much more about the *social*.**

THEOLOGY WITHOUT A NET

In my own parish work, I have taken to calling this practice of theology as conversation as doing "theology without a net"— without the net of a controlled environment, without the net of assumed authority, without the net of exclusive knowledge and information, without the net of a regular audience assumed to be already steeped in the faith, and without the net of neatly fixed and discrete theological categories. In my experience, theology without a net mostly happens in public—local or digital—spaces. It does not involve a presentation, PowerPoint slides, or a written text. It does not rely on the expert knowledge of professional ministry types. It does not promise neat answers. It is an open and ongoing conversation, which is shaped by whoever shows up online, in person, or the combination of both. It is responsive, not leading. It listens more than speaks. It needs to be authentic and rooted at the intersection of faith and life. Theology without a net is also done with great humility. Philip Clayton has called this "the *kenotic theological method*, one shaped by and around the self-emptying Christological picture of Philippians 2:5–8."[14] That passage begins, "Let the same mind be in you that was in Christ Jesus, who, though he was in the form of God, did not regard equality with God as something to be exploited, but emptied himself, taking the form of a slave. . . ." As ministry leaders, we need to divest ourselves in these conversations of the privilege of our position and the assumed authority that accompany it, recognizing the expertise of those gathered in the room, and accepting that we have as much to learn as we do to teach.

This humility and openness will only become more important as the number of religiously unaffiliated continues to grow year over year. We will increasingly engage with people for whom faith is not assumed, who do not hold the same commitments to certain traditional theological methods or frameworks, and who are not pre-disposed to make experience, belief, or spirituality fit into a preconceived religious, theological—let alone denominational—form. This does not mean they need to be educated in that method or those commitments, at least not at first. That may come later as they enter into a church or faith community. It means, however, that we have to hold our own conclusions and convictions more loosely. Although at first it may be uncomfortable, it can liberate us to think more broadly and deeply, without rushing to make everything and everyone fit into our Lutheran, Episcopal, Methodist, or Congregationalist boxes.

This all plays out for me when I lead God on Tap or our Coffee and Conversation. I convene a conversation about a topic for which I do not have any great answers. I don't even know which ways the conversation is going to go. I have to resist the temptation—and the unspoken expectations—that, as a pastor, I ought to have those answers, or have fully mastered the subject area before we gather. I have to consciously take my place on the edge of the conversation, facilitating the discussion, rather than being at its center. It requires humility and vulnerability, and a willingness to say, "I don't know. What do you think?" or not to jump in with a great insight from one of my seminary professors or a great book quote to wrap it all up neatly at the end of the hour's conversation. I have to be willing to leave loose ends, outstanding questions, and live with (or into) an unfinished theological product. And yet, when I take the risk of letting go of the pretense of being the expert in the room, amazing things happen. Insights I would have never considered emerge from the group, as people listen and share. They are not just learning from me, but each other.

This is the work of doing theology without a net: welcoming in a variety of people and perspectives, putting them and their ideas in relationship with another, and watching what emerges. This calls for a great deal of trust—perhaps, if we are honest, more trust than we have usually given to non-clergy and non-academics—to engage in the work of theology. This work also requires trust in the work of the Holy Spirit. For me, leading God on Tap is much more akin to leading Group Spiritual Direction than to leading an adult forum. In the practice of Group Spiritual Direction, the facilitator simply sets the conditions in which people can quiet themselves, listen for God and to each other, and reflect on God's work in their lives. The facilitator listens prayerfully, pays attention, and helps the group to name what is happening and the way they see the Holy Spirit moving within the conversation. It isn't leading or taking control, but simply making the space for people to encounter one another and

God. Ultimately, the director must deeply trust that God has something in store for the group and for each person.[15] I try to enter each conversation at the pub, coffee shop, and in social media with that same sense of openness and trust.

CONVERSATIONS ON THE WAY

For twenty years Pastor Paul Hoffman and the people of Phinney Ridge Lutheran Church in Seattle, Washington have employed a conversation in their practice of the ancient rite of Christian initiation called the adult catechumenate. At Phinney, they call it The WAY. The WAY is a yearlong process of faith formation that may lead seekers and inquirers to baptism or an affirmation of their baptism at the Easter Vigil. At the heart of The WAY is conversation around Scripture and sermon text. On Sunday nights people gather for a meal and then divide into small groups of six to eight people. Equipped with that morning's Gospel reading, the sermon text, and a few leading questions suggested by that Sunday's preacher, inquirers, their mentors and a catechist explore how God is at work in the text and in their lives. "This," Hoffman is careful to point, "is faith formation, not faith information." He writes,

> Among the hardest concepts to grasp for those new to the adventure of catechumenal ministry is that it is oral, relational, and without an off-the-shelf curriculum. . . . It is parish-based, person-to-person, and highly driven by laypersons, not pastors. . . . [it is] a way of being with one another and with our God that is dialogical, relational, and drawn from deep wells of the participants' real-life experiences and interactions with the Holy Scriptures.[16]

Faith is formed, engendered, and theological reflection is done in conversation among laity at various points on the winding road of faith. Hoffman says, "There are no planned outcomes, other than that the group have an open, honest, confidential conversation about their shared lives in Christ, springing from the morning's texts."[17] Instead, an insistence on outcomes is replaced by a deep trust in the work of the Holy Spirit as the One who ultimately forms us in faith, as these weekly conversations become the means for discovering the meaning of the Gospel for their lives and the congregation.

These conversations on The WAY have not only led many to baptism and deeper faith, they have also spilled over into every aspect of Phinney Ridge's common life, from meetings, to pre-marital counseling, and stewardship, and beyond.[18] Hoffman tells the story of leading a multi-generational Bible study on the story of The Road to Emmaus (Luke 24:13–35), where the risen Jesus walks unrecognized alongside two of his disciples on the road from Jerusalem to Emmaus. Hoffman divided the class into generational cohorts and asked each group to discuss what questions they bring to the text and then share them with the larger group. The oldest generational group began and said, "Why didn't the disciples recognize Jesus?" When he came to a group of young adults, they said, "Why was Jesus manipulating his disciples in that way?" The oldest group responded: "That's what we wanted to ask, but we didn't think we could." They had learned over the years that certain critical questions were off limits. Engaging with those less inculcated to a certain way or method of thinking opened them all to encounter and challenge the text in a new way.

Of course, conversational encounters have always been part of the work of ministry. Running into someone and striking up a conversation on the sidewalk, in the grocery aisle, or at the barbershop have been staples of ministry. Such conversations are the occasions for pastoral care, inspiration for sermons and deepening personal connection. Likewise, churches have long used conversational small groups and to a lesser extent offered or encouraged individual or group spiritual direction. The difference is that whereas once these relational, conversational encounters had been seen as an ancillary part of the ministry—happening in the spaces between programming, planning, and preaching—now they are at the center. While once they were seen as alternatives for people untrained in classic theology, now they are some of the most vital hubs of theological work in the church. This shift is reflected in the stories of the ministry leaders profiled throughout in this book, who are pursuing these encounters—and creating the conditions for these encounters—with great intentionality. For them, these encounters *are* the ministry itself.

Some may still object that this is not "real" theology, religious education, or church. However, every conversation—however brief or long, however deep or seemingly mundane—is an opportunity for engagement, understanding, learning, and yes, doing theology. Considering these paradigm shifts, Nicholas Knisely, the Episcopal Bishop of Rhode Island, reflects,

> I think it is really interesting that Jesus as his incarnational presence was a builder, a *technon*, and in his resurrection he appears as a gardener. It goes from the old man who is trying to impose order on nature and force a certain kind of outcome to the gardener who works with the chaos of everyday life and tweaks and prods and co-creates with the chaos of creation. And I think that's the paradigm we're heading to. We're giving up the idea that we can create these beautiful, logical structures that are going to make nature do our will and we're going to live more closely to the created order.

These are wise words for a church in the midst of its own time of death and resurrection. Rather than imposing theological systems in an attempt to quell the chaos of everyday life and make it fit our predetermined outcomes, we ought to engage with it, practicing theology according to the relational and networked character of our culture. Ministry leaders have been builders for so long, and many have become exhausted from it. Perhaps now is the right time to grab some fresh air and to get out into the garden.

OUR TASK: CONNECT, CONVENE, CONVERSE

The task of the ministry leader in this new digitally integrated and spiritually distributed environment is three-fold: to connect, convene, and converse:

Connect—Ministry leaders ought to be continually on the lookout for points of connection with others. We should seek to communicate our availability to others by being present in the places where they already gather, relinquishing the instinct to define the terms of those encounters. In social media terms, we need to be "discoverable." This means committing to a consistent presence on social media, actively seeking out local people, businesses, groups. Move some of your office hours outside the office. Get outside and spend some time on your sidewalk, whatever that place is for you in your context.

Convene—One of the most important and enduring roles of ministry leaders in a digital age is as conveners. Look for ways to bring people together, whether at the coffeehouse, pub, local gathering spot, or online. As Andrew Root writes, "The pastor, in this new era of sharing . . . should be the one thinking about how to set the space for facilitating these kinds of encounters. And this begins by finding ways for people to tell their stories, to share the relationships that make them them."[19] That can happen in someone's living room, or in a coffeehouse, barbershop, or pub, on social media, or in the park. It doesn't have to be sedentary either. Those conversations can happen while walking, running, or, as I have done for men's retreats, while climbing a high ropes course. Just bring people together, ask them to share their stories, and trust them and the work of the Holy Spirit.

Converse—Don't just make presentations. Host conversations. Give up your predetermined theological outcomes and focus on the relationships. The leader does not need to be the center of the conversation. Instead, the *kenotic* task is to listen prayerfully and be attentive to the work of the Holy Spirit. Trust the process of conversation, and recognize its theological import. For, as Kaufman writes, "only in the ongoing conversation as a whole is truth brought into being."[20]

FAiTH FORMATiON

Visual, Immersive, and Experiential

"Education must shift from instruction, from imposing of stencils, to discovery—to probing and exploration and to the recognition of the language of forms."

—MARSHALL MCLUHAN

". . . formation occurs all the time. It happens in the most unsubjective, information-filled and theory-driven classes as well as immersive experiences. It flows from daily life and practice. It occurs whether we are actively or passively engaged. It takes place whether or not we are aware of it."

—JULIE LYTLE

"Everything in a Gothic cathedral tells a story which in turn opens onto the narrative being spun by God."

—ROBERT BARRON

CATHEDRAL AS CATECHESIS

ON A GLORIOUS JULY DAY LAST SUMMER, my mom and I travelled to Washington, D.C. to visit Washington National Cathedral, the sixth largest cathedral in the world. We had come to celebrate an anniversary, of sorts. Twenty-five years earlier we had visited Washington National together, for the first and only time, as part of a field trip for my confirmation class. The experience of being in that beautiful cathedral space made a lasting impression on me as a teenager. So when it came time to reflect on the role of cathedrals in faith formation, visiting Washington National was the obvious choice, as was going once again with my mom. We started our visit of the cathedral by attending the noontime Eucharist in the Bethlehem Chapel in the easternmost point of the crypt—the lower level of the cathedral. It seemed a fitting way and place to begin our tour. It is where President Teddy Roosevelt laid the cornerstone of the cathedral in 1907, and where worship services have been observed nearly every day for just over one hundred years. The preacher that day reminded us that it was the Feast of St. Benedict, the father of medieval monasticism, and she recounted the opening line of his Rule, "Listen, O child, to the precepts of your master, and incline the ear of your heart."[1] She encouraged us to open the ears of *our* hearts to God. That is precisely why we had come to the cathedral—to experience its grandeur, to behold the beauty of its art, to marvel at its architectural achievement fashioned in Indiana limestone, to peer into the brilliant stained glass, and to drink in the experience of being in such a sacred space.

Following the Eucharist, we wandered through the three chapels in the crypt—Bethlehem Chapel, the Chapel of St. Joseph of Arimathea, and Resurrection Chapel. These chapels recount the three pivotal events of Jesus' life—his birth, crucifixion, and resurrection—through carvings and intricate mosaics. Upstairs, we walked slowly through the bays that line the sides of the nave, looking at the colorful modern stained glass, which communicated biblical stories as well as scenes from American history, like the windows of Lewis and Clark's expedition and the Space window, which contains a moon rock from the Apollo Eleven mission. Like all cathedrals, every carefully planned surface—whether stained glass, carving, statue, or chapel—even the kneeling cushions[2]—tells a story, connecting our lives and the life of faith to the community, the nation, and the world. Of course, we also enjoyed the occasional nods to popular American culture, including the gargoyle of Darth Vader on the Northwest Tower.[3]

One of the historic purposes of cathedrals is to teach the Christian faith. Medieval gothic cathedrals, the inspiration for

Washington National, were conceived in a time when most people were illiterate, so they learned the story of Scripture, faith, and the local community largely through the visual arts. In the late Middle Ages, they also served as a bulwark against heresy and so "each new cathedral was a concrete display and representation of orthodox Catholic theology."[4] In a cathedral you can, as we did on our visit, journey through the life of Jesus, and make your way through the canon of Scripture, from creation to revelation, all the while being reminded of the grandeur and majesty of God. If that weren't enough, later on in our visit, during the behind-the-scenes tour, we walked through the upper levels of the cathedral and stood above the great vaulted ceiling, one hundred and two feet high. Our tour guide emphasized that into each of the "boss stones"—the round stones that joined the ribs of the vaulted ceiling—were carved an element of the Nicene or Apostles' creeds. I took his point. The very spine of the cathedral is held together with the creedal faith.

A cathedral is an immersive experience of faith formation, with the images, architecture, people, music, and ritual all serving to form those who enter that space. Part of the genius of cathedrals is the way they affect and shape us simply by being inside them. Even as you trace a particular stone carving with your finger, stare up at a certain stained glass window, walk a labyrinth, or listen to a guided audio tour, the environment of the cathedral itself is shaping you. As Marshall McLuhan reminds us, "Environments are not passive wrappings, but are, rather, active processes which are invisible."[5] The spaces we inhabit (just as the media we use) affect us in ways we don't always notice. A friend of mine captured this well on her visit to another great church, Sainte Chapelle in Paris. At the same time we were exploring National Cathedral, she posted a panoramic picture of Sainte Chapelle's incredible stained glass windows on Facebook and wrote, "For me, this is the most beautiful, uplifting church in the world—though it's a big world and I've seen so little of it. . . . Still it's hard to image one more stirring, stunning, and gravity-defying than this."

That kind of reaction is just what the architects intended. While she was responding to the remarkable blue stained glass—created by processes innovative in its time—the overall feeling she had was one of weightlessness, as if being lifting heavenward.

A NEW OLD CULTURE OF LEARNING

This cathedral approach to faith formation lends itself to our digitally integrated environment, which is itself ubiquitous, immersive, highly visual, and has reshaped the way we connect, communicate, and live, whether or not we carry a smartphone in our pocket. When we embrace the idea that all of life, including these digital spaces, is lived *in cathedral*, we begin to see that faith formation is not something that happens solely within the confines of the church or cathedral building. It does not just happen in Sunday School, Confirmation, Adult Forum, or worship, but *everywhere* and *at all times*—in the precincts, the town, and, today, the globe, both online and off. We are continually being shaped and formed in multiple ways, whether we are aware of it or not.

Educators Douglas Thomas and John Brown, therefore, encourage us to "stop thinking of learning as an isolated process of information absorption and start thinking of it as a cultural and social process of engaging with the constantly changing world around us."[6] In a world where there is so much information that changes so rapidly, they argue, we must trade *memorizing* for *meaning making*. They write,

> In the new culture of learning, the classroom as a model is replaced by *learning environments* . . . [whereas] the teaching-based approach focuses on teaching us *about* the world . . . the new culture of learning focuses on *learning through engagement within the world*.[7]

If, as Thomas and Brown write, formation happens when we intentionally explore and engage our environments, then one of the tasks for today's ministry leaders is to create the conditions for and participate in the many and various ways formation happens. As Gordon Kaufman writes, "The central question for theology . . . is not primarily a speculative question, a problem of knowledge, at all. Most fundamentally it is a practical question: How are we to live?"[8] That question is discerned and answered as we engage the world together, and reflect appreciatively and critically on our experience. In this sense, then, the term formation is a more helpful descriptor than education. Whereas education connotes the transference of information, formation, for Christians, is about the shaping and sharing of Christian identity in durable but flexible fashion.

AND A CHILD SHALL LEAD THEM

Our four children have been steeped in this kind of formation by attending preschools inspired by the educational theory called *Reggio Emilia*, named after the Italian town in which it was created. The Reggio school, as it's known, states explicitly that the environment—the classroom, the playground, the physical and social surroundings—function as a third teacher. It is considered that important. When children come into the classroom at the start of school, there are various activities available from which they can choose. The children, not the teachers, decide what to engage and how to engage it. They can do activities the teachers have prepared, play with other classroom items, or create a completely new and different activity. The entire classroom is open to their curiosity. As the child begins to engage his or her environment, the teachers enter into the learning process alongside of them. They reflect with the child on what they are doing, why, and what they are discovering. There is a curriculum designed for each day, but it can and often does change based on the children's interests, curiosity, and input.

I was able to see this firsthand when I volunteered as a parent classroom helper. One day when I was helping in my oldest daughter's class, one of the activity choices was what they called "green gak," which is similar to Play Dough but more soft and gooey. That day, some kids were sticking small plastic animals in it, some cut it up with cookie cutters. My daughter took a large handful of gak and slapped in onto the edge of the table and said, "Daddy, watch!" and we watched as it ever so slowly oozed down to the floor. As we watched for several minutes, it became a moment of Sabbath in the midst of the chaos swirling around us. She did it several more times. As we watched, we talked about how slowly it moved and how peaceful it made us feel. That green gak brought us to a spiritual place, finding what T.S. Eliot once called "the still point of the turning world" even in a room full of preschoolers.[9]

The childhood Christian formation curriculum, Godly Play, works in much the same way.[10] As teachers tell the Bible story with the help of simple wooden figures and tactile items made from felt, stone, and sand, the teachers and students experience the Bible story together and ask wondering questions about the story. Afterward, the children can respond to that story by playing with the story pieces or other craft activities. One Sunday we experienced the lesson that included the "pearl of great value" (Matthew 13:45–46). After the story, I observed a little boy playing with a container full of beads. I noticed that he had seen one beautiful bead—opal colored, larger than the rest—and then he lost it in the sea of other beads. He spent the rest of the response time looking for that bead—just like the Gospel story. Finally, just before class ended, he found it. I said to him, "Hey, that was just like the story." He paused for moment and said, "Oh, yeah, like the guy who bought that pearl." He was so engrossed in finding his bead, he hadn't realized the connection. He didn't just learn about the parable. He lived it. He experienced the man's singular focus and utter desire for the pearl and, thereby, something of God's unrelenting love for him.

Both of these experiences were made possible because of the value placed on learning through experience, discovery, and engagement with our environments. They both value curiosity, the agency of the learner, and learning through play. But this kind of formation is not just for children and it doesn't just happen in a classroom.

LENT MADNESS

The website *Lent Madness* is an example of learning through social engagement and play, in this case, mediated by digital technologies. Begun in 2010 as the brainchild of Tim Schenck, rector of St. John Episcopal Church in Hingham, Massachusetts, Lent Madness is an ecclesiastical version of college basketball's March Madness.[11] Thirty-two saints face off in a single-elimination tournament, and the winner is crowned with the "Golden Halo." Church luminaries like Charles Wesley, founder of Methodism, contemplative Trappist monk Thomas Merton, and Anna Cooper, an African-American advocate for education and human rights, are pitted against each other, and people vote for which saint should advance. Throughout Lent, guest or "celebrity" bloggers detail the lives of these saints. Visitors to the site read the profiles, learning about each saint, and then vote for their favorite. In addition to the blog posts, Schenck and his colleague, Scott Gunn, whom he jokingly refers to as his nemesis, post weekly videos of their conversations on Skype, reflecting on how all the "Madness" is unfolding. All of this content is shared on their website and from there across various social media platforms. The combination of quality multimedia content, emphasis on participation through commenting and voting, and the good-natured campaigning for favorite saints has made Lent Madness into something of a phenomenon. In 2014, 50,000 people visited the site and it was profiled in national television, radio, and newspaper outlets. Schenck says of the site, "it's fun, whimsical, vaguely irreverent at times, but also at its core it is a devotional tool that takes formation and faith very, very seriously." Like Reggio or Godly Play, visitors to the website can freely explore and discover. They can read, comment, vote, and also share with friends what inspires them in the witnesses of these saints, all the while having fun. Schenck describes Lent Madness as a form of stealth Christian formation:

> I call it "stealth formation" because there are ways where it doesn't actually feel like Christian formation—like you're sitting in a class between services—but it is. My take is that faith formation takes many, many forms. Some of them are kind of overt, "Come sit in a classroom and we'll talk about the Gospel of Mark." Some are a little sneakier, like Lent Madness. People are learning a tremendous amount and they're having fun and they don't necessarily realize just how much they're learning until they're in the middle of it.

The action doesn't only happen online. The Lent Madness materials are available for people to adapt and use in creative ways within their local ministry setting. Schenk says that some churches:

> . . . will have people dress up as saints and have a debate with a particular matchup, or they'll do some kind of learning or craft, or they'll cook food from a particular culture of one of these battles. That's the thing about it that's kind of fun. There's a model that people can just take and use, but there's a degree of flexibility and it gives the freedom to be as creative as they want.

Lent Madness helps teach people about one of the church's great traditions and introduces them to inspirational figures from across church history. It broadly engages people who may never sit down to read through *Butler's Lives of the Saints* on their own, or attend a presentation on church history or the saints. Here, people are not passively receiving information through a book or a lecture. They are actively engaged with the material and each other. Together, they constitute a community and they, by their participation, are helping to share and shape the experience. Schenck may have dreamed up Lent Madness, but those who participate have helped to make it what it is today.

THE VISUAL WEB

Lent Madness exemplifies the kind of experiential, participatory, immersive formation that is made possible through social media. It also reflects the increasingly visual nature of the digital landscape.[12] Studies show that visual content has exploded in popularity in recent years and garners significantly higher levels of engagement across social media.[13] At the forefront of this move to the visual web are the social media sites Pinterest and Instagram, which Elizabeth Drescher has called "postmodern stained glass."[14] Like the stained glass of the cathedral, these technologies help ministry leaders tell a deeper story than text alone—an unfolding story that opens, as Robert Barron suggests, onto a larger narrative, both of their own lives, and, for many, God.[15]

Instagram, the elegant photo-sharing app, bought by Facebook in 2012, has quickly become one of the most popular social media platforms on the web, especially with younger users.[16] It boasts over two hundred million users, with sixty million photos uploaded every day and a total of over twenty billion photos shared on the site.[17] Users can apply "filters" to their pictures, giving them distinctive looks once only achievable using desktop photo-editing software. Instagram photos can be shared on Facebook, Twitter, Tumblr, and other social media platforms. I first understood the power of Instagram when on a mission trip with teenagers from our church to the Appalachia Service Project. There's nothing like hanging out with twenty-five teens for a week to learn about "what the kids are doing these days" in social media. They Instagrammed their entire experience, from beginning to end, posing with power tools, their work crews, and the families they served. All the while, they were telling a story to their friends and followers of living a life of service to others in response to the love of God.

Matthew Nickoloff of the South Wedge Mission has used Instagram to create a DIY (do-it-yourself) Advent series. For each day of Advent, Nickoloff posted an Instagram picture inviting viewers into a simple spiritual practice along the themes of Advent.

From there, he shared them on Facebook and Twitter. Each picture included an object or image, and a written note describing the practice. The series includes practices such as:

- Find out where your clothes for today were made. Pray for the laborers who made them, and for safe and just conditions for the workers in those lands.
- Talk a walk around the block. Don't wear a coat. Pray for those who are cold and naked.
- Leave your credit card at home one day.
- Start something new today. Something you've longed to try or do. Commit to it. As many fear the world's end, give thanks for Christmas beginnings, when God makes all things new.

Daily spiritual practice suggestion from South Wedge Mission DIY (Do-It-Yourself) Advent Instagram series. *Photo courtesy Matthew Nickoloff*

Especially poignant was a picture Nickoloff posted, which just happened to coincide with the shootings at Sandy Hook Elementary School in Newtown, Connecticut. It shows an image of the wounded Jesus with a note that says, "Take 10 minutes to really grieve today. Pray for all children of the world for whom violence is an everyday reality." People seeking some way to respond to the tragedy shared the image on social media hundreds, if not thousands, of times. It powerfully connected the liturgical season of Advent, spiritual practice, to our shared experience of grief over this terrible event.

Daily spiritual practice suggestion from South Wedge Mission DIY (Do-It-Yourself) Advent Instagram series. *Photo courtesy Matthew Nickoloff*

INSTAGRAMMING THE TEN COMMANDMENTS

At my congregation, we experimented with Instagram in our confirmation class as a way of deepening our understanding of the Ten Commandments. For each commandment we studied, we asked the students and adult leaders to post a picture on Instagram about it during the week. When we studied the first commandment, "Have no other gods before me," we asked people to post pictures of things they treat as gods in their lives. People posted pictures of things like an Apple icon for technology, a legal pad with notes propped up against a computer screen, and a collection of *Travel+Leisure* magazines. When we studied the third commandment, "Remember the Sabbath and keep it holy," we asked them to post pictures of places of Sabbath in their lives. People shared pictures of their home workshop, a piano keyboard, and their backyard garden.

A DIGITAL ADVENT CALENDAR

Along with Instagram, Pinterest has quickly become a popular image-sharing site. Pinterest describes itself as a "visual discovery tool" with over 70 million users. Users create "boards" onto which they "pin" content. These "pins" highlight the images from web pages while minimizing the text, thus creating a visually rich environment. People use Pinterest to collect recipes and home improvement ideas. Some use it to save and share inspirational quotes and images, while others use boards as ways to collect creative ministry ideas. Pinterest is an easy and aesthetically pleasing way to capture and collect images. A simple search for "Jesus" "cathedral" "prayer" offers reconfigured stained glass on the screen of your computer, phone, or tablet.

In another digital twist on an Advent practice, the Society of St. John the Evangelist created a Pinterest board that functioned as a digital Advent calendar. Each day a new picture and word of the day like "look," "remember," and "imagine," was revealed. The monastery invited people to help create a global Advent calendar

Pinterest Advent Calendar created by the Society of Saint John the Evangelist monastery as part of their #adventword initiative.

by posting their own pictures in response to those one-word prompts. People posted pictures on Pinterest, as well as Twitter, Facebook, and Instagram, using the hashtag #adventwords.[18] The result was an Advent calendar with thousands of images for each day. Altogether, there were 15,000 #adventword images on Instagram alone and it is estimated that fully 50,000 people participated in some fashion. Overall, the hashtag #adventwords was viewed across all social media 1.6 million times. Jamie Coats, director of the Friends of the SSJE who organized this initiative on behalf of the brothers, reflects: "It was like watching global prayer unfolding before your eyes."

Perhaps we shouldn't be surprised by this shift back from written text toward the visual. From cave paintings, to cathedrals, to YouTube and Instagram, human beings have always used images to communicate. Today the digital tools—software, mobile devices, and low-cost data storage in "the cloud"—are enabling us to communicate far more cheaply and easily than ever before. Even direct messaging has become more visual. Snapchat, increasingly popular with teenagers, is a photo-messaging application with 60 million users sending over 400 million photos and videos every day. The pictures only appear for a few seconds and then disappear. Here, as with Instagram and Pinterest, the picture is primary, with the text only appearing as a caption.

In an increasingly visual culture, we also need to give great care to the ways we incorporate visual elements in our ministries. Even one image displayed during the sermon can stir the listener's imagination and make a lasting impression.[19] Pictures on Instagram, Facebook, and blog posts, along with videos, help to win people's interest and enrich the stories we are trying to tell. Websites too are becoming more image than text driven. In some cases, the entire top of the webpage is a picture.[20] As Lutheran pastor Jay Gamelin has said, "We are moving from a *tell me* culture to a *show me* culture." Images on our social media platforms and in our class rooms and sanctuaries help us to show how we experience and share the Gospel.

PARTICIPATORY AND EXPERIENTIAL

Faith formation in the digital age is also participatory and experiential.[21] Bethany Stolle, a designer with a decade of experience developing Christian formation curriculum, recently traveled around the country interviewing ministry leaders, parents, and students about their confirmation experiences, and more generally, about what experiences have been most formative in their faith. She observes, "This is the first time I've seen such a significant articulation of experience and relationships in comparison to content and information." People have stressed servant projects, retreats, and hands-on, relational activities as most formative in their Christian faith and identity. She told me,

> One visual I've been operating with is thinking about confirmation as a campfire. The campfire is the gathering point, but what is really valuable about that time together is the experience, the

shared experience, the relationships, and the conversation. It's not so much about putting information on a pedestal, like "Here is the Small Catechism and it is on a pedestal and we must memorize it, and learn it, and study it." It's more about this being the gathering point where shared experiences can happen.

Inspired by Stolle's image of the campfire, I took a different approach to teaching the third commandment—"Remember the Sabbath and keep it holy"—in my own confirmation class. Rather than teach *about* Sabbath, we had a *shared experience of* Sabbath. We watched a short NOOMA video by Rob Bell[22] on getting in tune with God, and then offered the youth and adult leaders several options for engaging in Sabbath, including lighting candles, sharing art, praying with icons, engaging in conversation, and yes, being on their smartphones. We ended our time together with an informal celebration of the Eucharist, standing around a card-table-turned-altar, and singing *a cappella.* For teenagers who are heavily programmed, those twenty minutes of Sabbath time, bracketed by a video and the Eucharist, were a surprising and welcome experience of Sabbath, and far more lasting than just listening to me talk *about* it. I set the space, the conditions for Sabbath, and they help to fill and shape it as they were moved to do so.[23]

Jim Kast-Keat, associate minister for education at Middle Collegiate Church in Manhattan, says, "Education must grow and change as we grow and change." Kast-Keat, a digital and mobile native, told me that programs shouldn't be places to passively receive information, but training grounds for how we engage with the world in faithful ways. He explains,

> I'm a firm believer in practices over programs. I want to teach people the message, the practices, and not just show up. A program has a beginning and an end. That's its nature. But if I teach practices, those can transcend the program. If I have a container—a program—that has a start and an end time, how can I fill it with things that can outlive it?

One of the ways Kast-Keat has accomplished this is through a mindfulness practice he calls "stop and breathe." In his previous call, he says,

> . . . we would always do mindful breathing every single week. We called it "stop and breathe." Every week eighth graders would take a moment and "stop and breathe." We'd say those words together, and we'd take a deep breath in and a deep breath out and I'd hear from these kids over the years how they led "stop and breathe" at home.

The ability to slow down and just breathe is surely an important life skill for adolescents as well as adults. It is also a core spiritual practice in many faith traditions. In this instance, it enabled Kast-Keat to transcend the allotted program time and instill practices that helped his students and their families more mindfully and faithfully engage with each other and their world.

#HASHTAG FORMATION

In recent years, hashtags—words for phrases appended with the pound sign (#), like #digitalcathedral—have become ubiquitous in our culture. They appear at the bottom of the screen on television shows and sporting events. They even pop up in conversation where someone might throw in a hashtag, making the number sign with their fingers. During one of our confirmation lessons, we asked groups of our teenagers to rewrite articles of the Apostles' Creed. One group ended their version of the second article of the creed with #JesusRocks. Social media-savvy host of the Tonight Show, Jimmy Fallon, and singer Justin Timberlake created a hilarious video about the excesses of hashtag culture that illustrates in a sidesplitting way how ubiquitous this blend of textual and digital practice has become in popular culture.[24]

The hashtag, as we have come to know and use it, has an interesting history. Although it first came into common use on Twitter, it was not originally part of the Twitter platform. In 2007, a year after Twitter launched, a user named Chris Messina suggested the use of the hashtag for sorting tweets.[25] From the very beginning, then, hashtags have had an organic, open-source, and provisional nature. They are used for common themes and memes—popular content or ideas, topics, and events. Whether on Twitter or other social networks like Facebook and Instagram, which have both incorporated hashtags in their platforms, traditional media, or spontaneous conversations, hashtags are expressive symbols that are used to organize themes and gather people in certain ways. Like Stolle's campfire, they are connection points, at times created for a particular purpose and other times just for fun. As we saw in Tim Snyder's analysis of the Twitter responses to the shootings in Newtown in chapter two, although they may be makeshift, they can also be deeply profound.

Jes Kast-Keat, associate minister at West End Collegiate Church in Manhattan (and Jim's spouse), introduced the hashtag #MySixWordStoryOfFaith while crowdsourcing a sermon. (Crowdsourcing is when you pose a question to your social media contacts for feedback and ideas.) She was inspired by Jesus' resurrection appearance to his disciples in Luke 24, when Jesus tells them, "You are witnesses of these things" (Luke 24:48). While she was waiting to see whether she would be called for jury duty, she asked her contacts on social media to share their six-word story of faith. Within two hours, she says, the conversation took on a life of its own. The hashtag went viral with thousands of people, across denominations and religious lines, sharing their six words of faith. These are some of the tweets that were shared:

> It really is all a miracle. #MySixWordStoryofFaith
> —@peacebang
>
> God keeps welcoming me. You're invited. #MySixWord StoryofFaith —@nurya
>
> I don't know what I believe. #MySixWordStoryofFaith
> —@dankennedy_nu

Faith and doubt. Shaken not stirred. #MySixWordStory ofFaith —@jimkastkeat

In the abyss, you are there. #MySixWordStoryofFaith —@jeskastkeat

Listen. Learn. Love. Question. Try again. #MySixWordStory ofFaith —@wilgafney

Rejoice. His door is always open. #mysixwordstoryoffaith —@MousaSally

These are brief and yet deeply profound statements, any one of them worthy of further reflection and conversation. Of course, people don't need to be on Twitter or online to participate in a conversation like this. My local YMCA asked people to post six words describing what the Y means to them. They had people write them on a piece of paper to be displayed on a wall in the lobby. It was a great visual look at the various ways the Y enhances its members' lives. The same could easily be done for a church initiative, stewardship campaign, or Christian formation program. When I asked Jes to reflect on the experience, she said, "When people have the freedom to own their own formation and then have some mutuality involved in that, I think there's some real incredible possibilities for the church."

Holy Spirit Lutheran Church in Kirkland, Washington has taken this idea one step further with an initiative they call "Holy Spirit in the World." Pastor Katy McCallum Sachse explains that the theme was sparked by a Lenten book study—a traditional practice of congregational faith formation—of Barbara Brown Taylor's *Altar in the World*, a book about encountering God in a range of places in nature. McCallum Sachse explains their approach,

> We were looking for ways to engage people in ministries of the congregation and feel connected to the congregation and trying to reach out to people to understand that even if you're not in church every Sunday morning, that you are still a part of the ministry that this congregation is doing.

At the outset of their stewardship campaign, they mailed out to their members five hundred bright orange flags emblazoned with the church logo. Members were invited to hold up the flag in the various places in the world they saw God—their own altars in the world—and post the pictures on Instagram, Facebook, or Twitter, using the hashtag #HSLCintheworld. If they weren't technologically inclined, they could also email it to the church office or post printed photos on an old-school bulletin board in the fellowship hall. (They also had help stations available where youth could help adults unfamiliar with the technology.) They told the congregation, "It's one way to remind us that the church is not a building, but a people—not a place, but a way of life. And that way of life happens everywhere."[26] Ironically, McCallum Sachse said, "The first time we did it, people were taking pictures of themselves in the church building." Once they caught on and starting taking and posting pictures from *outside* the building, the theme went viral within their congregation and extended far beyond the scope and length of the annual stewardship drive. People liked it so much, they kept it as a theme in their ministry together. People continued to take pictures of themselves with the flags on their summer vacation travels, even from Europe. McCallum Sachse said,

> This is not just a stewardship campaign, but really a theological statement about the fact that God goes before us in the world, we encounter God in the world, we're not out there to bring God into the world. God's already there and we are learning to recognize that.

It is also an excellent way to affirm their members' vocations, their ministry in daily life, and to name the holy—quite intentionally pointing to where they see God outside their church building. This expands the notion of both where the Holy Spirit is at work, and where and how Holy Spirit Lutheran Church is engaged in the world. That engagement does not just happen through organized church activities, but in the daily lives of the members of its faith community. She observes that the visual nature of the campaign is a large reason for its success:

> Visual is big for people. For us as a congregation, and the Lutheran church in general, we're a very verbal, very wordy congregation. So we're not super visual. There's a lot of people who need, and rightfully so, a visual cue and I think that's been part of the fun of this. People can act or "talk" about their faith, but they can do it visually. They may not be comfortable going up to somebody and saying, "Hey, let me tell you about my church." But they might show them a photo. It increases the number of ways people can connect.

Hashtags like #MySixWordStoryofFaith and #HSLCintheworld can be fun, flexible, and multi-platform points of connection for faith formation. However, hashtags are only the beginning of conversations about how people understand and describe their faith, and where they see God in the world. Ultimately, it's not so much about the hashtags themselves, but what they represent. In terms of faith formation, they represent the way in which people co-create their environments or platforms for being formed in faith, in much the same way Reggio Emelia or Godly Play students shape theirs. Jes Kast-Keat and the stewardship team at Holy Spirit Lutheran Church may have come up with the idea, but, like the community that has formed around Lent Madness or Chris Messina and Twitter, those who participate help to make that conversation into something that far exceeds the imaginations of their creators. No one owns a hashtag—they can't be bought or copyrighted—and so they belong to everyone. Everyone can participate and adapt it, fueled by their own creativity and imagination, as they have need.

In the same way, cathedral visitors adapt the cathedral space to their own needs, whether it is for worship, art appreciation, faith formation, or quiet contemplation. In doing so, they help to make cathedral what it is too. Sometimes these great churches are quite literally reshaped by those who visit. I learned this on a visit many years ago to St. Peter's Basilica in Rome. One of the traditions of pilgrims who visit St. Peter's is to rub the foot of a bronze statue of St. Peter. The right foot of that statue has been rubbed so many times by pilgrims that the toes on that foot have been completely rubbed away. As I posed for a picture with my hand on that foot, I recognized that I stood in a long line of pilgrims who had also left their mark on that space.

Many years later on that July day at Washington National, the most memorable and formational moment for me during our visit was not looking at a sculpture or stained glass window, or even the boss stones on the ceiling high above, but watching a stranger, a woman, light a prayer candle, kneel down and pray. She seemed to be surrounded by friends or family, who stood vigil with her as she knelt there. Her hands were clasped and pressed against her forehead. As we walked by, I could see the wet pathways on her cheeks where tears had been. Seeing this woman pray moved me—and perhaps more than anything else on our visit—made the cathedral come alive for me. It also brought me to prayer—praying for her, for my own needs, for the world, for the gratitude of being in that space. Likewise, reprising that visit to the cathedral of so many years ago with my mom shaped my whole experience of the cathedral that day. Our conversation and reminiscences, the different observations we each made of the space formed us in a way that being there alone could not. The combination of nostalgia, shared appreciation, and wonder made the cathedral and its many treasures come alive for us both.

11
───

EVANGELiSM

Sharing the Gospel for the Sake of the Gospel

"Let the facade and doors of the Cathedral be so planned that their steps and approaches melt into the public sidewalk and the street. Thus those within the nave and on the sidewalk are not radically separated but conscious of each other's presence."

—*WILLIAM LAWRENCE*

"Cathedrals above all need to find ways of drawing their dispersed community together, even where this can lead to further dispersal: they are places of transit as well as stability."

—*JEREMY FLETCHER*

"[T]he real challenge of Christian evangelism for me is about how to attend. . . . How to be with other people and let their relationships with God evangelize us."

—*SARA MILES*

CATHEDRAL IN THE NIGHT

ON SUNDAY EVENINGS AT THE CORNER of Main Street and Center Street in Northampton, Massachusetts, a makeshift cathedral rises up from the sidewalk. It is called Cathedral in the Night, an ecumenical street ministry started by the Episcopal Church, the Evangelical Lutheran Church in America, and the United Church of Christ.[1] Here at their weekly worship service, four freestanding lamps illuminate the sidewalk as people gather around two tables.

The table at the center of the gathering is an altar covered with simple fabrics, bread and wine, and a cross. The other table is filled with food prepared by volunteers for the community dinner to follow. Gathered here are the homeless, the housed, local college students and professors, members of various congregations, and, among all of these groups, no few Nones. I asked one of the pastors of Cathedral in the Night, Steph Smith, why they decided to use the term cathedral for their name. She said,

> We really wanted to be a bit edgy and play with some of the church language in order to expand what church means. The cathedral is more than a building. It is the whole area and the neighborhood. We wanted to be evocative in the terminology to get people asking, "What is church?" Is it the big building or is it the people? We wanted to push the boundaries of what church is because we are a church that has no boundaries. We have no walls. Not only do we not have physical walls, a lot of what we do breaks down walls that we have inside ourselves, to really think about our own prejudices and stereotypes around poverty.

Founded in 2011, Cathedral in the Night stands in a long tradition of cathedrals serving the poor. For centuries, cathedrals have served as places of hospitality and refuge for those in need. As Tracey Lind, dean of Trinity Episcopal Cathedral in Cleveland, told me: cathedrals "have often been places of welcome for the hungry and the homeless, the destitute of the city, and the sojourner." Cathedral in the Night also embodies many of the characteristics of life and ministry in the Digital Cathedral, particularly for the way it envisions a networked community with a wide sense of belonging. It's not an outreach *to* the homeless; rather, it is focused on being a church community *together*—part of Smith's blurring the boundaries and deconstructing walls. She says,

> On an average night we really have a mixture of people. There are people who are homeless. There are a lot of people with homes who are just struggling with poverty in general. But then

there are people who are just looking for something different, and this is out of the box. Or they are committed to a Sunday morning church but they still want to come Sunday night. It really runs the gamut. And don't assume you know. You could look around and say, "I think that person is homeless." They could be a professor at Hampshire College. You don't know.

The worship is designed to reinforce this sense of unity. During the service, a microphone is passed around to anyone who would like to share a prayer, concern, song, or story. "People light up and see themselves as a leader and as having something to offer, which is not something they've really been told, felt, or lived into," says Smith. At the offering, people are given wooden tokens, shells, or rocks with the names of different gifts written on them like "humor," "being a good friend," "listening," or "sobriety." Congregants place them inside the hollow wooden cross on the altar. Smith says, "We don't want a monetary gift. We ask for something greater at Cathedral . . . we ask for you to become your own offering." In doing so, the service affirms the unique giftedness and contribution of each person, regardless of their means or the reason they came to be at Cathedral that night.

It's worth noting that the empowerment and affirmation that comes with passing the microphone and placing tokens in the cross echoes what happens online in social media spaces. Today people have their own personal digital platforms from which to share, speak, and advocate. They don't need to wait to be endorsed or recognized by a news outlet or church body. Equipped with a free blog, Facebook, or Twitter account, or a mobile phone, people can make their voice heard, tell their stories, and make change in the world. In this way, the practice of passing the microphone at Cathedral in the Night is not only contextually appropriate as well as just and compassionate, it is also culturally resonant in a digital age.

In its worship and wider ministry, Cathedral in the Night demonstrates a broad understanding of and appreciation for who is a part of the community. It includes those gathered for worship, those who hang around the edges of the assembly, as well as those who walk or drive by. It includes partner congregations who come from Massachusetts, Connecticut, and Vermont to assist with worship and supply food for the meal afterward. They are all *in cathedral*. Smith explains:

> People are walking by all the time when we are having church. One time when we were singing *This Little Light of Mine*, a woman belted out the song with us as she walked by. Or you'll notice people standing on the edge and never see them again. Or, they'll stay on the edge and over the course of a couple of weeks, they get closer and closer until one Sunday they want to lead the Lord's Prayer. And people will say that this is a place where they feel welcomed just as they are.

Cathedral in the Night is a ministry with those on margins— not only the margins of society, the poor and homeless, but also those on the margins of the church. It exists in between the traditional church and the world it often fails to engage as well as the various in-betweens of diverse, distributed religious and spiritual practice today. It beautifully demonstrates the ways in which, as Belden Lane writes, "the periphery often becomes the locus of the holy."[2]

Like Cathedral in the Night, congregations and ministry leaders must also cultivate a much broader sense of who is connected and belongs to our faith communities. Membership decline across the church has led many ministry leaders to fixate on the shrinking numbers of people in their church pews, which has blinded many of us to how, thanks to digital and mobile technologies, we are connected to more people than ever before. Even as our congregations have become smaller, our networks, and therefore opportunities for building community and sharing the Gospel, have become larger and more expansive. We need to let drop our binary and dichotomous classification of people as either member or non-member, affiliated or None, real or virtual, and shift to a more networked approach, recognizing that people are linked and belong to our churches in a variety of ways. For their part, Nones are not necessarily looking for a single faith community to join for the rest of their lives, and so the assumption or insistence on a singular durable mode of membership-based affiliation in the church misses the diverse ways in which the unaffiliated (as well as the affiliated) engage spirituality and religion. We need to conceive of our churches as broadly networked communities and the people in them as all falling *in cathedral*.

MODES OF BELONGING

In his research on church belonging, Bishop David Walker of the Diocese of Manchester in England has identified four modes of church belonging that unfold through *activities, events, relationships*, and *place*.[3] The first is belonging through *activities*—what we would associate with our traditional notion of church membership—like attendance at worship and Bible studies, or participation in church groups and committees. People who belong through activities are "the backbone of any organization," says Walker, however "the backbone isn't the whole body, especially if it's the Body of Christ."[4] While essential to the life of the church, activity belonging or formal membership is not the only meaningful way people participate, associate, or belong. He describes the other modes of belonging in this way:

> *Event* belonging is where people come to church for one-off occasions, baptisms, weddings, or special events. Walker has found that these people "are genuinely seeking spiritual refreshment and closeness to God, not just a cultural experience."[5]
>
> *Relational* belonging is having a sense of connection through the people—staff or lay—who are involved at the congregation.
>
> *Place* belonging is when people feel a draw or connection to a particular place, be it a church, cathedral, or holy site. These "particular locations heighten our awareness of God."[6]

Walker's categories became incarnate for me when I stopped into another vital local gathering place, my local barbershop. My regular barber was busy, so I decided to take a chance on a new, young barber. As he began cutting my hair, he asked what I do. I told him I was a Lutheran pastor and then paused to see what he would say. You never quite know how people will react. Surprisingly, this young, tattooed guy said, "I'm Lutheran too." It was my turn to be caught off-guard. It turns out he used to attend the Lutheran church just a few blocks away when he was a kid. His parents still go there, though he does not. But he still identifies as Lutheran and belongs to that church via *relational* and *place* modes of belonging. With Walker's categories in mind, I was able to recognize his connection to that church as a genuine form of belonging rather than viewing him as yet another fallen away Lutheran None. This helped me to keep the conversation open. I could affirm his connection to the church rather than, at least in my own mind, belittle it for not living up to that of belonging through *activity*, or pushing for him to start going every Sunday to that church or my own. Sure, he wasn't a member who would show up on the church database, but he *belonged.* He saw himself that way, and there was no good reason for me not to.

Walker's research offers an important corrective both to the narrow way we have understood church belonging—almost entirely through the lens of membership—as well as common perceptions of the motivations, practices, and beliefs behind the ways people engage with faith communities. He concludes,

> What seven years of studying belonging has taught me is that a preference for *events, people,* or *places* above *activity* is not a proof of nominal or weak faith, at least no more than is a preference for evangelical or catholic styles of worship. It reflects a different way of engaging with God. To the extent that it can be shallow, then the same is true for regular churchgoing. Whichever dimension of belonging motivates it, the engagement with God can be real and profound.[7]

Although they may make meaning, describe that meaning, and encounter God in different ways than those we have come to presume as normative for regular churchgoers, people who practice *event, relational,* and *place* belonging are also finding authentic and "real" ways of connecting faith communities, religious institutions, and God.

A HOUSE FOR ALL

Recognizing that people do not belong to faith communities in a uniform way, House for All Sinners and Saints in Denver, Colorado, which recently graduated from a mission start to a full-fledged congregation of the ELCA, adopted a congregational constitution, which includes a new, more expansive, category of membership called "participating members." In their denomination, the ELCA, the model constitution for congregations stipulates four categories of church member—baptized, confirmed, voting, and associate—all of which are predicated on having been baptized. Recognizing that many in their community are not baptized and come from a variety of religious or secular backgrounds, House added the category of "participating member," which according to the House constitution, is defined as "those persons who participate in the liturgy and receive the Eucharist and who have demonstrated a love for the community through prayer, work, and generosity." In this founding document, House recognizes that people have different modes of belonging to their community and expresses the value and importance of their presence and participation as the primary marker of membership. In fact, this is the *only* category House uses for its members. Everyone, from pastor to church pillars, to the newest members are all listed as *participating members.* For House, this single category is an expression of its expansive understanding of belief, practice, and belonging.

This was part of the culture at House well before they drafted their constitution. For instance, when you enter the worship space (the fellowship hall of an Episcopal church) on Sunday evenings, there is a table with worship bulletins marked with worship leadership roles for different parts of the liturgy like "greeting," "prayer of the day," "assisting minister," "chalice bearer," or "bread bearer." Anyone can pick up one of these bulletins and take on a leadership role for that night's service, as they feel so moved. The liturgical leadership, therefore, is distributed as a variety of voices emerge from across the assembly during worship. In this and many other ways, House demonstrates hospitality and wel-

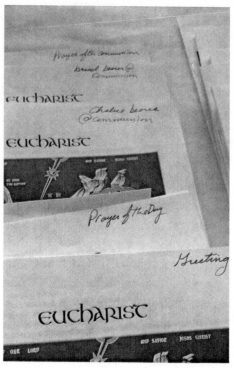

Sunday worship booklets at House for All Sinners and Saints in Denver, Colorado. Booklets have worship leadership roles written on the cover. *Photo: Keith Anderson*

come, as well as their broad understanding of who can participate, who belongs, and who is authorized to lead.

House also extends hospitality and inclusion through its significant digital presence, primarily through its founding pastor and best-selling author, Nadia Bolz-Weber. Bolz-Weber blogs her sermons each week and tells the story of her congregation with her trademark sarcastic wisdom and insight on Facebook and Twitter. Through this digital ministry, thousands of people who have never attended worship at House feel connected to the congregation's ministry, with many claiming it as a spiritual home and Bolz-Weber as pastor and spiritual leader.

DIGITAL BELONGING

We might add a fifth mode of belonging to Walker's model—*digital* belonging. After all, people can feel connected and have a sense of belonging to a congregation or ministry because of their online connection to the church through its website, social media platforms—or digital connections with the pastor, staff, or parishioners. Blog posts, sermon podcasts, and other social media activity can provide spiritual content and opportunities for engagement with what Jeremy Fletcher has called "the *dispersed community* of a cathedral."[8] Through digital social media we are meaningfully connected to and nurturing the faith of people we may never meet face-to-face, but again, those connections are no less real simply because they are digitally mediated. Rector Tim Schenk of St. John's Church and Lent Madness reflects, "Parishes that are going to grow and thrive in the future are the ones that see value in ministry to those they'll never meet in person. It's this globalization of church and it's welcoming the stranger, but it is the stranger that they probably won't ever meet." In my own experience, this thriving comes as a result of sharing the Gospel feely, without the expectation of anything in return. When we engage digitally with friends, acquaintances, or strangers that live beyond the geographical reach of our congregations, we are often able to set aside questions of membership and simply be in relationship and freely share the love and grace of God—not as an enticement to joining, but for its own sake.

WHAT DO WE MEAN BY EVANGELISM, ANYWAY?

A primary challenge to sharing the Gospel today is that the church often operates under a very narrow understanding of evangelism. We have reduced evangelism (sharing the Good News of new life through the death and resurrection of Jesus Christ) to a mere strategy or set of tactics by which we convert visitors into church members. We have narrowed our definition of success in our evangelism and our churches to the rate at which these conversions take place. By that limited measure, especially in our current environment, most of our congregations would be considered failures, and yet, as we have seen throughout this book, important and vibrant ministry is still happening in such places, regardless of whether it shows up in the annual statistical report.

For me, as a Lutheran, the Gospel means something very specific—the Good News of God's love, forgiveness, and grace in Jesus Christ. We receive that Good News in faith (which is itself a gift from God), and we respond to that Good News and gift of God's love through our actions towards our neighbors. Sharing the Gospel is about communicating the free and abundant grace and love of God, which does not necessarily result in church membership. Part of the problem is that we have mistaken evangelism for Good News about the *church*, rather the Good News of what *God* has done in Jesus Christ. They are related, but they are not synonymous—and the Good News of God should always come first. If the Gospel is a gift from God, then it makes sense to share it as a gift to others with no expectations in return. The Gospel is not a proprietary piece of software that requires a key code of my congregation or denomination to unlock it. It is a free download. It is to be given away freely to as many people as possible, in person and online. This approach to evangelism results, hopefully, in hearts set free to worship God, serve others, and love all. It is that generosity and the trust it builds that will draw people into community. A first and critical step, then, is to decouple *evangelism* from church *membership*, while preserving the important connection between the *Gospel* and *relationship*.

BARSTOOL EVANGELISM

In this approach, sharing the Good News doesn't necessarily require inviting people to church. At least, not at first, according to Emily Scott, pastor at St. Lydia's Dinner Church. She has said, "In a bar on the Lower East Side in New York City, the most powerful tool of evangelism is *not* inviting someone to church. In a bar on the Lower East Side of New York City, good evangelism does not have to be about preaching, proclaiming, pamphletting, or proselytizing. It is about relationships."[9] Rather than inviting people to church or trying to convert people, she looks to develop a relationship and start a conversation and lets things emerge from there. Scott describes how things might develop from that initial conversation at the bar:

> One, we wrap up our conversation and go our separate ways. My new friend has a new (and positive) impression of at least one Christian, which, in and of itself, is a work of the Spirit.
>
> Two, we wrap up our conversation, but run into each other again—even become friends. Somewhere along the line, my new friend and I start talking about life and how it unfolds, maybe God, maybe community, maybe doubt. It's not a formal relationship, but one day he begins to joke that I'm his spiritual advisor. I have a number of people like this in my life, and I've never once . . . invited any of them to church. This is not to say that they will never want to come. But I believe that they will tell me if they'd like to.
>
> Three, we continue talking. We talk a lot. About faith and doubt and God and relationships. And at some point he opens a door and says something like, "You know, I've really been looking for a place to have this conversation." And then I invite him to church. In context. These are the people who are coming to St. Lydia's.[10]

What Scott describes here is a networked, relational, and incarnational approach to evangelism. It values listening rather than broadcasting a message. It values relationship and staying connected over time, rather than making a one-time sales pitch to join a congregation. It allows the "church conversation" to come up later, organically, in context, if at all. When it does arise, it is with a real person, with real ideas, experiences, hopes, and fears, for whom faith is an integral part of life, and not a religious caricature. She writes,

Evangelizing—bringing the Good News—is not about convincing someone to believe in Jesus. It's about bearing witness to what God has done with the whole of our existence, within the context of our cultures and the patterns of our lives. . . .

I'm telling a story of how God doesn't need me to hide from the world within the confines of the Church, but to be a part of the whole of the world around me. I bear witness to my Good News every time I'm sarcastic, edgy, questioning, breaking the stereotype of a "good Christian girl." . . . I bear witness to my Good News every time I refrain from invitation, and try, instead, to listen. I'm telling a story of how God's love is so deep and so wide that she doesn't ask me to change people, but to walk with them, trusting that that she will do her work naturally, easily, in the context of relationship.[11]

Whether it starts on a bar stool, a barber's chair, or through social media, evangelism is not about messaging, marketing, or converting. It is about being in relationship over time and sharing your life, in which God has made a meaningful difference. Church is not a product to sell or consume. It is a community of people centered in God's grace with which to be in relationship.

THE DIGITAL GOSPEL:
STORYTELLING OVER TIME IN RELATIONSHIP

Digital social media and local third places provide the opportunity to tell our stories—both personal and congregational—over time in a variety of ways. We have the ability to reach a broader and more diverse group of people than ever before; however, messages and interactions in those spaces often seem fleeting. One-hundred-and-forty-character tweets hardly seem sufficient to share the life-altering Good News, though we can never discount how something small can make a profound difference in someone's life, especially when received at just the right time. **These episodic, seemingly ephemeral media—posts, tweets,**

Instagrams, check-ins—or conversations on barstools and bar-bers' chairs—have a cumulative effect as they are held together in the context of relationship. They help nurture, sustain, and enliven relationships in which we can share and experience the Gospel together. In a sense, this is not so different from the Gospels themselves, which are filled with Jesus' own episodic encounters—like with the woman at the well, the paralytic lowered through the roof by his friends, or the woman who grabbed the hem of his garment in the street—which take place in the context of relationship and the larger narrative of his own death and resurrection.

A notable and fun example is the Twible (rhymes with Bible) project undertaken by author Jana Reiss. Over the course of four years, Reiss tweeted a 140-character-or-less summary of each of the 1,189 chapters in the Bible, which were later collected into a book by the same name. The tweets are quick and witty looks at the Bible.

> Exodus 15: "Miriam's song. Oldest oral tradition in entire Bible? 'Our God is an Awesome God?' for the *1200 BCE WOW Gold Hits Album*. Now on iTunes."[12]

> Isaiah 6: "Isa [Isaiah] has a sentimental flashback about the moment he was first called to be a prophet and tell the people that they suck. Ah, happy day."[13]

> Mark 5: "JC [Jesus Christ] raises a girl from the dead! Good thing she was just 12. If she'd been a teen, she would have slept all day until *she* wanted to get up."[14]

Beyond the humor and the novelty of using Twitter to study and share the Bible, much of what made the Twible work was the relationships and connections that developed around it. Although each tweet on its own may have been fleeting, the consistency over time and the replies and retweets it generated helped to create engagement, conversation, and even community with friends, followers, and complete strangers around the Good News of Scripture.

KEEPING THE GOSPEL GOING

In a time when traditional models of religious affiliation and membership are in decline, these kinds of encounters perform an important function in engaging with both the religiously affiliated and Nones. Drawing on the work of sociologist Anthony Giddens, Elizabeth Drescher writes that these encounters across digital and face-to-face platforms help to create "narrative coherence . . . the capacity to keep a particular narrative going . . . from setting to setting, from relationship to relationship, from commitment to commitment."[15] She writes,

> This notion of narrative coherence has profound implications for the nurturing of religious and spiritual identities that historically were solidified in denominational and congregational membership and enacted in very specific locales at designated times. It means, for one thing, that traditional models of membership, with their associated denominational labels and worship practices, have less and less meaning in postmodern lives that play out in a largely postchristian, religiously plural world.[16]

Since we no longer construct our religious identities in the same way we once did, that is, by drawing on traditional modes of membership and participation in faith communities, we need an alternative to sustaining identity by keeping a cohesive narrative going across all areas of life. **In this new context, then, evangelism is not about manufacturing members, but about keeping the Gospel going through the various settings, relationships, and commitments in people's lives.** We meet in local gathering places to help keep a narrative going about God's presence in the neighborhood and in people's daily work and their leisure.

We gather in digital gathering spaces for the same reason. In digital social media we experience the convergence of various parts of our lives, which all come together on our Facebook wall, Twitter stream, or Pinterest boards. As we bear witness to the Gospel and share our stories of faith in these digital spaces, it touches on all these other parts of our lives. It keeps the Gospel going, strengthening that narrative coherence for ourselves and for others.

PREACH THE GOSPEL AT ALL TIMES; IF NECESSARY, USE TWEETS

Carolyn Clement and Laura Catalano, parish social media administrators at Episcopal churches in Connecticut and Missouri respectively, have invited people and congregations to tell their stories through a grassroots effort they called Social Media Sunday. They encouraged Episcopal churches to use the hashtag #episcopal and post about their congregations. Catalano explained, "People can take a selfie, or a picture of stained glass in their church or something fun going on and post them on Facebook, or Twitter. It's a neat way to get an idea of what's happening across the church."[17] They report, "There were 4,000+ posts on Twitter and Instagram and thousands more on Facebook. . . . we estimated that we reached 1 million+ on Twitter alone, and imagine there were millions more on Facebook! At approximately 10am EST we hit the top of the US Trends chart on Twitter."[18]

What distinguishes this approach to social media from some others is that it wasn't focused on marketing and messaging. It was about sharing the joy of being part of the church, sharing stories, and making new connections. It was grassroots, activated and fueled by social media, and not part of a branding campaign. The hashtag #episcopal became a campfire around which people could share stories from around the church with other far-flung Episcopalians as well those well beyond their faith communities in their social networks.

CHECKING-IN AT CHURCH

Of course, congregations can encourage their members to help share the Gospel and share their stories and those of their congregations every Sunday. Each Sunday as people enter our sanctuary, we project a PowerPoint slide that encourages them to check-in and hashtag their pictures, posts, and tweets. "If you have a Facebook or Foursquare profile, please check-in and let friends know you are worshipping with us today. If you are on Twitter, please hashtag your tweets with #udlc." Since then we have also added Instagram. We encourage this not just at worship, but on mission trips and other events and activities. In doing so, we encourage people to keep a narrative going about our congregation, but also their own lives, and for others.

We are extending the same invitation that the disciple Philip extends to his friend Nathaniel (John 1). After meeting Jesus, Philip seeks out his friend Nathaniel and tells him to come

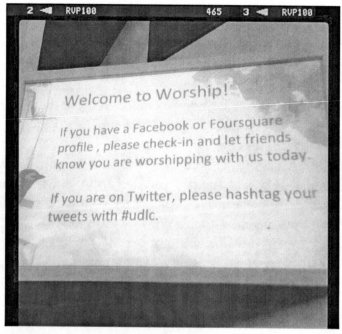

Welcome slide at Upper Dublin Lutheran Church, Ambler Pennsylvania. *Photo: Keith Anderson*

and see the long-awaited Messiah, who, incidentally, has come from Nazareth, then considered a cultural backwater. Nathaniel replies, "Can anything good come from Nazareth?" A growing number of people are asking that question in this way: *"Can anything good come from the church?"* Like Philip, our response is "come and see"—but not just "come and see" my church and its pastor, but "come and see" through local conversations and the online sharing of our lives, the role faith plays in our real lives. Alongside this invitation we may also need to include words of repentance for the hurt people have experienced at the hands of the church, and perhaps to debunk common misperceptions of churches as uniformly closed, ultra-conservative, homophobic, and hostile toward science. That message comes through best from members of the community, not clergy who can be dismissed as paid messengers.

When people do come to our churches, we can't shift back into well-worn models of member-making through classes that are information and transactional—some variation of "Welcome! This is who we are and what we do, go and do likewise, and, oh, and here are your offering envelopes." These encounters also need to be relational. Our congregation puts a high value on relationships, and the new-member classes are no different. We have two gatherings. The first is a social time in which newcomers and current members share their stories and what has brought them to the congregation. The second gathering builds on the relational groundwork. Newcomers meet the church staff and receive some information about the church. However, the focus remains on relationship building and exploring our spiritual gifts, which we share with the group, so everyone can get to know each other better. It's important to note that people should not have to wait to become members to participate in the life of the congregation. We encourage people to get involved as soon as they feel comfortable and not to wait for the imprimatur of membership before living out their faith and calling in our community.

Evangelism in a digital age is a highly networked and relational affair. It recognizes that we are connected like never before to broad networks of people, who belong to and connect with faith communities in a variety of diverse ways. It is focused on sharing the Gospel online and face-to-face in the context relationship, with an emphasis on listening and reconciliation rather than marketing and conversion. In the context of those relationships, we are able to share the Gospel through living our stories and demonstrating the difference God makes in our lives—to keep the Gospel going. This can undoubtedly be a more complicated, circuitous, and time-consuming process compared to what we imagine as the straightforward conversion of visitors to members. At Redeemer, my previous congregation, our mantra for connecting with people was, "Everyone is different and nothing is ever straightforward." Everyone has a different story, has followed a different path, and engages a faith community in different ways. That goes for people who visit and ultimately decide to join the church, as well as those who orbit around our faith communities—people, as Steph Smith from Cathedral in the Night described, standing just at the very edges, or far beyond the edges, of our congregations. "It's messy," says Smith. "You have to be comfortable with the mess, but through the mess comes amazing stuff."

12

A DiGiTAL RULE OF LiFE

"A rule sustains identity by mandating the rhythms of worship, spiritual discipline, prayer and rest, work and ministry. . . . And it connects the practices and ideals of the particular community or order with the gospel and the Christian mystery."

—*The Rule of the Society of St. John the Evangelist*

"Composing a rule is a very traditional thing to do; what is innovative is the freedom . . . in bringing into the Rule many themes that belong to our contemporary religious experience."

—*The Rule of the Society of St. John the Evangelist*

I FIRST VISITED THE MONASTERY of the Society of St. John the Evangelist in Cambridge, Massachusetts nearly twenty years ago at the invitation of a divinity school classmate. One snowy evening we walked across campus, then down Memorial Drive along the banks of the Charles River. When we finally arrived at the monastery, we stepped into a small square vestibule where we shook off the snow and cold. When we pushed open the door to the nave, the first thing I noticed (besides the welcome warmth) was the smell of incense—not newly burned incense, but the smell of incense that, like the prayers recited over the years, had seemingly seeped into the stone walls.

We walked into the Romanesque-styled sanctuary, with its marble floors, stone walls, rounded arches, and wood-beamed ceiling, and took our place in the chairs that lined either side of the nave. We sat quietly and waited for worship to begin.

Just a few minutes later, monks in black robes began appearing, bowing before the altar, and taking their places in their low-backed choir-stall chairs. At exactly eight o'clock, the brothers stood up, and the rest of us along with them, as worship began. We prayed, listened to Scripture, and sang. But the most transcendent part of the service was the brothers' signature plain-song chant, sung responsively back and forth from one side of the nave to the other. The beauty and simplicity of the liturgy and gentle countenance and welcoming smiles of the brothers immediately drew me in. I knew very quickly that I had discovered a spiritual home at SSJE, one to which I have returned many times over the years.

Later, as I began my life in ordained ministry, and before the arrival of our twins, I would spend many days in silent retreat at the monastery. In those visits, I gained a wider perspective and greater appreciation for the rhythm of life there. Each day revolves around worship: Morning Prayer, a Service for Noon-time, Evening Prayer, and Compline. In between services, a culture of silence is maintained throughout the monastery. Most communication with the brothers and other retreatants comes in the form of friendly nods. Meals are taken in silence as music plays or a brother reads from a book. While visitors like me make use of the quiet environment to rest, pray, reflect, or sleep, the brothers tend to a variety of duties that help sustain the community's life: community meetings, prayer, learning, sacred reading, preparing for preaching and worship, ministries of service, spiritual direction, and time of fellowship and Sabbath.

This rhythm of life at the monastery is guided by order's Rule, *The Rule of the Society of Saint John the Evangelist*. Like nearly every religious order, the brothers of SSJE have three overarching vows of poverty, chastity, and obedience. Each order has its own particular way of living out those vows, which they outline in their rule of life. The forty-nine short chapters of *The Rule of SSJE* describe and define the order's life, from the rhythm of worship, the culture of silence, the observance of their monastic vows, as well as prayer, Scripture, Sabbath, and navigating life in community. It also addresses more practical concerns like what the brothers should wear (a black robe, ring, and cross, in case you were wondering) and outlines the process for how one joins or leaves the order.

The Rule of SSJE is the spiritual descendent of *The Rule of St. Benedict*, written by Benedict of Nursia in the sixth century to help guide the community of monks that assembled under his leadership in Monte Cassino, Italy. The most influential monastic rule in the western church, Benedict's rule has served as a template for monastic practice and spiritual living ever since. To understand the Rule and its observance better, I spoke with Brother Dan Walters, a monk in the Order of St. Benedict, at Glastonbury Abbey in Hingham, Massachusetts. I first met Dan when he was serving as the chaplain at St. Francis House Homeless Shelter in Boston, a position he held for eighteen years. These days he serves as the Prior (the abbot's administrative assistant) and Director of Vocations at the monastery. I recently reconnected with Dan after about ten years when—you guessed it—he friended me on Facebook.

When I asked Dan about what it has been like living with the Rule over his forty-five years as a monk, he told me,

> We don't literally follow *The Rule of St. Benedict*. It's not that we're not keeping the Rule. I think we are keeping the Rule in our own way. When people read the Rule, they come [to visit the monastery] expecting us to be very severe and really separated from the world. St. Benedict's idea was that we would have nothing to do with the world, that we were self-sufficient, that we lived in our own little world. And even though we are separated in a way because we have a lot of land, we have people in and out of here all the time.

That wasn't always the case. As Dan recounted some of the changes at the monastery over time, he recalled that there once was a sign at the entrance to the monastery saying, "Monastic enclosure. Women are forbidden." Before signing on with the Benedictines, Dan spent a few years as a Trappist monk, inspired as he was by the work of Thomas Merton. Being one of the stricter religious orders, Trappists at the time were not allowed to have news or information from the outside world, except, Dan remembers, when President Kennedy was assassinated. Even then they only were given story clippings, not the whole newspaper. Dan speculates, "And that's probably only because he was Catholic." These days, Dan reads *The New York Times* and *The Boston Globe* on his computer in his monastic cell, along with Facebook and email. He says, "I've seen a lot of changes in my lifetime. And I think they are all good changes. I think it is for the best. It makes us a little more normal, more human."

Whether the ancient Rule of St. Benedict or more contemporary rules, such as *The Rule of Taize* (1953) or *The Rule of SSJE* (1997), monastic rules address common themes of community, prayer, humility, hospitality, worship, and Christian living. In this way, they are helpful guides for cultivating networked, relational, and incarnational life and ministry. They help to organize the life of the community and also serve as sources of spiritual wisdom for individuals and groups. They are "a description of the day-to-day living which revolves around Christ, both individually and corporately."[1]

Some individuals or groups choose to follow a particular rule of life, or create their own, as a way of expressing their spiritual values and pursuing God-centered lives. These rules can be trustworthy guides and supports for people and communities who want to lead lives shaped by prayer and a greater awareness of the presence of God. While the mention of a rule may conjure images of inflexible bureaucracy, as Brother Dan shared with me, they are not intended to be unchanging or oppressive, but instead guide and facilitate the spiritual lives of individuals and communities. As St. Benedict wrote, "This Rule is not meant to burden you. It should help you to discover and experience how great is the freedom to which you are called."[2]

Inspired by historic rules of life, this chapter offers fifteen rules for navigating life in the digital age—*a digital rule of life* as it were. These are ways to tend the heart, live faithfully in digital community, and stay spiritually grounded amidst the world's frenetic pace and many demands. What follows, then, are fifteen rules for life and ministry in the Digital Cathedral, ways to remain tethered to Christ our center in the midst of our wireless world.

1. Be Present
2. Listen
3. Welcome the Stranger
4. Pray Without Ceasing
5. Be Helpful
6. Be Humble
7. Get Rhythm
8. Curate Good Information
9. Convene Conversations
10. Participate in Meaning Making
11. Tell Good Stories
12. Disagree Amicably
13. Take Digital Sabbath
14. Meet in Person Whenever Possible
15. Commit All You Do to God

1. Be Present

> "Do not remember the former things, or consider the things of old. I am about to do a new thing; now it springs forth, do you not perceive it?" (Isaiah 43:18–19)

Ministry leaders in the Digital Cathedral should strive to be locally, digitally, culturally, and spiritually present.

As we have seen throughout this book, cultivating a consistent and gracious presence in local and digital gathering spaces enables us to encounter our neighbors and strangers, connect with our local communities, and engage our new digital neighborhoods. Where we choose to be present speaks volumes about our values and commitments. We need to demonstrate our genuine care and concern for what happens beyond our congregational enclaves by being present both locally and digitally.

While in these spaces, we need to be spiritually present and open. Our presence in these local and digital spaces is not a gimmick, not a bait-and-switch, and not a strategy. At heart, it is a spiritual practice. It is about deliberately relocating ourselves in order to encounter others and the sacred in the world. When we make ourselves open and vulnerable by entering these third places we do not manage or control, we are more open to the unpredictable ways the Spirit moves in us, in others, and in our world.

Finally, we need to be present to our world as it is, not as it once was. Brother Roger writes in *The Rule of Taize*, "Be present to your age; adapt yourself to the conditions."[3] Our lament for days-gone-by clouds our engagement with the world as it is and diminishes the quality of our presence. We ought not fear the present nor the future. For it too belongs to God.

2. Listen

> "You must understand this, my beloved: let everyone be quick to listen, slow to speak." (James 1:19)

We rightly recognize that social media can amplify our voice and the public witness of our faith, both individually and corporately. However, and more importantly, it also increases our capacity to listen. Social media and third places put us into daily contact with a wide range of people, who are sharing their lives through stories told in conversation, written text, images, and video. When we show up and login consistently, we are able to listen for what people are talking about, how they talk about it, and when they talk about it. We gain insight into the lives, hopes, and concerns of our friends and neighbors. Thus, the commonly accepted first rule of social media is to listen—or, in the words of the Prayer of Saint Francis, "to seek first to understand rather than to be understood."

More, we listen for God in others, listening deeply, below the surface, to hear and understand the ways in which people make meaning, engage their world, and struggle with their faith.

We should listen for the holy and the presence of God in what people share. When we listen consistently, patiently, and compassionately, we are able to respond with understanding and acknowledgement. This work of deep listening is at the heart of digitally integrated ministry and the spiritual life. As the Benedictine Joan Chittister writes, "The spiritual life is achieved only by listening to all of life and learning to respond to each of its dimensions wholly and with integrity."[4] The same goes for life in the Digital Cathedral.

3. Welcome the Stranger

"I was a stranger and you welcomed me." (Matthew 25:35)

Hospitality is one of the hallmarks of monastic rules. As St. Benedict instructed his monks, "Any guest who happens to arrive at the monastery should be received just as we would receive Christ himself. . . ."[5] When a guest entered the monastery in Benedict's time, the monks would pray and read Scripture with them, and the Superior, the second in command of the monastery, would wash the hands of the guest and then their feet. Some cathedrals (Canterbury, included) were administered by monks in the medieval period and have historically extended a similar hospitality to strangers, pilgrims, and the poor.

As fewer people affiliate with and attend our churches, and as that church membership and attendance become less culturally normative, we will encounter increasing numbers of Nones, who may appear to us as strangers. Nones are not problems to solve, or issues to be debated, but rather individuals to welcome as if they were Christ himself. As Benedict reminds us, we should seek to show honor and deference to the stranger—to listen, to learn, to affirm, to love, and to seek to be in relationship.

The hospitality we extend to Nones may take place within our congregations should they choose to visit us, but we should also practice a kind of hospitality that extends God's love and care beyond our church buildings, into the networked communities of which we are a part. We should accept the varied ways people choose to connect with us through different modes of belonging, and honor when people choose not to belong at all. Most of all, we should welcome them in our hearts, our lives, and our prayers. As Brother Roger writes, "It is Christ himself whom we receive as a guest. So let us learn to be welcoming and be ready to offer our free time; our hospitality should be generous and discerning."[6]

4. Pray Without Ceasing

> "This, then, is the beginning of my advice: make prayer the first step in anything worthwhile that you attempt."[7]
>
> —THE RULE OF ST. BENEDICT

Life in the digital age presents more opportunities, not fewer, for prayer. Treat your Facebook feed or Twitter stream as calls to prayer. Never miss an opportunity to say that you are praying when someone asks for prayer. A simple "Praying!" or "Holding you in prayer" will suffice. At times you may want to ask, "For what shall we pray today?" as an invitation for people to express their joys and concerns. When we offer or invite prayer, we are connecting with people through one of the most durable traditional religious categories. These moments of prayer requested and offered join us at deeply human and vulnerable levels.

Through prayer we recognize the sacred dimensions in life. As Joan Chittister writes, "To pray in the midst of the mundane is simply and strongly to assert that this dull and tiring day is holy and its simple labors are the stuff of God's saving presence for me now."[8] Praying for our friends, our communities, and our world are ways of naming them holy.

5. Be Helpful

"Love your neighbor as yourself." (Mark 12:31)

One of the easiest and most effective ways to demonstrate our love of neighbor and extend welcome to the stranger in the digital age is simply to be helpful. If someone calls or messages you asking for help, advice, or guidance, give it. Don't hesitate to help in any way you can. This book was made possible by the generosity of the people I have interviewed and chronicled in these pages. They are exemplars of ministry in the Digital Cathedral, not just for the remarkable work that they do, but their generosity in sharing that work with others—their best insights as well as their questions, their successes as well as their failures.

Seek to be open, generous, and helpful to others. Give away your best ideas, for in doing so you will gain the trust of others and build up the body of Christ. Share your favorite insights for this week's lectionary readings, your awesome plan for confirmation class, your own blog posts or videos with lessons learned and insights gained. Jamie Coats, director of the Friends of SSJE, a community that helps support and share the work of the monastery, says this is part of living in the "gift economy." He told me,

> Although I'm in charge fundraising and communication, 95 percent of my job is figuring out how to give away the brothers' wisdom. . . . How do we connect and give people wisdom that feeds them? If you understand you truly live in the gift economy and you're truly giving away God's gift for the sake of God's love, then it flows back.

In a time of shrinking membership and budgets, when we may be tempted to hold on to our best ideas and maintain what we imagine to be competitive advantage, we are called to give it away. More will be gained in giving away rather than in hoarding our best ideas and insights.

6. Be Humble

"Let the same mind be in you that was in Christ Jesus."
(Philippians 2:5)

One of the great temptations of the digital age is to think more highly of ourselves than we ought. There is something about posting something online and then getting immediate feedback that is seductive. It makes us feel liked, loved, and influential and can lead to mistakenly imagining ourselves to be the next church social media star. It can give us an inflated view of ourselves, our place in the church, and in the the world. At worst, it can cross into the realm of narcissism, as we continually check our friend and follower totals, likes, comments, retweets, and repins, as if that were the true indication of our value and influence.

Monastic rules place a high importance of humility in the spiritual life and community living. St. Benedict's rule on humility is one of his longest and describes twelve steps of humility, including the advice that "we should be ready to speak of ourselves as of less importance and less worthy than others, not as a mere phrase on our lips but we should really believe it in our hearts."[9] Echoing this, Brother Roger instructed the brothers of Taize, "In the work you do, do not compare yourself to other brothers. Your place is necessary for the witness of the whole community—in all simplicity, know how to keep it."[10] In a digitally integrated world, this means recognizing that we are just one part of a much larger network. We should fulfill our particular calling to the best of our ability and great humility.

7. Get Rhythm

"Seven times a day I praise you." (Psalm 119:164)

Monastic rules stress the importance of a rhythm of prayer, worship, study, work, and community. Esther de Waal observes, "The days of St. Benedict's monks were poised on the rhythmic succession of these three elements, prayer, study, work. Four hours of each day were devoted to liturgical prayer, four to spiritual reading, and six to manual work."[11] Not all of us are called to such structure. However, it is essential that we find a "rhythmic succession" that works for us, while understanding that our Rule can and will change over time.

Consider the rhythm—which will undoubtedly be different for each of us—between time spent online and face-to-face; how often we post and what we post about; and time spent away from the screen and ministry duties. In a world of immediacy, where we often find ourselves constantly reacting to things, consistency and equanimity over the long term is an underappreciated quality. Jamie Coats reflects, "Commit to a rhythm that you can absolutely promise and guarantee year in and year out." If that means you can only muster one blog post a month, then do that, but stick with it.

We must take this into account in our presence in local gathering places as well. In my parish, we are able to sustain a monthly theology pub, bi-monthly coffee shop conversations, the occasional Beer and Hymns night, and annual beer tasting charity event. Figure out what works for you. Create something people can come to expect, but leave time for yourself to renew your creativity. In a time when people's attention is so easily diverted, we cannot afford to be inconsistent. In a world of constant and sometimes confusing change, consistency is a quality that people seek in their spiritual leaders and faith communities.

8. Curate Good Information

"Set your minds on things that are above." (Colossians 3:2)

We live in a world of endless information, and not all of it is worthwhile. It is important that we function as curators of good information. We typically associate the term "curation" with museums and art galleries more than churches. Today, *curation* is a term that has been repurposed to refer to the management of digital content and communities. As we have seen, there is simply too much information to keep up with today. We need others to help sort and distinguish content that is worth our limited and valuable time and attention. Curators help to curate or filter good content worth reading or watching.

Seek to share good information in your particular areas of interest, whether the Bible, world events, church news, digital ministry, or spiritual living. Choose material that is thoughtful and well reasoned. Lift up important voices, however small their social media platform may be. Provide a variety of distinctive content. Share things that build up and edify your digital community, instead of dividing it. Avoid inflammatory and reactionary posts.

Develop strategies to manage information without becoming overwhelmed by it—without feeling that you need to be on your computer or mobile device all the time. Consider your options in how you access and receive content such as email subscriptions, RSS (real simple syndication) readers, or Twitter lists.[12]

9. Convene Conversations

"For where two or three are gathered in my name, I am there among them." (Matthew 18:20)

In addition to being curators of information, we need to be conveners of conversation in which people can reflect on their experience of life and faith. We should host conversations that allow individuals to reflect together on what all this information means for them, for their community, and for the world. In an increasingly polarized world, we need meeting places for people to explore their values and the way they make meaning and make sense of an ever-changing world. As Jodi Houge has said, this can be a "healing thing." These conversations can happen at church, locally, on Facebook, using hashtags, and beyond.

Hosting these kinds of conversations is an extension of our practice of hospitality and humility, in that we offer a safe space for people to gather and share. Resist the impulse to dominate or make yourself the center of the conversation. Instead, facilitate and make yourself at home at the edge of the discussion. Do not presume to impart answers, but help others discern how God is at work in their lives and the world. Model good listening. Leave it open ended. God knows we don't have all the answers, but we can bring a particular wisdom shaped by our experience and perspective. Bryan Berghoef writes that this can make a world of difference, "between an indoctrination approach to faith (where the focus is on getting it right) and an exploration approach to faith (where the goal is to experience God in a way that is life-affirming, gracious, and for the good of those around us)."[13]

10. Participate in Meaning Making

> "The praise of Christ expressed by the liturgy permeates us
> insofar as it is maintained throughout our humble daily tasks."[14]
>
> —THE RULE OF TAIZE

As we have seen, people are making meaning all the time. Support and engage with them in the activities and practices they find meaningful. Look at what people share through the eyes of faith and help them to do the same. Affirm them in their daily vocation.

Help people to see their lives holistically as a way of countering the fragmentation caused by our frenetic pace of living. Help them plumb the hidden depths, and encounter the God that is always right there, but who sometimes seems hidden or absent. People are hungry to know God sees them, knows them, and loves them. People are harried, stressed, tired, and anxious. They are carried along by rapid change and an always-on, plugged-in world. They want to know that things like packing their kid's lunch for school, doing the dishes, heading off to work while it's still dark in the morning, and the other work they do matters. They want to know it makes a difference.

11. Tell Good Stories

> "Storytelling reveals meaning without committing the error of
> defining it."
>
> —HANNAH ARENDT

Be aware that in a digital world we are always telling a story. We tell stories in long-form blogs and video, but also tell a story with our accumulated likes, comments, check-ins, and more. We are constantly telling a story or multiple stories through our activity on social media and with our physical presence—or for that matter, our absence.[15] These stories are shaped by what we share and how we share it and with whom we interact. Today many of these activities are available for public consumption. Whereas once you might have worried about running into a parishioner or two at the grocery store, now hundreds of people are now paying attention to your physical and digital footsteps.

Become a good digital storyteller—spin a narrative of God in your life and the life of the world. Use a variety of media, text and images. Don't just share your great success stories, but stories of redemption and unexpected graces. These stories are told over time in the context of relationship. Look back regularly on your tweets and posts. What story are you telling?

12. Disagree Amicably

> "Make the unity of the body of Christ your passionate concern."[16]
>
> —THE RULE OF TAIZE

The authors of monastic rules were well aware that any time you have a community of people who hold various viewpoints, perspectives, and convictions, conflict is inevitable. The same goes for social media. Just as there are seemingly endless opportunities for wider and broader connections and relationships, the potential for hurtful and harmful is also amplified. A recent study shows that 40 percent of people have personally experienced some form of bullying online.[17]

Give people the benefit of the doubt. Sometimes it is hard to judge people's tone and intent in digitally mediated spaces. Remember that in social media there is no final word. There is only the *next* word. Don't delude yourself into imagining you will have the final say. Whenever possible, seek to disagree amicably.

Sister Julie Vieira, IHM, says we can even have compassion for trolls—people whom it seems only live to disrupt life online. She asks, "Can you create a space big enough in yourself to care even for those people? It's too easy to hit the delete or ban button sometimes. It's the presumption that the person isn't a troll, they're a person." Although we might need to delete a comment or block someone as a last resort, we can still hold them in prayer.

13. Take a Digital Sabbath

"But who is not daunted by this silence, preferring to be distracted when it is time for work, fleeing prayer to wear himself out at useless tasks, forgetful of this neighbor and himself?"[18]

—*The Rule of Taize*

In our always-on digital culture, it is entirely too easy to be swept away in the stream of comments, issues, and information. Take time to step out of the digital stream with technology Sabbaths. For, if we are constantly driven by the fear of missing out (FOMO) on digital content, we'll end up missing out on the world that is right in front of us. We must take time to step away from the screen if we want to cultivate our incarnational imagination.

Try to take long stretches of screen Sabbath, but if you can't do that, take mini-Sabbaths. As a wise preaching professor once said, interesting sermons are preached by people who lead interesting lives. Live stories worth telling. Sometimes that means getting away from your screen. Go ahead. We'll be here when you get back. When you do take Sabbath, leave a note on your social media platforms saying you are logged off for a little while, just as you would with an email vacation reply.[19] Taking regular times for the practice of Sabbath-keeping helps to avoid digital burnout and keeps things fresh and fun. As Brother Dan told me, "It takes something from people to be always connected and have all that social media happening in their lives and checking their iPhone messages all the time."

14. Meet in Person Whenever Possible

"... we are to aim at eucharistic living that is responsive at all times and in all places to the divine presence."[20]

—*The Rule of SSJE*

Accept the invitation to meet digital friends in person whenever possible. As we have seen throughout this book, these moments greatly reinforce and enhance online relationships. Whether it is over coffee, dinner, at a conference, or during a short layover, be intentional about connecting with people in person. In this way, we embrace the incarnational dimensions of ministry and engage in "Eucharistic living" in a digital age.

15. Commit All You Do to God

"... be faithful with Christ's help to this small Rule which is only a beginning."

—*St. Benedict*

Finally, commit all you do to God. We live in exciting and challenging times, times full of trial and error, successes and failures. We are all finding our way. Trust that the God who has called you to this work of ministry, the God who has begun a good work in you and the Church, will bring it to fulfillment.

Conclusion

"This is a precarious and dangerous project, repairing and rebuilding the very boat which keeps us afloat. But of course it is even more dangerous simply to sit complacently in that boat as it sinks, or to oppose or otherwise obstruct those seeking to rebuild it. If it has gotten into waters which it cannot manage, something must be done."

—GORDON KAUFMAN

"Cathedrals are (or should be) places for the best kind of Christian risk."

—CHRISTOPHER LEWIS

A TRANSITIONAL CATHEDRAL

On February 22, 2011, a 6.3-magnitude earthquake rocked the southeastern coast of New Zealand. Among the buildings damaged in the quake was the beloved ChristChurch Cathedral. The stone cathedral—the only one in Australasia—had long served as a center for civic and religious life in ChristChurch as well as a symbol of the city itself. In just a matter of minutes, a cathedral that took forty years to build and had stood for another one hundred and ten was completely devastated. The tower, spire, and western wall that formed the front of the cathedral were irreparably damaged and eventually reduced to rubble.

Plans are slowly taking shape to build an entirely new cathedral, but in the meantime, just a few blocks away, a temporary cathedral has risen from the proverbial ashes. It is officially called the ChristChurch Transitional Cathedral, but is better known to residents and pilgrims to ChristChurch as the "Cardboard Cathedral."[1] Designed by architect Shigeru Ban, renowned for his style of emergency or disaster architecture, the cathedral is so called because it is built substantively out of cardboard. Ninety-eight cardboard tubes form the a-frame ceiling of the cathedral and are overlayed with a polycarbonate translucent roof, allowing light to pour in between the cardboard cylinders. The sides of the nave are lined with eight shipping containers, which serve as offices and side chapels. On the eastern wall, a cardboard cross hangs above the altar, which, along with the other liturgical furnishings, is also made of cardboard. On the western end, there is a large multicolored triangular stained glass window composed of smaller triangles each imprinted with an image from the old cathedral's rose window. The whole project was completed in just two years at a cost of $7 million, remarkably fast and comparatively inexpensive as cathedrals go.

Just as the old stone cathedral was representative of the city and the devastation it experienced in the earthquake, the new cardboard cathedral is a symbol of the city's resilience and recovery. As Andrew Barrie, professor of architecture at the University of Auckland, has written, "The cardboard cathedral is a symbol of moving on."[2]

The Cardboard Cathedral is a powerful metaphor for Church, which has suffered its own kind of earthquake and subsequent shockwaves amidst the profound changes in life, religion, culture, and technology at the dawn of the twenty-first century. The Church is struggling profoundly with new patters of belief and practice, the rising number of religiously unaffiliated, and new communication technologies, slowly coming to grips with the way people live out their digitally integrated lives and faith. The preceding pages have chronicled the ways ministry leaders are living into this new time, facing its challenges and seizing its opportunities—and how, as Gordon Kaufman describes, we are repairing the very boat that keeps us afloat.[3]

Kaufman's observation calls to mind a story Steve Jobs once told about Gil Amelio, the CEO of Apple prior to Jobs' return. Amelio, according to Jobs, would say, "Apple is like a ship with a hole in the bottom, leaking water, and my job is to get the ship pointed in the right direction."[4] The joke, of course, is that no matter which direction you point it, if you don't address the leak, the boat is still going to sink. You have to do both. And so it is with the Church. Many of the strategies being proffered around the Church today are trying to point the ecclesiastical ship in the right direction, all the while ignoring the leak at our feet.

In these pages, I have sought to weave together a narrative of creative and innovative ministry leaders and faith communities that are fueled by a passion for their local and digital communities and for sharing the Gospel. Like medieval cathedral builders, they and we each have a role to play, a story to tell, and a mark to make. For today,

> The answers cannot come from on high. The world needs distributed leadership because the solutions to our collective challenges must come from many places, with people developing micro-adaptations to all the different micro-environments of families, neighborhoods and organizations around the globe.[5]

Much of the work we will do in this time, like the Cardboard Cathedral itself, will undoubtedly be transitional and provisional. We are in a time of experimentation and iteration, learning together as we go, discerning what to keep and what to let go. We are searching Scripture, our history and tradition, and our hearts and minds to find our way forward. Social media platforms will undoubtedly change. New digital devices will continue to emerge. Changes in religious affiliation, practice, and belief will persist and bear close watching. Perhaps at the end of this journey we will wind up with an entirely new boat. More likely, like most cathedrals, we will arrive with elements of both old and new. In either case, Kaufman reassures, "We are quite capable . . . of living in a world"—and for that matter, a Church—"even while it is being reconstructed. . . ."[6]

Like cathedral builders of old, we will not see the finished work—truly, cathedrals, be they stone, cardboard, or digital, are never finished—but may we, in the time we have been given, dedicate ourselves to the arts of ministry and the work of the Gospel, and, finally when our work is run, entrust the church we love to future generations of cathedral builders.

Notes

Foreword

1. Danièle Hervieu-Lége, *Religion as a Chain of Memory* (Cambridge: Polity Press, 2000), 24.

Introduction

1. Theos, "Spiritual Capital: The Present and Future of English Cathedrals," accessed November 1, 2014. Available online at *http://www.theosthinktank.co.uk/publications/2012/10/12/spiritual-capital-the-present-and-future-of-english-cathedrals*

2. Robert A. Scott, *The Gothic Enterprise: A Guide to Understanding the Medieval Cathedral* (Berkeley: University of California Press, 2003), 235.

3. Pew Research, "'Nones' on the Rise," October 9, 2012. Available online at *http://www.pewforum.org/2012/10/09/nones-on-the-rise/*

4. See Lee Rainie and Barry Wellman, *Networked: The New Social Operating System* (Cambridge, MA: The MIT Press, 2012), 1–108.

5. Scott, *The Gothic Enterprise*, 233.

6. This is a leadership model Elizabeth Drescher and I introduced in *Click2Save: The Digital Ministry Bible* (New York: Morehouse Publishing, 2012), 176.

7. Jane Shaw, "The Potential of Cathedrals," *Anglican Theological Review* 95(1) (2013). Available online at *http://www.questia.com/read/1P3-2883105911*

8. On this see David Kinnaman and Gabe Lyons, *Unchristian: What a New Generation Thinks About Christianity . . . and Why It Matters* (Grand Rapids, MI: Baker Books, 2007), and George Barna and David Kinnaman, eds., *Churchless: Understanding Today's Unchurched and How to Connect with Them* (Carol Stream, IL: Tyndale Momentum, 2014).

Chapter 1 ▪ Canterbury Cathedral c. 1167

1. Take the Canterbury Cathedral tour for yourself at *http://www.canterbury-cathedral.org/visit/tour/*

2. Keith Anderson, Twitter post, March 4, 2014, 7:28 a.m., *https://twitter.com/prkanderson/status/440826105436848128*

3. NB is an abbreviation for *note bene*, to mark something as important.

4. Michael Sandgrove, Twitter post, March 4, 2014, 7:42 a.m., *https://twitter.com/Sadgrovem/status/440829754825265152*

5. Keith Anderson, Twitter post, November 5, 2014, 10:24 a.m., *https:// twitter.com/prkanderson/status/530017855136620544*

6. Patrick Collinson, Nigel Ramsey, and Margaret Sparks, eds., *A History of Canterbury Cathedral* (Oxford: Oxford University Press, 1995), 44.

7. View a color reproduction of the Waterworks drawing at the Canterbury Cathedral website. Canterbury Cathedral, "The Waterworks Drawing from the Eadwine Psalter," February 1, 2014. Available online at *http://www.canterbury-cathedral.org/2014/02/01/the-waterworks-drawing-from-the-eadwine-psalter/*.

8. Collinson, Ransey, Sparks, eds., 59.

9. Francis Woodman, "The Waterworks Drawings of the Eadwine Psalter," in *The Eadwine Psalter: Text, Image, and Monastic Culture in Twelfth-Century Canterbury*, edited by Margaret Gibson and others, *Publications of the Modern Humanities Research Association, vol. 14* (London: The Modern Humanities Research Association, 1992), 171.

10. Michel de Certeau, *The Practice of Everyday Life* (Berkeley: University of California Press, 1984), 129.

11. William Urry, *Canterbury Under the Angevin Kings* (London: The Athlone Press 1967), 162.

12. *Ibid.*, 39.

13. Anne Duggan, "Canterbury: The Becket Effect," in *Canterbury, A Medieval City*, Catherine Royer-Hemet, ed. (Newcastle upon Tyne: Cambridge Scholars Press, 2010), 80.

14. Scott, *The Gothic Enterprise*, xi.

15. Cynthia M. Baker, *Rebuilding the House of Israel: The Architectures of Gender in Jewish Antiquity* (Palo Alto, CA: Stanford University Press, 2002), 44–46.

16. Certeau, *The Practice of Everyday Life*, 93.

17. *Ibid.*, 107.

18. Visit the Humans of New York blog at *http://humansofnewyork.com*

19. Jon Groat, "Video Profile: Photographing the 'Humans of New York,'" *New York Magazine* (August 1, 2012). Available online at *http://nymag.com/ daily/intelligencer/2012/08/video-photographing-the-humans-of-new-york.html*

20. See *http://www.humansofnewyork.com/post/91356515896/she-got-pregnant-with-another-man-then-asked-me*

Chapter 2 ▪ Make Your Neighborhood Your Cathedral

1. Learn more about Humble Walk at *humblewalkchurch.org*

2. Drescher and Anderson, *Click2Save*, 157.

3. Robin Johnson, "Best Creative Burgers in Minnesota," *Minnesota.cbslocal. com* (February 19, 2014). Available online at *http://minnesota.cbslocal.com/ top-lists/best-creative-burgers-in-minnesota/*

4. Belden C. Lane, *Landscapes of the Sacred: Geography and Narrative in American Spirituality*, revised edition (Baltimore: The Johns Hopkins University Press, 2001), 48.

5. Jeanne Halgren Kilde, *Sacred Power, Sacred Space: An Introduction to Christian Architecture and Worship* (Oxford: Oxford University Press, 2008), 7.

6. Sarah Miles, *City of God: Faith in the Streets* (New York: Jericho Books, 2014), 59.

7. Susannah Fox and Lee Rainie, "The Web at 25 in the U.S.," *Pew Research Internet Project* (February 27, 2014). Available online at *http://www.pewinternet.org/2014/02/27/the-web-at-25-in-the-u-s/*

8. Maeve Duncan, Nicole B. Ellison, Cliff Lampe, Amanda Lenhart, and Mary Madden, "Social Media Update 2014," *Pew Research Internet Project* (January 9, 2015). Available online at *http://www.pewinternet.org/2015/01/09/social-media-update-2014/*

9. "Religion and Electronic Media: One-in-Five Americans Share Their Faith Online," *Pew Research Religion and Public Life Project* (November 6, 2014). Available online at *http://www.pewforum.org/2014/11/06/religion-and-electronic-media/*

10. Timothy K. Snyder, "Twitter and Tragedy: A Revamped American Religious Experience," *ReligionNewsService.com* (September 13, 2013). Available online at *http://www.religionnews.com/2013/09/13/twitter-tragedy-revamped-american-religious-experience/*

11. *Ibid.*

12. Jeffrey Stalley, "Sneakers, But Not Being Sneaky, for Sarah (Who's an All-Star)," *jefferyt20.wordpress.com* (September 20, 2013). Available online at *http://jeffreyt20.wordpress.com/2013/09/20/sneakers-but-not-being-sneaky-for-sarah-whos-an-all-star/*

13. Learn more about Ashes to Go at *ashestogo.org*

14. Ronald Thiemann, *The Humble Sublime: Secularity and the Politics of Belief* (New York: I.B. Tauris, 2013), 41.

15. Miles, *City of God*, 39.

Chapter 3 ▪ Shifting from Newton to Networks

1. Melissa Massello, "Maker Moment: Crafting to Build Community with Pastor, Lobbyist, and Bike-Commuting Yogi Reverend Laura Everett," *Boston.com* (October 17, 2013). Available online at *http://www.boston.com/lifestyle/blogs/diyboston/2013/10/maker_moment_crafting_to_build_community_with_pastor_lobbyist_and_bike-commuting_yogi_reverend_laura.html*

2. Drescher and Anderson, *Click2Save*, 168–171.

3. Massello, "Maker Moment."

4. Margaret Wheatley, *Leadership and the New Science: Discovering Order in a Chaotic World* (San Francisco: Berrett-Koehler Publishers, 2006), 6.

5. The Episcopal Church in Minnesota, "The Rev. LeeAnne Watkins: The Way We Do Formation Is Not Working," *EpiscopalStoryProject.org* (February 16, 2012). Available online at *http://episcopalstoryproject.org/2012/02/16/ the-rev-leeanne-watkins-the-way-we-do-faith-formation-is-not-working/*

6. Rob Bell, *What We Talk About When We Talk About God* (San Francisco: HarperOne, 2013).

7. Wheatley, *Leadership and the New Science*, 144.

8. Dwight Friesen, *Thy Kingdom Connected: What the Church Can Learn from Facebook, the Internet, and Other Networks* (Grand Rapids, MI: Baker Books, 2009), 109.

9. Rainie and Wellman, *Networked*, 11–20.

10. *Ibid.*, 55.

11. *Ibid.*, 6.

12. Pew Research, "Millennials in Adulthood: Detached from Institutions, Networked with Friends," *PewSocialTrends.org* (March 7, 2014). Available online at *http://www.pewsocialtrends.org/2014/03/07/ millennials-in-adulthood/*

13. Jon L. Wergin, "Leadership in Place," *The Department Chair* 14(4) (Spring 2004), 1–3.

14. Howard Rheingold, *NetSmart: How to Thrive Online* (Cambridge, MA: The MIT Press, 2012), 209.

15. Pew Research, "Mobile Technology Fact Sheet," *PewInternet.org*. Page accessed on November 1, 2014. Available online at *http://www.pewinternet. org/fact-sheets/mobile-technology-fact-sheet*

16. Rainie and Wellman, *Networked*, 101.

17. Stephen Platten, "Introduction—Dreaming Spires?" in *Dreaming Spires?: Cathedrals in a New Age*, Stephen Platten and Christopher Lewis, eds. (London: Society for Promoting Christian Knowledge, 2006), 7.

18. Graham James, "Masks and Mission: Cathedrals and Their Communities," in Platten, *Dreaming Spires?*, 17–18. Emphasis mine.

19. Rainie and Wellman, *Networked*, 29.

20. Abby Day, "Varieties of Belief over Time: Reflections from a Longitudinal Study of Youth and Belief," *Journal of Contemporary Religion* 28(2) (2013): 290.

21. *Ibid.*

22. See Heidi Campbell, *Exploring Religious Community Online: We Are One in the Network* (New York: Peter Lang Publishing, 2005), 35–36, and Elizabeth Drescher, *Choosing Our Religion: The Spiritual Lives of America's Nones* (Oxford: Oxford University Press, 2015).

Chapter 4 ▪ Practicing Relational Ministry

1. "Oxford Dictionaries Word of the Year 2013," *Oxford Dictionaries* (November 19, 2013). Available online at *http://blog.oxforddictionaries. com/press-releases/oxford-dictionaries-word-of-the-year-2013*

2. "Newlyweds Pose for Selfie with Pope Francis Himself," *The Huffington Post* (March 20, 2014). Available online at *http://www.huffingtonpost. com/2014/03/20/pope-selfie_n_5002167.html*

3. Keith Anderson, "@Pontifex Signs Off: Exploring Benedict's Digital Media Legacy," *New Media Project* (February 15, 2013). Available online at *http:// www.cpx.cts.edu/newmedia/blog/new-media-project/2013/02/15/pontifex-signs-off-exploring-benedicts-digital-media-legacy*

4. "'Communication at the Service of an Authentic Culture of Encounter'— Pope's Message for World Communications Day," *News.va* (June 1, 2014). Available online at *http://www.news.va/en/news/communication-at-the-service-of-an-authentic-cultu*

5. "Digital native" is a term coined by Marc Prensky in his article, "Digital Natives, Digital Immigrants," *On the Horizon* 9(5) (2001). Available online at *http:// www.marcprensky.com/writing/Prensky%20-%20Digital%20Natives,%20 Digital%20Immigrants%20-%20Part1.pdf*

6. Andrew Root, *The Relational Pastor: Sharing in Christ by Sharing Ourselves* (Downer's Grove, IL: IVP Press, 2013), Kindle location 255.

7. *Ibid.*, Kindle location 405.

8. Campbell, *Exploring Religious Community Online*, xiv.

9. *Ibid.*, 187.

10. Wheatley, *Leadership and the New Science*, 11.

11. Listening, attending, connecting, and engaging is the LACE model developed by Elizabeth Drescher in *Tweet if You Heart Jesus: Practicing Church in the Digital Reformation* (New York: Morehouse Publishing, 2011), 17–22.

12. Root, *The Relational Pastor*, Kindle location 596.

13. Elizabeth Drescher, "Quitting Religion But Not the Practice of Prayer," *Religion Dispatches* (March 28, 2103). Available online at *http://religion dispatches.org/quitting-religion-but-not-the-practice-of-prayer/*

14. Kristofer Lindh-Payne, "Faith in the Public Arena: An Experiment in Healing Prayer on a Suburban Sidewalk," *Epiphany Episcopal Church* (January 28, 2014). Available online at *http://www.epiphanybaltimore.org/ faith-public-arena-experiment-healing-prayer-suburban-sidewalk/*

15. David Weinberger, *Everything Is Miscellaneous: The Power of the New Digital Disorder* (New York: Times Books, 2007), 230. Emphasis mine.

Chapter 5 ▪ Excercing Incarnational Imagination

1. Jim Hazelwood, "Hammo Text and Talk with the Bishop—Follow Up," (September 9, 2012). Available online at *https://www.youtube.com/watch?v=kokBv2q8NDA*

2. Jim Hazelwood, "Why Talk and Text Works at Hammo," *Bishop on a Bike* (September 10, 2012). Available online at *http://bishoponabike.squarespace.com/blog/2013/9/10/why-text-and-talk-works-at-hammo.html*

3. *http://bishoponabike.com*

4. *http://instagram.com/jimhazelwood*

5. Campbell, *Exploring Religious Community Online*, 6–10.

6. Thiemann, *The Humble Sublime*, 4.

7. See Kirsten Purcell, "Online Video 2013," *Pew Research Internet Project* (October 10, 2013). Available online at *http://www.pewinternet.org/2013/10/10/online-video-2013/*, and Maeve Duggan, "Cell Phone Activities 2013," *Pew Research Internet Project* (September 19, 2013). Available online at *http://www.pewinternet.org/2013/09/19/cell-phone-activities-2013/*

8. Thiemann, *The Humble Sublime*, 41.

9. Learn more about the South Wedge Mission at *http://southwedgemission.org*

10. The advanced Twitter search allows you to search for tweets near you. See *https://twitter.com/search-advanced*

11. Learn more at *http://thads.org*

12. Krysta Fauria, "Laundry Love Provides More Than Just Free Cleaning to Southern California's Poor, Homeless," *The Huffington Post* (August 31, 2014). Available online at *http://www.huffingtonpost.com/2014/08/31/laundry-love-southern-california_n_5736934.html*

13. "Video Explores the Ministry of Laundry Love," *The Episcopal Church*. Available online at *http://www.episcopalchurch.org/notice/video-explores-ministry-laundry-love*

14. *Ibid.*

15. Antonia Blumberg, "Los Angeles Deacon Ordained in Laundromat as Part of Street-Based Ministry," *The Huffington Post* (May 2, 2014). Available online at *http://www.huffingtonpost.com/2014/05/02/deacon-ordained-in-laundromat_n_5248371.html*

16. Peter Rollins, *Insurrection: To Believe Is Human to Doubt, Divine* (Brentwood, TN: Howard Books, 2011), 112.

Chapter 6 ▪ Everyday Sacred: Locating God in Daily Life

1. Jon Kabat-Zinn, *Full Catastrophe Living: Using the Wisdom of Your Body and Mind to Face Stress, Pain, and Illness* (New York: Delta Trade Paperbacks, 1991).

2. Sue Bender, *Everyday Sacred: A Woman's Journey Home* (San Francisco: HarperOne, 1996).

3. Learn more about the Shalem Institute for Spiritual Formation at *http:// shalem.org*

4. Charles Taylor, *Sources of the Self: The Making of the Modern Identity* (Cambridge, MA: Harvard University Press, 1992), 211ff.

5. *Ibid.*, 218.

6. *Ibid.*, 218–219.

7. Martin Luther, "The Estate of Marriage," *Luther's Works*, Vol. 45 (Philadelphia: Muhlenberg Press, 1962), 47.

8. Martin Luther, "Lectures on Genesis 17:9," *Luther's Works*, Vol. 3 (Philadelphia: Muhlenberg Press, 1962), 128.

9. Martin Luther, *Weimarer Ausgabe* 32, pp. 495–496 (The Sermon on the Mount).

10. David Lose, *Preaching at the Crossroads: How the World—and Our Preaching—Is Changing* (Minneapolis: Fortress Press, 2013), 71–72.

11. Wendy Wright, *Seasons of a Family's Life: Cultivating the Contemplative Spirit at Home* (San Francisco: Jossey Bass, 2003), 17–18.

12. Kathleen Norris, *The Quotidian Mysteries: Laundry, Liturgy and "Women's Work"* (Mahwah, NJ: Paulist Press, 1998), 3.

13. Thich Nhat Hanh, *Peace Is Every Step: The Path of Mindfulness in Everyday Life* (New York: Bantam Books, 1991), 27.

14. Scott, *The Gothic Enterprise*, 148.

15. *Ibid.*, 160–161.

16. *Ibid.*, 152.

17. For a vivid, if fictional, depiction of life in a cathedral town, read the novel by Ken Follet, *Pillars of the Earth* (New York: Morrow, 1989).

18. Robert Barron, *Heaven in Stone and Glass: Experiencing the Spirituality of the Great Cathedrals* (New York: Crossroad Publishing, 2000), 47.

19. Christopher Lewis, "Glory and Pride: The Church and its Cathedrals," in Platten, *Dreaming Spires?*, 60.

20. Alisa Roth, "Blessed Be Thy Bicycle," *npr.org* (May 5, 2014). Available online at *http://www.npr.org/2014/05/05/309653656/blessed-be-thy-bicycle-new-york-riders-roll-into-church*

21. "Candler: 'We're Trying to Replicate What a Cathedral Was in the Middle Ages,'" *reporternewspapers.net* (April 7, 2011). Available online at *http://www.reporternewspapers.net/2011/04/07/candler-replicate-cathedral-middle-ages/*

Chapter 7 ▪ Naming It Holy: Common Ground for Nones and the Affiliated

1. Patricia O'Connell Killen, ed., *Religion and Public Life in the Pacific Northwest: The None Zone* (Charlotte, NC: Rowman & Littlefield, 2004).

2. See Drescher, *Choosing Our Religion*.

3. William Lawrence, *The American Cathedral* (New York: The Macmillan Company, 1919), 26.

4. *Ibid.*, 27.

5. Pew Research, "'Nones' on the Rise."

6 On this see Kinnaman and Lyons, *Unchristian*, and Barna and Kinnaman, eds., *Churchless*.

7. Drescher, "Quitting Religion. . . ."

8. *Ibid.* For further detail on the study, see Drescher, *Choosing Our Religion*.

9. In a talk given at the BTS Center Annual Convocation, "Hand, Heads, Hearts, and Smartphones, January 20–22, 2014, Portland, Maine.

10. Leslie Albrecht, "'Dinner Church' Where Parishioners Eat While They Worship Coming to Gowanus," *DNAinfo* (February 13, 2014). Available online at *http://www.dnainfo.com/new-york/20140213/gowanus/ dinner-church-where-parishioners-eat-while-they-worship-coming-gowanus*

11. Michael Pollan, *The Omnivore's Dilemma: A Natural History of Four Meals* (New York: Penguin, 2007), 407–408.

12. Nancy Ammerman, *Sacred Stories, Spiritual Tribes: Finding Religion in Everyday Life* (Oxford: Oxford University Press, 2013), 76.

13. The Pew Forum on Religion & Public Life, "U.S. Religious Landscape Survey—Religious Affiliation: Diverse and Dynamic" (February 2008). Available online at *http://religions.pewforum.org*

14. Ammerman, *Sacred Stories, Spiritual Tribes*, 46.

15. *Ibid.*, 40–41.

16. Elizabeth Drescher, "No to Church, Yes to Jesus?" *Religion Dispatches* (January 31, 2014). Available online at *http://religiondispatches.org/ no-to-church-yes-to-jesus/*

17. Mark Allan Powell, *Chasing the Eastern Star: Adventures in Biblical Reader-Response Criticism* (Louisville, KY: John Knox Press, 2001), 8, 71.

18. See Sanctuary's Fence online at *http://sanctuarymarshfield.org/creating/ beliefsandvalues*

Chapter 8 ▪ God on Tap: At the Intersection of Life and Faith

1. Trey Popp, "Philadelphia Restaurant Review: Forest & Main," *Philadelphia Magazine* (November 27, 2012). Available online at *http://www.phillymag.com/articles/philadelphia-restaurant-review-forest-main/*

2. John Burnett, "To Stave Off Decline, Churches Attract New Members with Beer," *NPR.org* (November 3, 2013). Available online at http:// www.npr.org/blogs/thesalt/2013/11/03/242301642/to-stave-off-decline-churches-attract-new-members-with-beer. Sally Quinn, *Pub Theology: Beer, Burgers and a Side of Spirituality in D.C., The Washington Post*

(November 8, 2013). Available online at http://www.washingtonpost.com/national/on-faith/bar-theology-beer-burgers-and-a-side-of-spirituality-in-dc/2013/11/08/025bdb16-47e3-11e3-a196-3544a03c2351_story.html.

3. Ray Oldenburg, *The Great Good Place: Cafés, Coffee Shops, Bookstores, Bars, Hair Salons and other Hangouts at the Heart of a Community* (Cambridge, MA: Da Capo Press, 1999), 16.

4. Carter Lindberg, *The European Reformations*, second edition (Hoboken, NJ: Wiley-Blackwell, 2009), 285.

5. Lane, *Landscapes of the Sacred*, 41.

6. Oldenburg, *The Great Good Place*, 33

7. *Ibid.*, 34.

8. *Ibid.*, 38.

9. *Ibid.*, 41.

10. James, "Masks and Missions," 20.

11. Sarah Miles, *Take This Bread: A Radical Conversion* (New York: Balantine Books, 2008).

12. "Community Contemplative Space," *Calvary United Methodist Church.* Accessed November 3, 2014. Available online at *http://www.allmeansall.org/contemplative.html*

13. "At a West Philly Church, a Breather from the Multitasking Life," *Newsworks* (September 18, 2014). Available online at *http://www.newsworks.org/index.php/local/newsworks-tonight/72928-at-a-west-philly-church-a-breather-from-the-multitasking-life*

14. Dutch Godshalk, "Upper Dublin Lutheran Church Pastor Holds 'God on Tap' at Forest & Main Brewing Co.," *Ambler Gazette* (November 27, 2013). Available online at *http://montgomerynews.com/articles/2013/11/27/ambler_gazette/news/doc52961d252bd4a556852962.txt?viewmode=fullstory*

15. Dan Flanagan, "Wesley Pub," *YouTube* video, 5:47, August 16, 2010, *https://www.youtube.com/watch?v=8I7XCm1OwVA*

16. To see all the topics we've covered, visit the God on Tap blog at *http://godontap.net/blog*

17. Adam Walker Cleaveland, "Theology Pub (2.0) in Ashland, Oregon," *Pomomusings* (August 29, 2012). Available online at *http://pomomusings.com/2012/08/29/theology-pub-2-0-in-ashland-oregon/*

Chapter 9 ▪ Theology without a Net: Conversation at the Core

1. Learn more about accompaniment as mode for ministry at the ELCA Global Mission website, *http://www.elca.org/Our-Work/Global-Church/Global-Mission*

2. Marshall McLuhan and Quentin Fiore, *The Medium Is the Massage: An Inventory of Effects* (Berkeley, CA: Gingko Press, 1967), 63.

3. MG Siegler, "Eric Schmidt: Every 2 Days We Create as Much Information as We Did Up to 2003," *TechCrunch* (August 4, 2010). Available online at *http://techcrunch.com/2010/08/04/schmidt-data/*

4. Weinberger, *Everything Is Miscellaneous*, Kindle location 1625.

5. Drew DeSilver, "Facebook Is a News Source for Many, But Only Incidentally," *Pew Research Center* (February 4, 2014). Available online at *http://www.pewresearch.org/fact-tank/2014/02/04/facebook-is-a-news-source-for-many-but-only-incidentally/*

6. Amy Mitchell and Emily Guskin, "Twitter News Consumers: Young, Mobile and Educated," *Pew Research Journalism Project* (November 4, 2013). Available online at *http://www.journalism.org/2013/11/04/twitter-news-consumers-young-mobile-and-educated/*

7. Danielle Fuller and DeNel Rehberg Sedo, "'And Then We Went to the Brewery': Reading as a Social Activity in a Digital Era," *World Literature Today* (May–August 2014). Available online at *http://www.worldliteraturetoday.org/2014/may-august/and-then-we-went-brewery-reading-social-activity-digital-era#.VFeVrofaGOd*

8. Drescher, *Tweet if You Heart Jesus*, 61–64.

9. Philip Clayton, "Theology After Google," *Princeton Theological Review* (XVII)(2) (2010),14.

10. Gordon D. Kaufman, *In Face of Mystery: A Constructive Theology* (Cambridge, MA: Harvard University Press, 1993), 64.

11. *Ibid.*, 64.

12. Marshall McLuhan, *Understanding Media: The Extensions of Man (Critical Edition)* (Berkeley, CA: Gingko Press, 2003). First edition published 1964.

13. Clayton, "Theology After Google," 14.

14. *Ibid.*, 17.

15. For more on group spiritual direction, see Rose Mary Dougherty, S.S.N.D., *Group Spiritual Direction: Community for Discernment* (New York: Paulist Press, 1995).

16. Paul Hoffman, *Faith Forming Faith: Bringing New Christians to Baptism and Beyond* (Eugene, OR: Wipf & Stock, 2012), 32–33.

17. *Ibid.*, 9

18. See Paul Hoffman, *Faith Shaping Ministry* (Eugene, OR: Cascade Books, 2013).

19. Root, *The Relational Pastor*, Kindle location 1136.

20. Kaufman, *In Face of Mystery*, 67.

Chapter 10 ▪ Faith Formation: Visual, Immersive, and Experiential

1. A good contemporary translation of *The Rule of St. Benedict* can be found in Patrick Barry et al., *Wisdom from the Monastery: The Rule of St. Benedict for Everyday Life* (Collegeville, MN: Liturgical Press, 2006), 7–97. Here, the first line of the Prologue is translated, "Listen, child of God, to the guidance of your master."

2. Kathleen Smith, "Notes on Needlepoint," *Washington National Cathedral* (April 30, 2013). Available online at *http://www.nationalcathedral.org/pdfs/NeedlepointHistory.pdf*

3. "Darth Vader: The Star Wars Villain on the Northwest Tower," *Washington National Cathedral*. Available online at *http://www.nationalcathedral.org/about/darthVader.shtml*

4. Robert Scott, *The Gothic Enterprise*, 74.

5. McLuhan, *The Media Is the Massage*, 68.

6. Douglas Thomas and John Seely Brown, *A New Culture of Learning: Cultivating the Imagination for a World of Constant Change.* (CreateSpace Independent Publishing Platform, 2011), 47.

7. *Ibid.*, 37–38.

8. Kaufman, *In Face of Mystery*, 15.

9. T.S. Eliot, *Four Quartets* (Boston: Houghton Mifflin Harcourt, 2014), 18.

10. Learn more about Godly Play at *http://www.godlyplayfoundation.org*

11. Lent Madness is now done in conjunction with Forward Movement, a ministry of the Episcopal Church, *http://forwardmovement.org*

12. Len Sweet has written extensively about an EPIC (Experiential, Participatory, Image Driven, Connected) model for churches in *Post-Modern Pilgrims: First Century Passion for the 21st Century World* (Nashville: Broadman & Holman Publishers, 2000) and *The Gospel According to Starbucks: Living with a Grande Passion* (Colorado Springs: WaterBrook Press, 2007).

13. See U.S. Department of Commerce and National Telecommunications and Information Administration, "Exploring the Digital Nation: Embracing the Mobile Internet" (October 2014). Available online at *http://www.ntia.doc.gov/files/ntia/publications/exploring_the_digital_nation_embracing_the_mobile_internet_10162014.pdf*; and Ekaterina Walter, "The Rise of Visual Social Media," *Fast Company* (August 28 2012). Available online at *http://www.fastcompany.com/3000794/rise-visual-social-media*

14. In a talk given at the BTS Center Annual Convocation, "Hand, Heads, Hearts, and Smartphones, January 20–22, 2014, Portland, Maine.

15. Barron, *Heaven in Stone and Glass*, 10.

16. Bianca Bosker, "Facebook's Rapidly Declining Popularity with Teens in 1 Chart," *The Huffington Post* (October 23, 2013). Available online at *http://www.huffingtonpost.com/2013/10/23/facebooks-teen-trouble-in_n_4150940.html*

17. Available online at *http://instagram.com/press/*

18. See the Advent Calendar Pinterest board at http://www.pinterest.com/iamepiscopalian/advent-calendar/ and the Instagram version at *http://instagram.com/adventword*

19. For good insight in using images, I recommend Nancy Duarte, *Slide:ology: The Art and Science of Creating Great Presentations* (Sebastopol, CA: O'Reilly Media, 2008).

20. See, for example, *God on Tap* at *http://godontap.net*, and *The Narthex* religion magazine at *http://medium.com/the-narthex*

21. Len Sweet has called this EPIC—Experiential, Participatory, Image-Driven, and Communal. See Sweet, *Post-Modern Pilgrims*, and Sweet, *The Gospel According to Starbucks*.

22. The NOOMA video series by Rob Bell is a collection of twenty-four short ten-minute videos. Learn more at *http://nooma.com*. We watched the video, "Rhythm," *http://nooma.com/films/011-rhythm*

23. For more details and resources, see *http://pastorkeithanderson.net/item/keeping-sabbath-with-my-confirmation-class*

24. For a good laugh, check out the Jimmy Fallon, Justin Timberlake, and Quest Love skit called "#Hashtag." The Tonight Show with Jimmy Fallon, ""#Hashtag" with Jimmy Fallon & Justin Timberlake (Late Night with Jimmy Fallon)," *YouTube* video, 2:00, *https://www.youtube.com/watch?v=57dzaMaouXA*

25. Liz Gannes, "The Short and Illustrious History of Twitter #Hashtags," *GigaOm* (April 30, 2010). Available online at *http://gigaom.com/2010/04/30/the-short-and-illustrious-history-of-twitter-hashtags/*

26. Katy McCallum Sachse, "#HSLCintheworld," *Holy Spirit Lutheran Church* (May 22, 2014). Available online at *http://www.hslckirkland.org/blog/hslcintheworld*

Chapter 11 ▪ Evangelism: Sharing the Gospel for the Sake of the Gospel

1. Learn more about Cathedral in the Night at *http://www.cathedralinthe night.org*

2. Lane, *Landscapes of the Sacred*, 48.

3. David Walker, "Four Types of Belonging," *Church Times* (March 28, 2014). Available online at *http://www.churchtimes.co.uk/articles/2014/28-march/comment/opinion/four-types-of-belonging*

4. *Ibid.*

5. *Ibid.*

6. *Ibid.*

7. *Ibid.*

8. Jeremy Fletcher, "Liturgy on the Frontiers: Laboratories for the Soul," in Platten, *Dreaming Spires?*, 51.

9. Emily M. D. Scott, "Refraining from Invitation: Evangelism in Context," *Episcopal Café* (June 1, 2009). Available online at *http://www.episcopalcafe. com/daily/evangelism/refraining_from_invitation_eva.php*

10. *Ibid.*

11. *Ibid.*

12. Reiss, *Twible*, 17.

13. *Ibid.*, 157.

14. *Ibid.*, 222.

15. Elizabeth Drescher, "Who Do You Say that You Are? The Stories of Spiritual Selves in the Postmodern, Postchristian World," *Bearings* (October 30, 2014). Available online at *http://www.thebtscenter.org/who-do-you-say-that-you-are-the-stories-of-spiritual-selves-in-the-postmodern-postchristian-world/*

16. *Ibid.*

17. Pat McCaughan, "#Episcopal 'Social Media Sunday' a Digital Invitation," *Episcopal News Service* (June 26, 2014). Available online at *http://episcopaldigitalnetwork.com/ens/2014/06/26/episcopal-social-media-sunday-a-digital-invitation/*

18. "#Episcopal Social Media Sunday," *EpiscopalShare.org*. Available online at *http://episcopalshare.org*

Chapter 12 ▪ A Digital Rule of Life

1. Esther de Waal, *Seeking God: The Way of St. Benedict* (Collegeville, MN: Liturgical Press, 2001), 31.

2. Quoted in de Waal, *Seeking God*, 48.

3. Brother Roger of Taize, *The Rule of Taize* (London: Society for Promoting Christian Knowledge, 2012), 6.

4. Joan Chittister, OSB, *Wisdom Distilled from the Daily: Living The Rule of St. Benedict Today* (San Francisco: HarperOne, 1990), 16.

5. Barry et al., *Wisdom from the Monastery*, 74.

6. Brother Roger, *The Rule of Taize*, 52.

7. Barry et al., *Wisdom from the Monastery*, 10.

8. Chittister, *Wisdom Distilled from the Daily*, 31.

9. Barry et al., *Wisdom from the Monastery*, 32.

10. Brother Roger, *The Rule of Taize*, 23.

11. de Waal, *Seeking God*, 86.

12. Drescher and Anderson, *Click2Save*. For more on RSS, see pages 182. Twitter lists explained on page 82.

13. Bryan Berghoef, *Pub Theology: Beer, Conversation, and God* (Eugene, OR: Wipf & Stock, 2012), Kindle location 1536.

14. Brother Roger, *The Rule of Taize*, 10.

15. Drescher and Anderson, *Click2Save*, 53–59.

16. Brother Roger, *The Rule of Taize*, 7.

17. Maeve Duggan, "Online Harassment," *Pew Research Internet Project* (October 22, 2014). Available online at *http://www.pewinternet.org/2014/10/22/online-harassment/*

18. Brother Roger, *The Rule of Taize*, 25.

19. Visit website for the National Day of Unplugging for more on digital Sabbath: *http://nationaldayofunplugging.com*

20. Society of Saint John the Evangelist, *The Rule of the Society of Saint John the Evangelist* (Cambridge, MA: Cowley Publications, 1997), 44.

Conclusion ▪ A Transitional Cathedral

1. Learn more about the ChristChurch Transitional Cathedral at their website: http://www.cardboardcathedral.org.nz

2. Charles Anderson, "How Temporary 'Cardboard Cathedral' Rose from the Ruins to Become Most Recognised Building in ChristChurch," *The Guardian* (September 17, 2014). Available online at *http://www.theguardian.com/cities/2014/sep/17/temporary-cardboard-cathedral-ruins-christchurch-new-zealand-earthquake*

3. Kaufman, *In Face of Mystery*, 52.

4. Kara Swisher, Steve Jobs, Bill Gates (May 30, 2007). "Steve Jobs and Bill Gates Together: Part 2, All Things Digital 5." *The Wall Street Journal* (video). Event occurs at 5:20. Retrieved February 15, 2010. Available online at *https://www.youtube.com/watch?v=lK_HThS8DZo*

5. Ronald Heifetz, Alexander Glashow, and Marty Linski, *The Practice of Adaptive Leadership: Tools and Tactics for Changing Your Organization and the World* (Boston: Harvard Business Press, 2009), 3.

6. Kaufman, *In Face of Mystery*, 51.